Anatomy, Physiology and Pathology *for* the Massage Therapist

Anatomy, Physiology and Pathology *for* the Massage Therapist

Su Fox and Darien Pritchard

CORPUS PUBLISHING

First published in 2001. This second edition published in 2003, reprinted in 2004, 2007 and 2011.

Corpus Publishing Limited
PO Box 8 Lydney Gloucestershire GL15 6YD United Kingdom

Disclaimer
This publication is intended as an informational guide. The techniques described are a supplement to, and not a substitute for, professional tuition. While the information herein is supplied in good faith, no responsibility is taken by either the publisher or the author for any damage, injury or loss, however caused, which may arise from the use of the information provided.

British Library Cataloguing in Publication Data
A CIP record for this book is available from the British Library
ISBN 1 903333 07 5

Dedication
To Frankie Armstrong for belief. Many thanks to Gina Barker for her love and support. Also to Jane Crabtree, Lucy Lidell, Celia Webb, Andy Fagg and Ann Pritchard for support and encouragement. To Richard Leadbeater, Charlene Penner, Sally Morris, Anja Saunders, Vicky Gaughan, Anne Whall, Jude Gooden, Rob Ranzijn, Carolan Evans, Kate and David Fox for their useful suggestions.
Su Fox and Darien Pritchard

Text and Cover Design Sara Howell
Cover Photography Darien Pritchard
Drawings Amanda Williams
Printed and bound in Great Britain by Short Run Press

Contents

Introduction

Because some massage students have no prior experience in studying anatomy, physiology or biology, the initial purpose of this book is to describe the physical make-up of the body, giving a broad introduction to the body's physical functioning. The emphasis here is on the body systems and aspects most relevant to the dynamics of massage, muscle activity, stress response, tension and relaxation, and the effect of touch. This means primarily the muscular, skeletal and nervous systems, and the skin, with reference also to the respiratory and cardiovascular systems (breathing and blood circulation). We will look at the interrelationships of all these aspects, and connect them with the practical concerns of massage and the dynamics of stress and relaxation.

We will follow the usual method of study, which is to divide the body into its component functioning systems, looking individually at each system. Keep in mind however, that this is an artificial division for the purposes of study. The parts cannot function independently, so we will also look at how they connect with, and are interdependent with, one another.

Living bone, for example, is dependent on the circulation to bring it nutrients from the food we eat for repair and maintenance, and to carry away discarded materials for elimination, usually via the kidneys and urinary system or the skin. Bones are also sites for the storage of minerals and fats, and for the development of blood cells.

Bear in mind that this is a study only of the physical body. This is crucial for understanding certain aspects of human functioning. However, you cannot X-ray a person's vitality, or necessarily explain in medical terms why one person recovers from a certain disease and another doesn't. What massage practitioners need is to comprehend and be familiar with common medical terms, and have the ability to research these in reference books.

It is important that you keep this knowledge and understanding in perspective. Ultimately, it needs to be at the service of your hands and the feeling you have already developed for massage.

The Role of Anatomy, Physiology and Pathology in Massage

At present, anatomy, physiology and pathology sit uneasily in much massage training and practice. Some practitioners, for example, are reluctant to question clients about medical matters as they believe it is irrelevant to the massage. Others go through a detailed medical check list with the client but this information may have little effect on the hands-on treatment.

One of the major challenges to a beginning massage practitioner is getting the balance right between knowledge, sensing what is under your hands and the intuitions that come to you as you gain experience. The ideal that we aspire to is an interweaving of science and art. That is the appropriate knowledge applied in a way that acknowledges and works with the client's needs and comforts.

The teaching texts that have preceded this book were written in response to the demands of massage students who wanted information geared to the particular concerns of their profession. The present text is designed for both students and massage practitioners in the early years of professional practice.

Appropriate Knowledge

What are the needs of the beginning massage practitioner? Obviously practitioners need a basic understanding of anatomy, kinesiology and some physiology. However, not as much physiology or pathology is required as in the modalities that are designed to affect the functioning of the body systems, such as Shiatsu and Reflexology, or the body's chemistry, such as Aromatherapy.

In recent decades, the upsurge of research on stress management has highlighted useful information that should be part of a practitioner's repertoire, as two aspects of massage can benefit from an understanding of the physiological dynamics of stress and relaxation. Helping the client to relax is an important component of most treatments, either by teaching relaxation or at least by creating a relaxed working atmosphere. Professionals should also be able to explain to clients the body's responses to short-term and long-term stress.

It has often been assumed that massage practitioners do not need to ask clients about their health, apart from any obvious injuries, aches or pains. If this was satisfactory in the past, it is certainly not so now. The wide publicity and growing interest in massage means that the practitioner is seeing a clientele with a wider range of conditions than a decade ago.

In fact many people now seek out massage (and other treatments) because they are unhappy with the response of the 'mainstream' medical profession to their problems. Thanks to the work of some pioneering individuals, massage practitioners are beginning to work in hospitals, hospices and other medical, support and rehabilitative settings.

This highlights the role of anatomy, physiology and pathology knowledge in massage therapy. It is crucial in determining guidelines on contra-indications (i.e. when not to treat), cautions to be exercised and parameters within which to work with a client.

This knowledge also serves the practitioner's searching hands and intuition, as they sense and adapt to responses in the client's body.

So it is important to have a basic grasp of the body's structure, functioning and common problems. However, to be useful, training needs to go beyond being just a catalogue of these facts. Although diagnosing medical conditions is outside the scope of training, practitioners should be able to make sense of the information that the client gives them.

If the client has already had a medical diagnosis, the practitioner needs to be able to make use of this. Therefore, there should be familiarity with the terminology of human biology and how the words are built up. There should also be the ability to refer to medical books and make sense of relevant information – particularly concerning likely effects on the relevant body tissues and areas.

This understanding will also lead to further questions about how the condition affects the client and to determine how it will shape the treatment session. This may include matters such as a client's difficulty in lying down comfortably, or areas of the body that should not be touched.

Having an understanding of the client's condition may also highlight the need to elicit 'safety' information. For example, if the client is diabetic, is his blood sugar level presently steady and likely to remain so? What are the symptoms that will indicate if he is becoming hypoglycaemic and what does he need the practitioner to do in that case?

Practitioners should be able to question the client, if necessary, to make some sense of undiagnosed conditions and, if appropriate, to work out which professionals to refer clients to. Massage practitioners should also be able to talk to other professionals in medical language, to share information and to explain relevant aspects of their work.

Role of Teaching Methods

This book attempts to bring anatomy, physiology and pathology to life, by making connections with everyday understanding and massage experience and concerns. However, the way that it is taught in a class can be an important factor in shaping the beginning practitioner's attitude to it.

Information becomes most useful and memorable for a massage student when it can be grounded in experience. Therefore it is hoped that this book will be used in conjunction with the palpation of structures that can be readily felt, e.g. muscles, bones and joints in action, ideally on a number of people, to get a broad understanding and with imaginative teaching of the less readily palpable aspects.

Applying the Information

There are two potential sources of conflict between anatomy and physiology information and practical massage that we, as massage teachers, have learned to address.

Many beginning students fear that this information will overwhelm their fragile, newly emerging palpation skills. A teacher can encourage the development of a healthy relationship between the two types of input by presenting information that can be investigated and reinforced by 'hands-on'. This could involve investigating the structure of a joint, by feeling it on oneself and fellow students, or identifying the muscles in which tension was found. These are essential abilities that practitioners need to develop.

There can also be a tendency to view massage purely in medical terms, particularly as the struggle for formal national recognition and registration increases the pressure to 'medicalise' massage, leading to the downgrading or ignoring of the importance of friendly, nurturing touch. The concern is that intuition will be discounted, and the importance of the interpersonal connection between practitioner and client will be ignored. Massage practitioners, it is feared, could lose larger perspectives on their work and come to see themselves only as medical 'problem-solvers'.

This is where the practitioner's personal preparations for working come into play to help put this information into perspective. These can include physical preparations such as energising, grounding and centring exercises, an understanding of the nurturing and relaxing elements of massage as well as the remedial aspects, and an appreciation of the dynamics of the professional relationship. These are all crucial elements beyond the scope of this present book.

While this book attempts to place anatomy, physiology and pathology in relation to the concerns of the massage practitioner, it is only ultimately through experience that practitioners will find for themselves where this information fits within the massage session and how to use it to inform their practical work.

The ideal is to incorporate the intelligent use of this information into one's overall development as a well-rounded practitioner. This will enable you to marry sensing and knowledge, analysis and intuition, and take into account medical conditions that will influence the intentions and shape of a treatment session, and thus deliver the best service to clients.

Section 1
Building Blocks

Chapter 1 Introduction to Terminology

This book calls upon a number of disciplines within the study of the human body:

Biology (*"study of life"*) is the science of living things, including plants (botany) and animals (zoology). This book is concerned with human biology, particularly the aspects most relevant to massage.

Anatomy (*"dissection"* – from Greek) is the study of the structure of the body – the naming of the parts. For massage practitioners this will be primarily **surface anatomy** (studying the 'landmarks' that give reference points on the surface of the body), **gross anatomy** (structures visible to the naked eye), and **histology** (the study of tissues).

Physiology (*"study of nature"* – from Greek) is the science of the functioning of cells, tissues and organs – the chemical processes of the body.

Kinesiology (*"study of motion"*) covers the movements of the body, the actions of the muscles in moving the bones at the joints.

Pathology is the study of problems, disorders and diseases which involves changes in the structure or functioning of the body.

General Terminology

Anatomical language is largely derived or adapted from classical Greek or Latin names so that, with the common English language name, there are often two or three names for the same body part.

Many of the longer terms, which can be daunting to the beginning student, are made up from smaller words or prefixes and suffixes. These compound words, like any new language, will become sensible to you as it becomes familiar to your ear and tongue.

It is important to learn the terminology because, like any technical language, it provides a useful way of talking to colleagues and other professionals. So do begin to use it, even if you stumble at first. Note that the precise meanings of some terms can differ from everyday usage. The terms are covered in the text. There are a few prefixes and suffixes that are used very commonly:

General

-logy   refers to the study of a topic, e.g. biology, psychology.

-metry   refers to measurement, e.g. geometry.

Position

Ec-, ecto-, exo-   out, on the outside of, e.g. exodus.

En-, endo-   within, inside, e.g. encase, encapsulate.

Peri-   around, e.g. perimeter.

Sub-   under, e.g. submarine.

Condition

Hyper-, hypo-   above/below, e.g. hyperactive, hypothermia.

-itis   inflammation of tissues, e.g. arthritis, appendicitis.

-otomy   to cut, usually describes surgery, e.g. tonsillectomy, appendectomy.

One other term is important for massage students:

Palpate   to examine by touching.

Note About Personal Pronouns

Many writers have deplored the fact that in English there isn't a pronoun that can be used to refer to a person, when they could be either male or female. Apart from the awkward 's/he', 'him/her', 'his/hers', etc.

In this book we have decided to refer to 'she' and 'her' on some occasions and 'he', 'him' and 'his' on others. Wherever this occurs, it should be understood to also stand for an individual of the opposite sex (except in reference to the reproductive systems).

Chapter 2 Chemistry of the Body

In this section, you are introduced to some basic scientific ideas; those that are necessary for you to understand before moving onto those aspects of the body's structure and function that are of interest to the massage practitioner. We start with the building blocks that make up all living and non-living material and from there to the basic unit of all living organisms, the cell. Cells in the human body are grouped into tissues. The organs of the body are composed of different kinds of tissue, and these organs grouped into systems, each with its own particular role in the overall functioning of the body. In reality, these systems are not separate at all but work as a complex interrelated whole.

Chemicals

From a scientific point of view, all matter, both living and non-living, is made up of chemicals called elements. One group of elements are called metals, e.g. iron, zinc and sodium. The other group are the non-metals, e.g. oxygen, hydrogen and carbon. The smallest part of an element is called an atom.

Elements often combine together to form chemical compounds. A chemical containing more than one atom is called a molecule. A single molecule of water is a compound made of one oxygen atom and two hydrogen atoms. Hormones, neurotransmitters, carbohydrates, and haemoglobin, which are a few of the many chemicals involved in the physiology of the body, are all complex chemical compounds containing four or more elements. There is a unique shorthand used to describe elements and compounds in written form, called the chemical formula. The formula of an element is the first letter (or two) of the word, or of its Latin equivalent. The formula of a compound describes the elements that make it up, and how many atoms of each.

Element	Compound	Formula
Carbon		C
Oxygen		O
	Carbon Dioxide	CO_2
Hydrogen		H
	Water	H_2O
	Glucose	$C_6H_{12}O_6$
Sodium		Na (Latin: Natrium)
Chlorine		Cl
	Salt	NaCl

Elements and compounds occur in one of three states:

1. Gas
2. Liquid
3. Solid

Of the compounds in the table above, water is usually a liquid, although it can become solid, as ice, or gaseous, as steam. Salt and glucose are solids and carbon dioxide is a gas. Many, but not all solids will dissolve in water, and for this reason it is known as the universal solvent.

It takes energy to change the state of an element or compound. For example, we heat water to turn it into steam. When we sweat, we use up some of our body energy to turn some of the body's water to sweat, thus cooling the body.

The chemical bonds between the elements that make up the compounds are one of the ways that our bodies store energy. If the elements in a compound are separated, and the bonds broken, there is a release of energy. This can be used in a variety of ways. Some of the compounds in our bodies are very stable, and it takes considerable energy to change them. Others are unstable and separate easily. The energy released is used in many different ways, including heat production, muscle and nerve activity, tissue repair, and cell growth.

In addition to the energy that we receive through the food that we eat (chemical energy), we take in energy from other sources. Sunlight gives us warmth and also stimulates chemical processes, such as the manufacture of vitamin D in the skin. Light and sound waves that reach our bodies through our eyes and ears stimulate activity in our nervous system.

When used to describe physiological processes in the body, the term 'energy' has very different and precise meanings compared to its usage within a healing context. Energy is used by massage therapists to refer to a variety of phenomena including the state of the therapist or client's being (grounded), the atmosphere in the environment, a spiritual quality (higher energy), or the energy fields around and within the body (the chakra and aura). It is used to describe the quality of movement or stagnation in tissues. There is an experiential understanding of energy within this context, sometimes with an emotional component.

Used scientifically, energy always has a specific meaning, defined as the capacity of a system to do work, and is always measurable in some way. Forms of energy are heat, light, sound, gravity, electromagnetic, mechanical and hydraulic.

Living Organisms

The world is made up of living and non-living matter. All living organisms share certain characteristics that make them different from non-living things. Consider what makes daffodils, butterflies, oak trees, frogs, and people different from butter, stones, computers, and windows.

All the organisms in the first category, plant and animal, share certain characteristics. They all:

1. Require food of some kind to fuel basic life processes. This food is taken into the organism, broken down and used to create energy.
2. Have methods of eliminating the waste material left over from this energy making process.
3. Use energy to grow.
4. Have the means of reproducing themselves.
5. Are sensitive to, and can adapt to, changes in both their external and internal environments.
6. Have the ability to move. In the case of most animals, this means being able to move around in the environment. In the case of most plants, this means the ability to move in response to the environment.

Chapter 3 Cells, Tissues, Organs and Body Systems

The Structure of Living Organisms

The basic unit of all living matter, plant and animal, is the cell. Some organisms, such as the amoeba, a microscopic aquatic creature, consist of just one cell, but more commonly, cells are grouped together with lots of other more or less identical cells supported by non-cellular material, to form tissues. The tissues that make up the human body are epithelial and connective tissues, muscle tissue and nervous tissue. The organs of the body are formed from several tissues grouped together. One such organ, the heart, consists of cardiac muscle, lined with epithelial tissue, full of blood (a connective tissue) and powered by nerves. Organs and tissues that function together for a particular purpose within the body are called a system. So, the heart together with the blood vessels and the blood is known as the cardiovascular system.

The Cell

Key Words

Intercellular fluid	Endoplasmic reticulum
Diffusion	Nucleus
Osmosis	Mitochondria
Filtration	Golgi body
Exocytosis	Lysosomes
Endocytosis	Cellular respiration
Pinocytosis	ATP (adenosine triphosphate)
Phagocytosis	Mitosis
Cytoplasm	Neoplasm
Organelles	Cilia
Cell membrane	

Although there are many different types of cells, plant and animal, each type being designed for a particular function and varying according to its location, all cells share some common features, and are able to perform all the functions of living creatures listed in Chapter 2. All cells take in and metabolise food, excrete waste, grow and reproduce, are sensitive to and can adapt to their environments.

The cellular environment: More than half of the human body is composed of water, and all cells are surrounded by a constantly moving fluid, called **intercellular fluid**. The other major fluids of the body are the blood, the lymph and the cerebrospinal fluid that bathes the nervous system. These are all interchangeable with the intercellular fluid that bathes the cells, and contains within it all the components necessary for the maintenance of life.

Because of its ability to dissolve so many substances and to move around the body, water is crucial for life processes. A substance dissolved in a fluid will tend to spread evenly through that fluid by **diffusion**, moving from the areas where it is most concentrated to those of lowest concentration. (This is how sugar disperses through a cup of tea, even without stirring). When two chemicals are dissolved in water, they will diffuse, mix together and more readily react with one another (like adding water to the dry ingredients of a cake mix).

Water is the medium that transports materials around the body. When the water passes passively through a membrane such as the cell wall, attempting to equalise the concentration of dissolved substances ('solutes') on each side of the membrane, the process is known as **osmosis**. Oxygen, salts, simple sugars and amino acids (the building blocks of proteins) are carried into each cell because the cell is constantly using up its supply of them; carbon dioxide and other wastes are carried out of cells into the blood where there is a lower concentration of them.

Wherever possible, the body does this using as little energy as possible. Many of the nutrients that pass from the blood circulation into the intercellular spaces and then into the cells, and the waste products which are carried in the opposite direction are transported by processes that use no energy, such as osmosis and filtration. **Filtration** is the process by which water and its dissolved solutes are forced through a membrane by applied pressure to a place of lower pressure (in the way that fluid drips through a coffee filter under the weight of gravity). Much of the blood fluid is pushed by the pressure of the pulse out of the tiniest blood vessels and into the spaces around the cells.

Sometimes a cell has to use energy to move large molecules across its membrane or to move material in the opposite direction. Nerve cells, for example, do this to keep their sodium and potassium molecules separate until they need to use them to fire messages.

Cells make parcels of material that they wish to actively expel by **exocytosis** (out of the cell). Cells also surround and take in the material that they need by using a section of the cell wall, a process called **endocytosis** (into the cell). **Pinocytosis** (cell drinking) is the routine activity of cells in capturing liquids that contain dissolved proteins or fats. A similar process is also used by the white blood cells to engulf bacteria or dead body cells and destroy them, in which case it is called **phagocytosis** (cell eating).

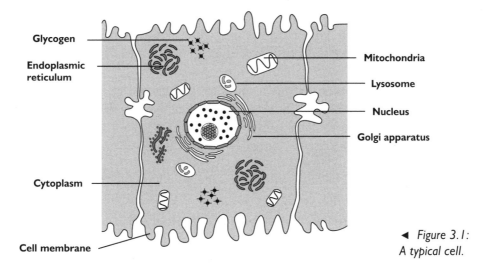

Glycogen
Endoplasmic reticulum
Mitochondria
Lysosome
Nucleus
Golgi apparatus
Cytoplasm
Cell membrane

◄ *Figure 3.1:*
A typical cell.

Cell Structure

Although cells come in many forms, all have certain aspects of their structure in common. All consist of an outer boundary, the **cell membrane**, containing a semisolid substance called **cytoplasm**, and the working parts of the cell, the **organelles**.

The cytoplasm: This is a jelly-like substance, about 70% water, filling the space between the cell membrane, in which the **organelles**, or little organs, of the cell are suspended.

The cell membrane: This is an elastic, porous membrane (skin) which encloses the cell, helps it maintain its structure, and allows the passage of different substances in or out of the cell. It consists of two membranes with a thin layer of fatty substance sandwiched between them. Receptor sites, where large molecules can 'land' and interact with the cell are found on the surfaces of the cell membrane. It separates the internal medium of the cell, the cytoplasm, from the surrounding intercellular fluid.

The endoplasmic reticulum: The cell membrane is continuous with the endoplasmic reticulum, a transportation network of tubular canals running throughout the cytoplasm. Much chemical activity takes place in the endoplasmic reticulum. Chemicals such as fatty acids and hormones, needed for cell activity, are made here, and others are broken down.

The nucleus: The nucleus is the largest of the organelles, often located centrally in the cell. It contains the genes, the coils of chemicals called DNA (deoxyribonucleic acid) and RNA (ribonucleic acid), which encode the genetic information of the cell. The genes are responsible for determining the activity of each cell, as well as the characteristics which are passed on from parent to child in the reproductive cells.

The mitochondria: There are a number of mitochondria in each cell, sometimes called the 'powerhouses', because in these organelles a process called **cellular respiration** takes place, which releases energy. Muscles cells, which are required to work hard, need lots of energy and so contain many more mitochondria than other types of cells.

The Golgi body: The Golgi body is the name for little sacs which absorb waste material from the cell, swell and eventually move to the cell membrane where the waste is released out of the cell into the intercellular fluid.

Lysosomes: These sacs contain enzymes which digest foreign material and are capable of destroying the cell at the end of its useful life, or if it becomes damaged. They are sometimes called 'suicide sacs'. When muscles are not used, they atrophy. This shrinkage happens because lysosomal action has destroyed the non-functioning muscle cells.

Cellular Respiration

There are two substances that our bodies need to take in from outside on a regular basis for all the essential life processes – growing, adapting, moving, reproducing – to take place. One of these, oxygen, we obtain from the atmosphere around us just by breathing, which is also called external respiration. The other, food, we have to go to greater lengths to obtain, and need at much less regular intervals. Oxygen is absorbed straight into the blood, but food has to be broken down into smaller components before it can be absorbed. Both are carried round the body in the blood supply, diffuse into the intercellular fluid, are absorbed into the cell and used in the process called cellular, or internal, respiration, which takes place continuously in the mitochondria of every cell in the body.

When the nutrients, either glucose, fatty acids or amino acids, combine with oxygen, they help to create a complex chemical compound called **adenosine triphosphate**, or **ATP**, and water and carbon dioxide. This chemical reaction is written as:

Food + Oxygen > ATP + Water + Carbon Dioxide

ATP is sometimes referred to as the 'energy currency' of the body because it contains the energy required to power the cellular functions of the body, including muscle contraction. Each molecule is one part adenosine to three parts phosphate. The bond between the third phosphate part and the rest is very unstable, and when it breaks, energy is released, and the compound becomes adenosine diphosphate, or ADP. During cellular respiration, the split off third phosphate part is reconnected, so ADP becomes ATP again. Water and carbon dioxide are the by-products of the reaction, and are removed from the cell.

$$\text{ATP} \qquad \rightarrow \qquad \text{ADP}$$

\(\widetilde{\text{Adenosine}}\) Ⓟ Ⓟ Ⓟ ➜ \(\widetilde{\text{Adenosine}}\) Ⓟ Ⓟ + ENERGY ➜ Ⓟ

Cell Reproduction

Most cells reproduce themselves through a process called **mitosis**. First, the genes in the nucleus divide into two equal halves, followed by the rest of the nucleus through the four stages of prophase, metaphase, anaphase, and telophase. Then, as the cytoplasm and organelles divide, the cell membrane moves in and separates the contents into two distinct and identical cells.

Abnormal Cell Growths

Normally, there are many controls on the rate of cell reproduction. When these do not operate as they should, cells can suddenly multiply and form an abnormal cell mass called a **neoplasm**. Some of these are benign. Cysts, for example, grow within a capsule and merely put pressure on local structures as they grow; they can be surgically removed without problems. Others, such as cancer cells, can infiltrate into other cells and tissues and disrupt normal functioning and destroy tissues; they can also spread to distant parts of the body.

Cell Movement

Most cells remain embedded in their surrounding tissue, but a few types, for example white blood cells, are able to wander throughout the tissues. They do this through ameboid movement. The cell membrane extends an 'arm', the cytoplasm flows into it, followed by the rest of the cell. Certain other cells have the potential to create movement in the intercellular fluids by waving the hair like projections, called **cilia**, on the external surface of the cell membrane. The cells lining the inside of the nasal passages move the mucus secretions in this way (*see* figure 3.2).

Tissues

Tissues are groups of cells that are similar in form and similar in function. Tissues cover, support and move the body and convey information. There are four categories:

1. Epithelial tissue, which covers the surface of the body, and lines the internal surface of the vessels, tubes and organs.
2. Connective tissue, which binds, connects and supports all the internal structures of the body.
3. Muscle tissue, which has the property of contraction, and creates movement.
4. Nervous tissue, which has the ability to carry information.

Epithelial (lining) Tissue

Key Words

Epithelial: squamous / columnar / cuboid / cilia / simple / stratified / transitional / glandular
Membranes: serous / mucous / synovial

Epithelial cells are arranged in flat sheets of epithelial tissue, sometimes only one cell thick, which form the outer layer of the skin and line the inner surfaces of the vessels,

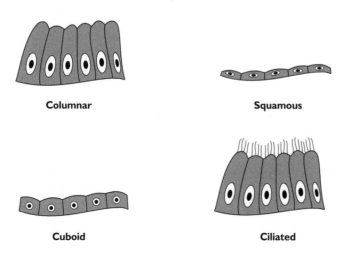

Columnar

Squamous

Cuboid

Ciliated

◄ *Figure 3.2: Different types of epithelial tissue.*

tubes and organs. They have no internal blood circulation, but receive nourishment in the fluid that diffuses from blood vessels in the underlying connective tissue.

Epithelial cells vary in shape depending on the location and their function. **Squamous** epithelium, found lining the heart and blood vessels, for example, consists of flat squashed cells that allow for rapid movement of gases in and out. It also forms the serous membranes (described below). **Columnar** epithelial cells, found in the intestine, which absorb and secrete foodstuffs, are column-shaped. Some columnar cells produce mucus from a central cavity; these are called goblet cells. In the kidneys, **cuboid** epithelium is made up of cube shaped cells. Some epithelial cells have cilia on their external surface. In the windpipe, the **cilia** move mucus, and in the Fallopian tubes, move the egg cell from the ovary to the womb.

Epithelium tissue that is only one layer of cells thick is called **simple** epithelium. This type occurs where there is rapid passage of gases or fluids, for example, in the air sacs of the lungs and the section of the digestive tract from which foodstuffs are absorbed. In the skin and the first part of the digestive tract, where there is more wear and tear, the epithelium contains more than one layer of cells, usually of squamous tissue, and is called **stratified** epithelium. The cells here are formed from the underlying blood vessels, so that the deepest layer of the tissue is renewed as the outer layer is worn away.

The largest sheet of epithelial tissue in the body is the outer layer of the skin (*see* Chapter 12).

Transitional epithelium is multi-layered tissue that forms the lining of the urinary system – the bladder and the urinary tubes. At rest, it is quite thick but, as the bladder and tubes fill, it stretches and thins. Exocrine and endocrine glands are made of **glandular** epithelial tissue.

Membranes

Sheets of epithelial tissue inside the body are sometimes called **membranes**. There are three kinds:

1. Serous
2. Mucous
3. Synovial membranes

They all secrete a lubricating fluid that reduces friction. **Serous** membranes are those that line the body cavities that have no connection with the outside of the body. In the chest or thoracic cavity, the lining around the heart is a serous membrane called the pericardium and the lining around the lungs is called the pleural membrane; the abdominal cavity is lined by the peritoneum. **Mucous** membranes line body spaces that have an opening to the outer world, like the respiratory and digestive and reproductive tracts. **Synovial** membranes line joints (*see* Chapter 6).

Connective Tissue

Key Words

Bone
Blood
Matrix: sol / gel
Fibroblasts
Fibrous: areolar / adipose / dense / elastic / reticular
Fibres: collagen / elastin
Cartilage: hyaline or articular / fibrocartilage / elastic

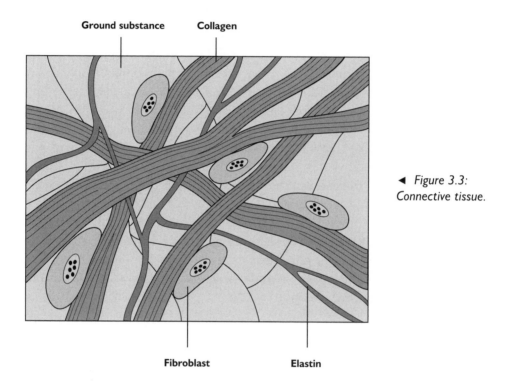

Ground substance   **Collagen**

Fibroblast   **Elastin**

◄ *Figure 3.3: Connective tissue.*

Connective tissue wraps every muscle, nerve, bone and organ in the body. It is packed round cells in the tissues, joins muscle and bone, and joins skin to underlying tissue. It wraps, binds, supports, connects, stores and facilitates movement. It can be either elastic or inelastic, liquid or solid. It includes the hardest substance in the body, **bone**, and one of the fluids, **blood**. The factor that all types have in common is their structure.

Structure of Connective Tissue

All connective tissue has three components. There is a **matrix**, or ground substance, containing cells called **fibroblasts**, and fibres made of protein. The matrix is not living matter, and varies in texture. It can be like a runny syrup or a gel, or, like the matrix of bone, so full of minerals that it is solid. The consistency of the matrix can change from a fluid – **sol** – state, to a jelly – **gel** – state if heated. Some connective tissues tend to harden and dry up with age, and lose this ability to shift from sol to gel. The cells, the living component, are called fibroblasts. These secrete both the matrix and the fibres, and are able to migrate around the body as needed. Scar tissue, for example, is formed by fibroblasts that have travelled to the site of the injury. Other types of cell are found in some connective tissues. Fat cells make up the bulk of the adipose tissue of the skin, for example, and white blood cells involved in defending the body against infection are found in reticular tissue in the liver.

The solidity and pliability of the tissue depends on the type, density and arrangement of the **fibres**. The most common sort are the long white collagen fibres. These are tough, and rope-like, and can bend, but not stretch. They give strength and structure to tissues. The yellowish elastin fibres are stretchy and rubbery. Reticulin fibres are much finer than both of these, and usually found packed round and supporting groups of cells in tissues. The fibres in blood are those involved in clotting.

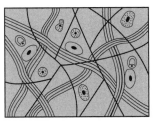

Areolar tissue

Dense connective tissue

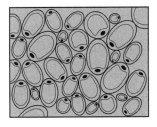

Adipose connective tissue

◄ *Figure 3.4: Different types of connective tissue.*

The categories of connective tissue are blood, bone, the fibrous connective tissues and cartilage (*see* Chapters 6 and 16 for more detail on bone and blood).

Fibrous Connective Tissue

Areolar tissue, also called loose connective tissue, is soft and pliable, consisting of a loose network of fibres with lots of open spaces between. To the naked eye, it looks like a cross between white tissue paper and cling film. It connects the skin to tissue underneath in a continuous sheet throughout the body. This is called the superficial fascia. It also wraps round the muscles, vessels and nerves, the internal organs, and the individual fibres within the muscles.

Adipose tissue (fatty tissue) is packed with fat cells, and is found under the skin, forming a protective cushion around organs, and in the marrow of long bones.

Dense connective tissue contains many **collagen** fibres arranged in wavy bundles, giving a glistening white appearance. It is very strong, inelastic and stretches only very slightly. Most ligaments and all tendons are made of dense connective tissue.

Elastic tissue contains more **elastin** fibres arranged randomly, and can stretch and return to its normal size. The lungs, respiratory tubes and blood vessels are made of elastic connective tissue. Some ligaments, such as those between the vertebrae, are elastic tissue.

Reticular tissue is a mesh of tissue, which forms the framework for some organs, such as the liver, spleen and lymph glands. Within reticular tissue are specialised cells to fight infection, called phagocytes.

Cartilage

The matrix in cartilage is both hard and flexible, making it a supportive rather than binding connective tissue. There is no blood supply, so cartilage heals very slowly if damaged. There is also no nerve supply, so cartilage is insensitive.

Hyaline or **articular** cartilage is the smooth, glassy cartilage found at the ends of bones in synovial joints, where it eases movement. It also forms the template for bones during embryonic development.

Fibrocartilage is found in the discs between the vertebrae, and between the pubic bones. **Elastic cartilage** contains more elastin, making it tough but flexible and is found in the external ear, the end of the nose and the larynx.

Muscle Tissue

Key Words

Skeletal / striated
Smooth / visceral
Cardiac

All muscle cells have the ability to contract, which gives muscle tissue its elasticity and power to move. Muscle tissue also contains blood vessels to supply the food and oxygen required for the work of the muscle cells, and nerves which stimulate the muscle tissue to move, and nerves which transmit messages to the brain about the state of the tissue. There are three types of muscle tissue. (There is more detail about the structure and function of all these in Chapter 7):

1. **Skeletal**, or **striated** muscle which attaches to and moves the skeleton.
2. **Smooth**, or **visceral** muscle which is found in internal organs with elastic walls such as the stomach and the bladder.
3. The heart, or **cardiac** muscle.

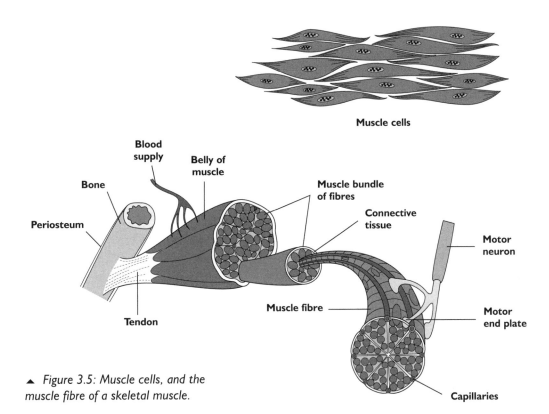

▲ Figure 3.5: Muscle cells, and the muscle fibre of a skeletal muscle.

Nervous Tissue

Key Words

Neuron
Glial cell

Nervous tissue consists of nerve cells, or **neurons**, which have the ability to transmit messages via the many long thin extensions arising from the cell body, and **glial** cells, which surround, and may provide nutritional support for the nerve cells within the central nervous system. Nervous tissue is found in the brain, spinal cord and the nerves (*see* Chapter 9).

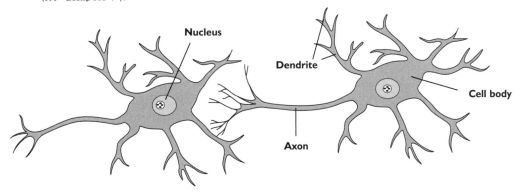

▲ Figure 3.6: Nervous tissue.

Body Fluids

As well as the four types of tissue that make up the organs of the body, there are the body fluids that transport essential chemicals, heat and some cells, around the body. These are the liquid part of the blood, called plasma; the lymphatic fluid; the liquid that bathes the central nervous system, called the cerebrospinal fluid, and the intercellular fluid. These fluids move as a continuous watery medium, although the chemical balance in each varies.

Organs

All the organs of the body are composed of a mixture of these four basic types of tissue. For example, the wall of the heart is cardiac muscle, covered with areolar connective tissue, and supplied with blood, another form of connective tissue. The cavities are lined with epithelial tissue, and the activity of the whole organ is maintained by the action of nerve tissue. The brain, however, is an organ with a very different structure. Here, the main tissue is nervous tissue, with the nerve cells and nerve fibres arranged in complex multilayered structures, covered by three layers of dura mater, which is made of connective tissue, and bathed in cerebrospinal fluid, one of the body's specialised fluids. The walls of the intestines, another example, are smooth muscle, lined with epithelial tissue, and covered with connective tissue.

Systems of the Body

Although the body works as an integrated whole, and no one part can function independently, it is divided into systems for ease of understanding. There are systems responsible for growth and repair, movement, transmission of information, transportation, defence against infection or disease, removal of waste and reproduction. Each system contains organs or tissues designed to carry out its function. Some systems, such as the cardiovascular system, have more than one main role.

Key Words

Skeletal system   Digestive system
Muscular system (musculoskeletal system)   Cardiovascular system
Nervous system   Urinary system
Endocrine system   Integumentary system
Immune system   Reproductive system
Respiratory system

Movement Systems

The **skeletal system** comprises the bones, the joints and the ligaments that hold them together. It provides a supporting framework for the body and provides points of attachments for the skeletal muscles so that movement can occur. The bones store fat and minerals, and blood cells are made in some bone cavities.

The **muscular system** includes all three types of muscle tissue with the unique property of contraction. These types are skeletal muscles that attach to and move bone, smooth muscles lining the organs, blood vessels and digestive tract, and cardiac muscle forming the wall of the heart.

Sometimes these two systems are referred to together as the **musculoskeletal system**.

Transmission of Information

The **nervous system**, the brain, spinal cord and nerves, receives messages from the internal environment of the body, and from the outside world through the senses. The brain receives information and sends messages to the muscles and glands to act. The information is transmitted both by electrical impulses and messenger chemicals called neurotransmitters. The **endocrine system** consists of glands that secrete chemicals called hormones, which also transmit information around the body. The **immune system** alerts and mobilises the body to deal with damage to tissues from foreign organisms, trauma or homeostatic failure through a complex system of specialised tissue in the lymphatic system, the spleen, specialised white blood cells and messenger chemicals called cytokines.

Growth and Repair

The substances needed for growth and repair are oxygen and food, and responsibility for absorbing these into the body lie with the **respiratory system** and the **digestive system**. The nose, respiratory tract, lungs and diaphragm are the organs of respiration and gaseous exchange.

The digestive system, consisting of the digestive tract (mouth, oesophagus, stomach, intestines, rectum and anus) and the associated organs (liver, pancreas and gall bladder), is responsible for breaking down, absorbing and storing food.

Transportation

Oxygen, carbon dioxide, hormones, antibodies, foods, heat, and wastes such as urea, are transported round the body by the **cardiovascular system**. This includes both the circulatory system, a closed loop of arteries, veins and capillaries using the heart as a pump, and the lymphatic system, a network of fine vessels that drain intercellular fluid from the tissue spaces and return it to the blood circulation, and the lymph nodes and spleen.

Removal of Waste

The **urinary system** has two kidneys that filter the blood, via a pair of tubes called the ureters, to the storage bladder. The bladder has a tube, called the urethra, to the outside, for the secretion of the urine. A large component in urine is urea, a protein by-product of many physiological processes. The kidneys also regulate the water and salt content of the body.

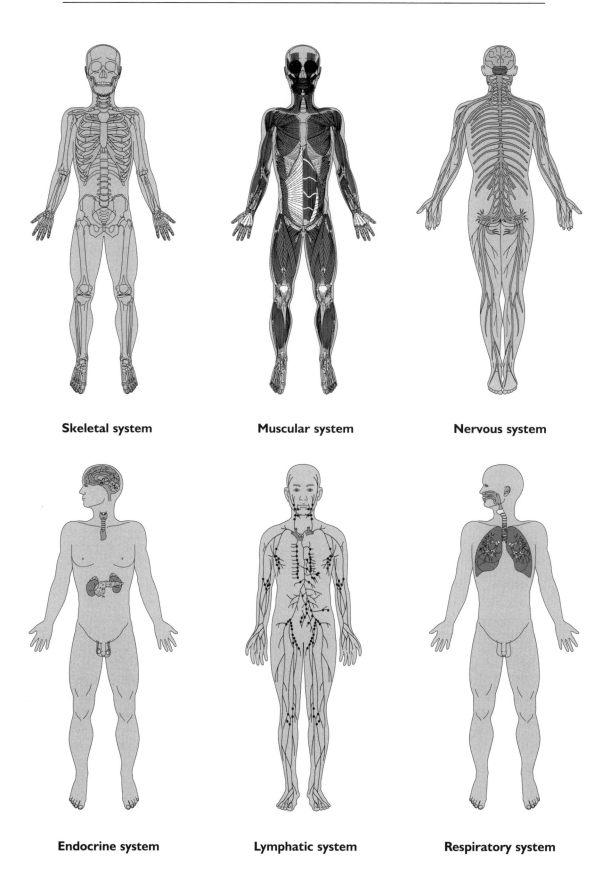

Skeletal system

Muscular system

Nervous system

Endocrine system

Lymphatic system

Respiratory system

▲ *Figure 3.7: The systems of the body.*

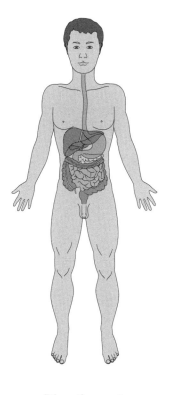

Digestive system

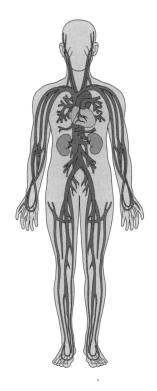

Circulatory system

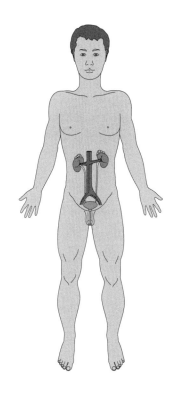

Urinary system

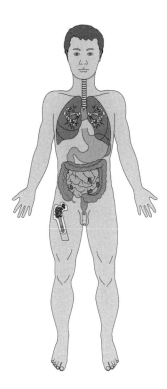

Immune system

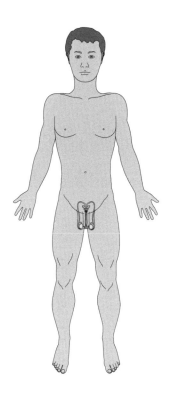

Reproductive system (male)

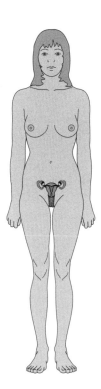

Reproductive system (female)

Holding it all together is the **integumentary system**, the skin and its appendages which surrounds the body and is the boundary between it and its environment. The skin has a sensory function, transmitting information about heat, touch and pain, and a waste removal function, as small amounts of waste are secreted in sweat. As a protective membrane, it helps defend the body against invaders. But its most important function is homeostatic, as it helps regulate body temperature through sweating or shivering, combined with dilation and constriction of blood vessels at the surface of the body.

Reproduction

Finally, there are the **reproductive systems** (both male and female), responsible for the creation of new human beings, the development of the secondary sexual characteristics at puberty, and the changes that occur during menopause. The ovaries produce egg cells, or ova, which are shed monthly into the uterus in a woman. If an ovum connects with a sperm cell from a man, conception occurs and the cells bed down in the uterus wall for nine months until the foetus is ready to come into the world. The development of the reproductive systems at puberty, and subsequent activity, is regulated by the endocrine system.

Section 2
The Movement Systems

Movement of the body is provided by the musculoskeletal system – the muscles moving the bones – activated, monitored and co-ordinated by the nervous system (*see* Chapter 9). This section firstly covers the names and anatomical landmarks of the main bones and joints, which are reference points for locating the muscles and the other soft tissues that cover them. The general structure and function of bones, joints and muscles are then considered, their most common disorders and considerations for massage. There is also a chapter on the main muscles that are relevant to the massage practitioner, focusing particularly on locating their position and understanding the movements that they produce.

As you study the musculoskeletal system, it is worth bearing in mind that the diagrams and descriptions that follow, and those in other books, refer to a body of average proportions, with the skeleton and musculature on the right and left sides being of equal size.

However, not everyone is born with the same number of muscles and bones. For example, about 10% of the population do not have the palmaris longus muscle, a muscle of the forearm that extends into the palm. The authors of this book have also had massage clients who were born with other musculoskeletal variations, e.g. people with six toes on each foot, or with an additional vertebra in the neck or lower back.

Additionally, our bodies are affected by the way that we use them in everyday life. Most people, for example, have a dominant hand that is used more than the other hand and consequently develops more. This difference will be most marked in a person who consistently uses only the dominant hand, for example a professional tennis player. In such a person, the massage practitioner will be able to see and feel the extra muscle development in the dominant arm, shoulder and the upper back. X-rays would also reveal some thickening of the bones in these areas, and greater density in the bone tissues, when compared to the other side of the body.

While the contrasts are not as obvious in most people, everyone has some small differences that will be palpable to the massage practitioner and may be due to postural habits, adaptations to work situations and leisure activities, or in response to accidents, injuries or emotional traumas.

Chapter 4 Terms of Position and Movement

Key Words

Position	**Movement**
Anatomical position	Flexion
Anterior	Extension
Posterior	Hyperextension
Superior	Abduction
Inferior	Adduction
Proximal	Lateral flexion
Distal	Rotation
Medial	Circumduction
Lateral	Supination
Superficial	Pronation
Deep	Dorsiflexion
Prone	Plantar flexion
Supine	Inversion
	Eversion

To help understand the bones and muscles, it is useful to know some of the terms that are used to locate parts of the body in relation to one another and to describe the movements of the body.

Anatomical Divisions of the Body

Some terms have a precise meaning in anatomical terminology that differs from their common language meaning. You will be able to work out from the context which way the words are being used.

The body is divided into head, trunk, upper limbs and lower limbs. The upper limb is divided into the upper arm (sometimes just called the 'arm'), the forearm and the hand. The lower limb is divided into the thigh, the lower leg (often just called the 'leg'), and the foot.

Anatomical Terms of Position

The **anatomical position** is the position of the body to which all the terms of position and movement refer. It is defined as the body standing erect, facing forwards, with the arms hanging at the sides and palms facing front. This is probably based on the position of dissections – a corpse lying on a table with palms up. The terms of position are grouped in pairs. Each of the paired terms is relative to the other.

ANTERIOR. Towards the front surface of the body **OR** the front surface of a body part.
POSTERIOR. Towards the back surface of the body **OR** the back surface of a body part.

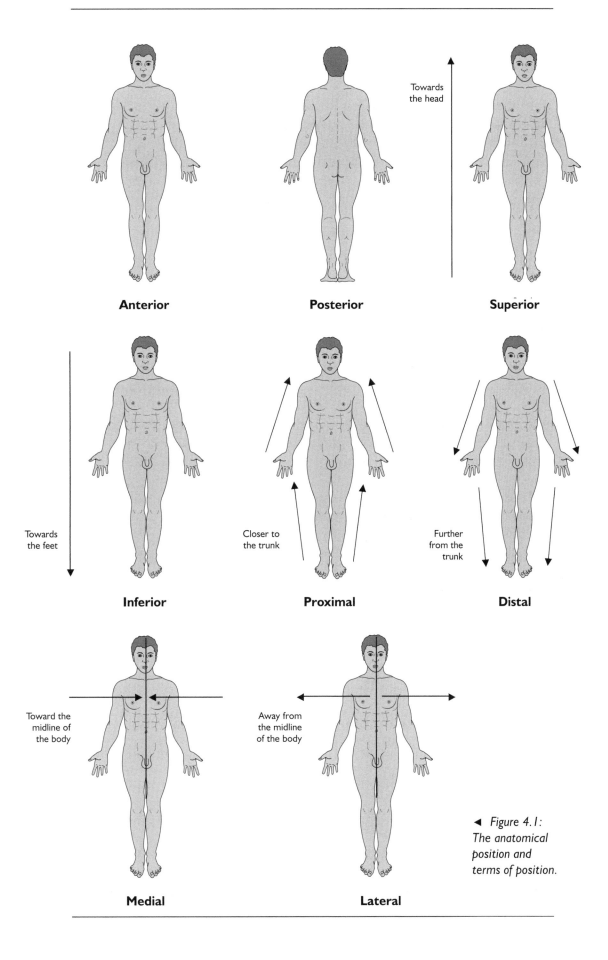

Anterior

Posterior

Towards
the head

Superior

Towards
the feet

Inferior

Closer to
the trunk

Proximal

Further
from the
trunk

Distal

Toward the
midline of
the body

Medial

Away from
the midline
of the body

Lateral

◄ *Figure 4.1:*
The anatomical
position and
terms of position.

Examples: In the foot, the toes are anterior to the heel. The anterior and posterior surfaces of the knee (the front and back).

Note that the back surface of the body is sometimes also referred to as the **DORSAL** surface. This term is particularly used in relation to the trunk.

This terminology can also be used for the hands and feet. The back surface of the hand is called the dorsum of the hand; the top of the foot is called the dorsum or dorsal surface. Conversely the palm of the hand is called the **PALMAR** surface, and the sole of the foot is called the **PLANTAR** surface.

SUPERIOR. Above **OR** the top end or top surface of a body part.
INFERIOR. Below **OR** the bottom end or bottom surface of a body part.

Examples: The chest is superior to the abdomen, but inferior to the head. The superior and inferior ends of the windpipe.

Note that this terminology is in relation to the anatomical position, and always remains the same, no matter the position of the body. Even if you are hanging upside down, the head is always considered superior to the ribs – in the same way that we consider the left hand to always be the left hand, even when we place it on the right side of the body. Inferior and superior are used in describing the trunk and the head. In the limbs, a different terminology is generally used.

PROXIMAL. Closer to the root of the limb (where the limb joins the trunk).
DISTAL. Further away from the root of the limb.

Example: The proximal or distal end of the shinbone.

The bones in each section of the toes, fingers and thumbs are called 'phalanges'. The bone in each finger nearest to the hand is the proximal phalanx; the furthest section is the distal phalanx.

There is an imagined midline between the right and left sides of the body. The next terms describe positions in relation to that line.

MEDIAL. Towards the midline of the body.
LATERAL. Away from the midline of the body.

Example: The arms are lateral to the trunk.

In the limbs, the medial surface is the surface closer to the midline of the trunk, and the lateral surface is furthest away.

Note that the lateral surface of the forearm (the thumb side) is always referred to as the lateral surface, even when the forearm is turned so that the thumb is closest to the body.

SUPERFICIAL. At, close to **OR** closer to the surface of the body.
DEEP. Away from the surface of the body.

Example: The lungs are deep to the ribs. The skin is superficial to the muscles. The superficial (outer) surface of the cranium, and the deep surface (inner).

There are two terms for the position of the whole body when it is lying down.

PRONE. Is lying with the front (anterior) surface downwards.
SUPINE. Is lying with the back (posterior) surface downwards.

This terminology also applies to the forearms and hands – prone is palms down; supine is with palms up (*see* figure 4.6).

Movement Terminology

Many of the movement terms are also in pairs. One term is applied to a movement in a certain direction and the other applied to the opposite movement. They are all used in relation to the anatomical position.

FLEXION. Bending of the trunk or bending at a joint – bringing it towards the foetal position.
EXTENSION. Straightening a limb – towards the anatomical position.
HYPEREXTENSION. Extension of the trunk or neck that takes it backwards beyond the anatomical position.

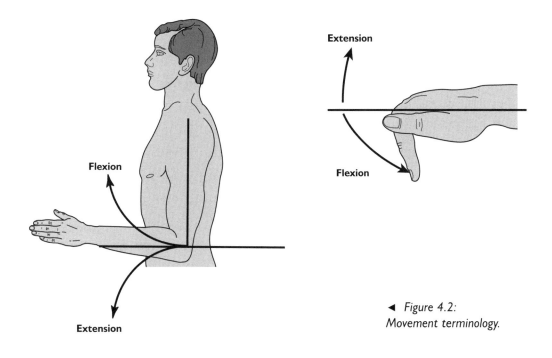

◄ *Figure 4.2:*
Movement terminology.

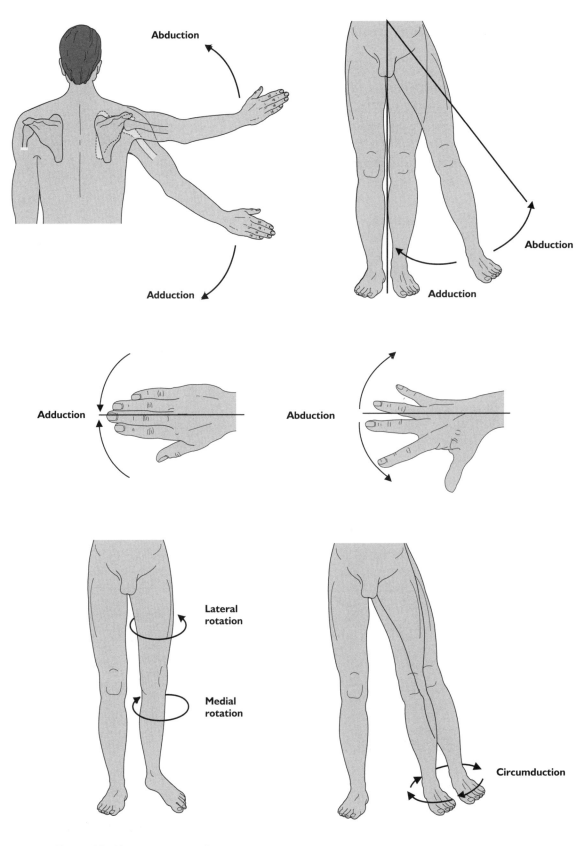

▲ Figure 4.3: Movement terminology.

Examples: Bending up the forearm at the elbow, curling up the fingers or bending the lower leg back, are all described as flexion. Straightening the elbow, the fingers or the knee are called extension. Curling the trunk towards the foetal position is called flexion.

Note the terminology used at the shoulder and hip joints, as it can be confusing. Flexion of the arm, which can also be described as flexion at the shoulder, is lifting the arm forward; extension is lifting the arm backwards. Flexion at the hips, which can also be described as flexion of the leg, is lifting the leg forward; extension is taking the leg backwards. There is also special terminology for the movements of the foot – plantar flexion, dorsiflexion, inversion and eversion (*see* page 38).

ABDUCTION. Moving a limb away from the midline of the body.
ADDUCTION. Moving a limb towards the midline of the body.

Examples: Lifting the arm out sideways from the body (abduction), and lowering it back to the side of the body (adduction).

Note that the term adduction also describes moving the limb across the midline (e.g. taking the arm across in front or behind the body towards the opposite shoulder).

These terms are also used within the hand and foot to describe fanning out the fingers or toes from the midline (abduction) or bringing them together (adduction).

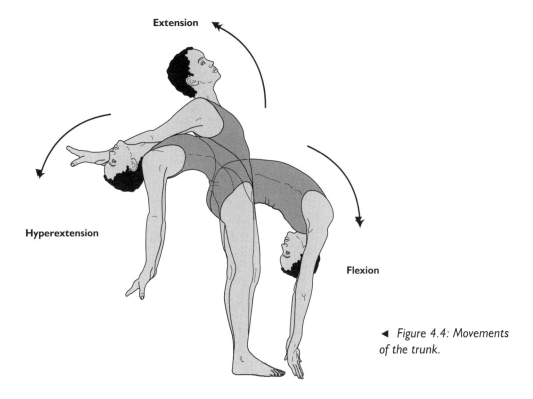

◄ *Figure 4.4: Movements of the trunk.*

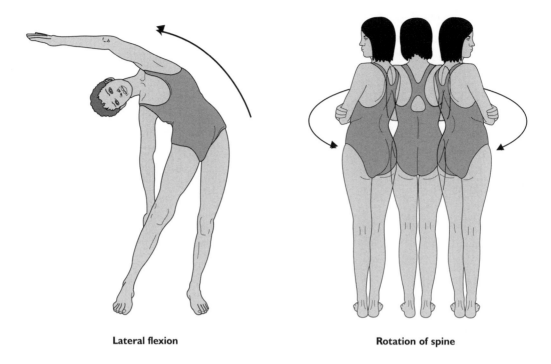

Lateral flexion   **Rotation of spine**

▲ *Figure 4.5: Movements of the trunk.*

LATERAL FLEXION. Side bending of the trunk.

ROTATION. Twisting of the trunk or a limb around its own axis. The limbs can be rotated either medially or laterally.

Examples: Turning the head to look behind oneself (rotation of the neck). Turning the leg so that the foot turns outwards is called lateral rotation (or sometimes, external rotation). Turning the leg so that the foot turns inwards is called medial rotation (or internal rotation).

CIRCUMDUCTION. Sweeping a limb through a cone shape in space, that incorporates flexion, extension, abduction and adduction.

There are two terms that distinguish the turning movements of the forearm from rotatory movements of the whole arm (at the shoulder joint).

SUPINATION. Turning the forearm so that the palms turn upwards ('for soup').
PRONATION. Turning the forearm so that the palms turn downwards.

To avoid possible confusion, there are specific terms for movements of the feet.

DORSIFLEXION. Bending up the top of the foot (the dorsal surface).
PLANTAR FLEXION. Bending down the sole of the foot (the plantar surface), pointing the toes downwards.

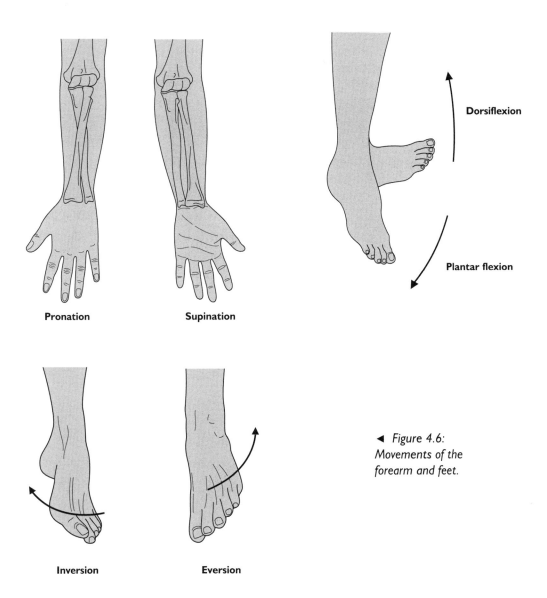

Pronation   Supination

Dorsiflexion

Plantar flexion

Inversion   Eversion

◀ *Figure 4.6:*
Movements of the
forearm and feet.

INVERSION. Turning the foot so that the sole faces inwards.
EVERSION. Turning the foot so that the sole faces outwards.

Chapter 5 Main Bones of the Skeleton

The human skeleton is bilaterally symmetrical (the same on the left and right sides). It has two main parts called the axial and appendicular skeletons, which are distinctly different in structure and function.

The **axial skeleton** forms the central axis of the body. It consists of the bones of the skull, the neck and the trunk (the spine, the ribs and the breastbone).

The **appendicular skeleton** is the appendages – the limbs. This part consists of the bones of the limbs themselves, and the bones that connect them with the axial skeleton. The arm is connected by the shoulder girdle (the collarbone and the shoulder blade) and the leg by the 'hip' bones (the innominate bones of the pelvis).

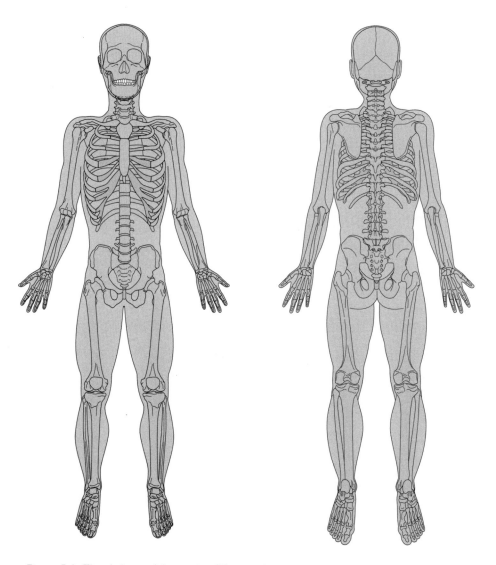

▲ *Figure 5.1: The skeleton, (a) anterior, (b) posterior.*

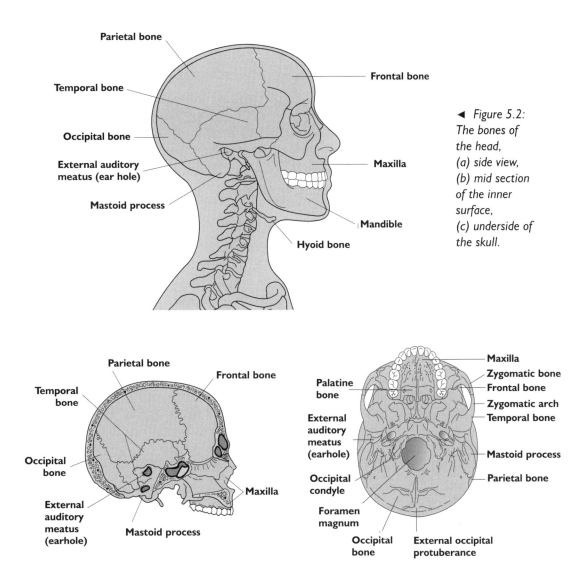

◀ *Figure 5.2: The bones of the head, (a) side view, (b) mid section of the inner surface, (c) underside of the skull.*

Axial Skeleton

The **head** is made up of eight cranial bones, fourteen facial bones, the hyoid bone in the throat and three tiny bones called ossicles in each ear, which are part of the hearing mechanism. Each ear and most of the external parts of the nose are made of cartilage.

The **cranial bones** form a solid container, the brain 'box' that surrounds and protects the brain. The inner surface is lined by membranes, the meninges, that in turn contain a fluid. Together, these cushion the brain from jarring against the bony cranium in the course of ordinary daily activities. There are many small holes through the bones for the passage of nerves that connect mainly to the muscles and sensory organs of the head.

At birth, these bones have soft areas of membrane called 'fontanelles' between them to allow the baby's head to adapt to the birth canal. As the child grows, all the bones of the skull gradually grow together along 'sewing' lines called 'sutures', except at the connection between the upper and lower jaw. The bones of the top of the skull are relatively smooth and evenly curved. At the front, the **frontal bone** makes up the forehead and the upper part of the eye socket. The cranial bones below it spread back under the brain, forming part of the nasal cavity and connecting to many of the facial bones.

The back surface of the skull, from about halfway down, is formed by the occiput (**occipital bone**) which also forms the posterior part of the underside of the skull. This under-shelf extends quite some way under the skull, providing a large area for the attachment of the many layers of muscles in the neck that hold the head upright and move it around.

Towards the front of this under-shelf is the large hole called the foramen magnum through which the nerves of the brain stem exit from the cranium to form the spinal cord. In four-legged animals, this hole is much higher on the back of the skull. Because we humans stand upright, it is directly under the skull. In front of the foramen magnum, there are two small bumps called condyles on either side, via which the occiput sits on the first vertebra. The head can rock on these to give a small nodding movement – nodding 'yes'.

Between the frontal bone and the occiput, two **parietal bones** join at the top and extend about halfway down each side. Below them at each side of the head, a **temporal bone** extends from the temples back to the occiput, and some distance under the head. It contains the ear hole and also forms the back part of the cheekbone. Just behind the ear, there is a lump of bone under the skull called the mastoid process, which serves as an attachment place for muscles. 'Process' is a general name for a bony projection and this one looks a little like a breast, so it is called mastoid, meaning 'breast-shaped'.

The front of the skull is formed by the **facial bones**. They are all strongly interlinked with each other, apart from the lower jaw, forming the bony surface underlying the face, the front of the cheek bone, the bony parts of the nose, the upper palate of the mouth, and the upper jaw – the **maxilla**.

Many of these bones contain sinus cavities that make the bones lighter. These are hollow spaces, some of which are lined with mucus producing membranes. Those close to the nasal cavity are connected to it and contribute to a person's vocal quality. 'Sinusitis' is the condition in which they become inflamed, usually due to upper respiratory tract infections.

The lower jaw, the **mandible**, is the largest and strongest of the facial bones. It is the only bone of the head with any significant mobility, apart from the hyoid. There are two large muscles that move it for the important activity, in terms of survival, of chewing. It forms a joint with the temporal bone – the temporomandibular joint (TMJ). When the jaw is held tight, TMJ problems can develop, including grinding the teeth, aching jaw and headaches.

The **hyoid** is a small, horseshoe shaped 'floating' bone. It is not attached to any other bones, but is held in place by small muscles that form the base of the mouth and the front of the neck. These muscles move the hyoid when a person swallows. It also serves as a base for some of the muscles of the tongue. Because it is commonly removed with the muscles in dissection, it is often missing from display skeletons.

The breastbone at the front and twelve pairs of ribs that attach to the spine at the back make up the **ribcage**. In four legged animals, it hangs down between their front legs, being narrow from side to side and quite deep from the spine forward to the breastbone. By contrast, in humans, it is wide from side to side and narrow from front to back.

The **breastbone**, called the **sternum**, is at the front of the chest. It is only present in creatures that have front limbs, as it gives leverage for the muscles that move these limbs in front of the body. This is most obvious in the skeletons of large-winged birds, where it forms the central keel of the bird's chest to anchor its wing muscles. In humans it is a flat, dagger-like bone, made up in the adult of three fused parts, although the lower one (the xiphoid process) which forms the 'point' of the dagger may remain as cartilage, or even be absent.

The **ribs** are long, flat 'straps' of bone, which are higher at the front, curve down at the side of the body and rise up again at the back where they connect to the spine. At the back they form joints with the ribs, which allow some movement. Of the twelve pairs of ribs, only the upper seven pairs join directly to the sternum at the front by flexible **costal cartilage** ('costal' meaning 'of the ribs'). These are described as 'true ribs'.

The lower five pairs are called 'false ribs'. Pairs eight to ten usually have cartilage at the front that joins onto the cartilage of the seventh pair. The eleventh and twelfth pairs are

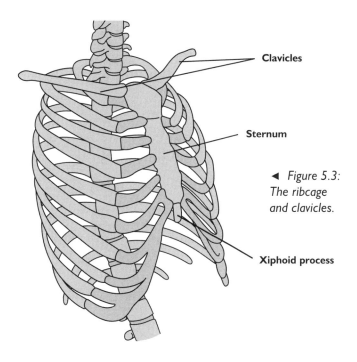

Clavicles

Sternum

◄ *Figure 5.3:*
The ribcage
and clavicles.

Xiphoid process

'floating ribs', the lowest one being much shorter. They do not extend to the front of the body but end in the muscular wall of the waist.

The ribs maintain the integrity of the chest wall, and protect the lungs, heart and the organs of the upper abdomen. The ribs play a part in breathing, in that they are lifted by muscles to help expand the chest for inhalation and drop back down again in exhalation. This action is often compared to that of lifting and lowering the handle of a bucket. There are occasional variations in the number of ribs. Some people have only eleven pairs, or some have a cervical rib or a lumbar rib. These extra ribs are usually short and can be problematic as they may interfere with the free movements of muscles.

The **spine** is the 'backbone' of the body and can be viewed as the physical core of the body, the central axis around which everything else balances. This centrality of the spine begins in our individual development in the womb, where the forerunner of the spine forms a distinct shape quite some time before limb buds appear. Many systems of bodywork, particularly those that use physical activity as a path to self-development, emphasise the role of the spine. In Yoga, for example, it is said that keeping the spine supple keeps the body young.

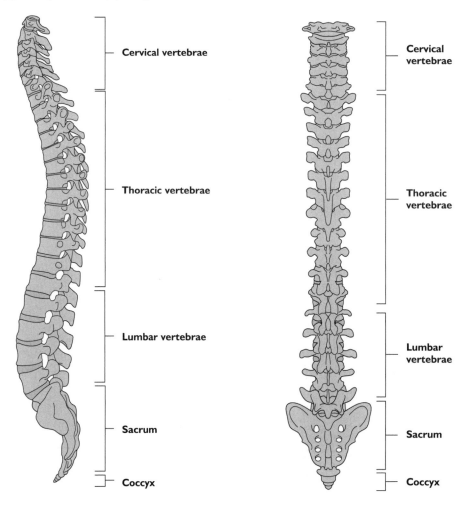

▲ *Figure 5.4: The spine, (a) lateral view, (b) posterior view.*

Adults usually have twenty-six separate bones in the spine. These consist of thirty-three bony segments called vertebrae. In adults, the upper twenty-four remain separate, but the sacrum consists of five fused vertebrae and the coccyx of four fused vertebrae (*see* below). The spine is divided into sections, according to the structure and functioning of the vertebrae.

There are seven small vertebrae in the neck – the **cervical** region. This is the common number for all mammals, even giraffes, whose cervical vertebrae are very large. The name 'cervix' means neck and is the same one used for the 'neck' of the womb in the female reproductive system.

Next, there are twelve **thoracic** vertebrae, each with a pair of ribs attaching to it with one rib on each side. This is the equivalent area to the thorax of an insect such as a bee.

Five **lumbar** vertebrae make up the lower back. These are the largest single vertebrae.

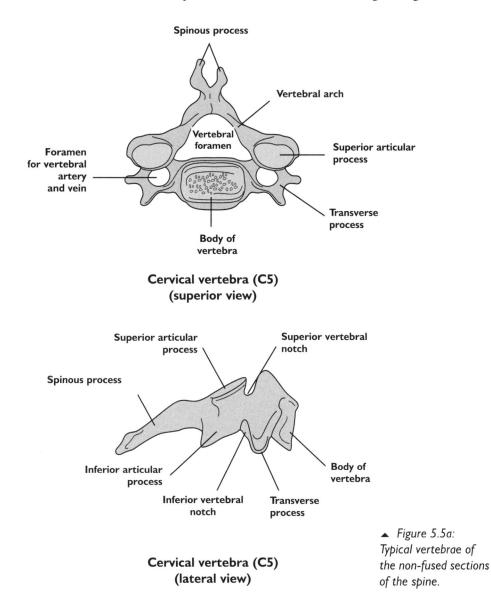

Spinous process

Vertebral arch

Vertebral foramen

Foramen for vertebral artery and vein

Superior articular process

Transverse process

Body of vertebra

Cervical vertebra (C5)
(superior view)

Superior articular process

Superior vertebral notch

Spinous process

Inferior articular process

Inferior vertebral notch

Transverse process

Body of vertebra

Cervical vertebra (C5)
(lateral view)

▲ *Figure 5.5a:*
Typical vertebrae of the non-fused sections of the spine.

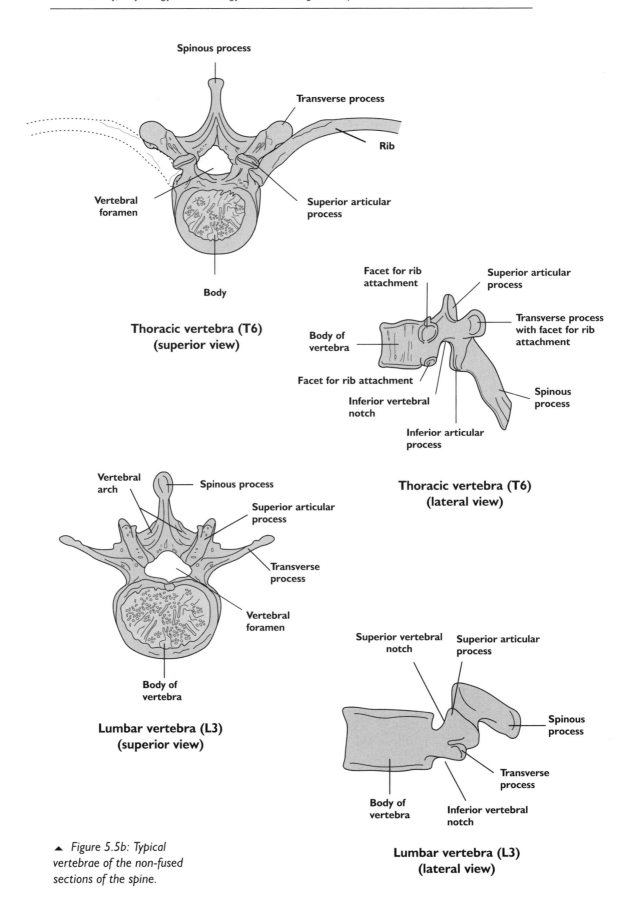

Spinous process

Transverse process

Rib

Vertebral foramen

Superior articular process

Body

Thoracic vertebra (T6) (superior view)

Facet for rib attachment

Superior articular process

Body of vertebra

Transverse process with facet for rib attachment

Facet for rib attachment

Inferior vertebral notch

Spinous process

Inferior articular process

Thoracic vertebra (T6) (lateral view)

Vertebral arch

Spinous process

Superior articular process

Transverse process

Vertebral foramen

Body of vertebra

Lumbar vertebra (L3) (superior view)

Superior vertebral notch

Superior articular process

Spinous process

Transverse process

Body of vertebra

Inferior vertebral notch

Lumbar vertebra (L3) (lateral view)

▲ *Figure 5.5b: Typical vertebrae of the non-fused sections of the spine.*

The **sacrum**, the back part of the pelvis, is made up of five vertebrae that fuse together in the first years of life, to form a triangular spade shape. The sacrum joins together with the two hipbones to form the pelvis (*see* figure 5.12). It needs to be strong for supporting the weight of the body and transferring it via the pelvis to the legs, and also for the reciprocal role of transmitting the force of leg movements up to the trunk in walking, running and jumping.

Sacrum means 'sacred bone', a terminology which developed from mediaeval theology. On judgement day, according to the Bible, everyone who was worthy would be resurrected 'in the flesh' – the body would be resurrected from the grave. It was noted that the sacrum was the longest lasting bone in the ground. Hence, it was seen as the sacred bone from which this resurrection would be possible.

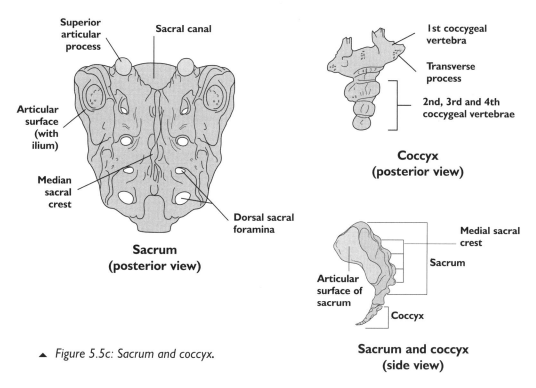

▲ *Figure 5.5c: Sacrum and coccyx.*

The lowest part of the spine is usually made up of four small fused vertebrae which form the tailbone or **coccyx** (pronounced 'koksix'), although the number can vary from three to five, and the top one sometimes remains separate.

Although it is not weight bearing, the coccyx plays an important part in the stability of the pelvis. Many ligaments run between it and the other bony parts of the pelvis, giving stability, without the weight of solid bone, to the 'bowl' of the pelvis, which supports the abdominal contents.

To distinguish the individual vertebrae, each one is given a label derived from its location consisting of a letter and a number – the initial of the section to which the vertebrae belong and their number in that section, counted from the top. For example, the vertebra immediately under the skull is labelled C1, and the lowest lumbar one is labelled L5. The thoracic vertebrae are usually labelled T1–T12.

The vertebrae protect the spinal cord, support the trunk and head, provide support for the actions of the arms, and transmit the weight of the body to the legs. Because humans stand upright, the vertebrae carry an increasing load from the highest to the lowest, so they are progressively larger from the top down (apart from the non-weight bearing coccyx).

A small proportion of people have an extra vertebrae, most commonly in the lumbar area. Very occasionally, a vertebra develops at the junction between regions of the spine that has features common to both regions; the lowest cervical vertebra occasionally has mini 'ribs', or the lowest lumbar vertebra can partly fuse with the sacrum. These transitional vertebrae can cause problems by interfering with the movements of local muscles.

Curves of the Spine

The spine has four curves in the anterior-posterior plane (from front to back). The neck is concave (curves forward), the thoracic section is convex, the lumbar section is concave, and the sacrum and coccyx form a convex curve.

In the womb, the foetus' spine is curled up like the letter 'C', with the head folded into the front of the body and the legs also curled up in front. After birth, this curve remains in the thoracic and pelvic (sacral and coccygeal) sections of the spine. These are known as the 'primary curves'. As the crawling baby lifts the head and pushes with the back legs, 'secondary curves' develop in the opposite direction in the cervical and lumbar sections. These small curves make the spine potentially more flexible and resilient than if it were a rigid vertical pole.

Bone diseases, habitual poor posture and congenital problems can cause exaggerations or imbalances in these curves. They can also be affected by both pregnancy and obesity. Many people develop slight lateral imbalances due to overuse of their dominant hand or via repetitive activities.

Movements of the Spine

Small movements in various directions between consecutive vertebrae add up to the large movements of which the whole spine is capable. These movements can be in a range of directions, and simultaneously be in varied directions in different parts of the spine.

Spinal movements can be defined in terms of three groups of movement in 'pure' anatomical directions, most movements being composites of these:
1. **Flexion** and **extension** – each vertebrae tilting forward or back to curl up or uncurl the spine; **hyperextension** is extension which continues beyond the anatomical position, i.e. back bending;
2. **Lateral flexion** to either side – side bending;
3. **Rotation** to either side – twisting the central axis of the spine, e.g. turning to look behind yourself.

The greatest movement possible in all directions is in the neck. The lumbar spine can flex and extend much more than the thoracic. Although many people assume that the thoracic spine is rigid because of the ribs, it has a range of movement in all directions.

Common Structure of the Non-fused Vertebrae

The cervical, thoracic and lumbar vertebrae (apart from C1) have a common general structure, with an additional element in C2 (described below). The special features of the sacrum are described at the end of this section.

The largest part of the vertebra is the **body**, a solid cylinder at the front of the vertebra that is the main weight bearing part.

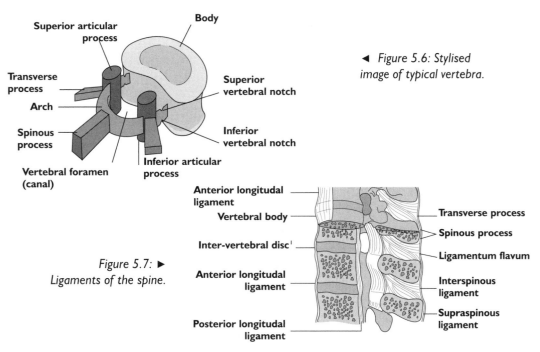

◄ *Figure 5.6: Stylised image of typical vertebra.*

Figure 5.7: ►
Ligaments of the spine.

Most vertebrae are separated by an **intervertebral disc**, that lies between the bodies of the consecutive vertebrae from the second cervical vertebra to the sacrum. Together, the discs make up about one fifth of the length of the spinal column. Each disc has an outer capsule of tough, stringy cartilage surrounding a softer jelly-like inner core (see page 74). This structure makes them 'squashable' under pressure and able to expand again when the pressure is off.

Water and nutrients pass to and from the disc which, in adults, is usually about two thirds water. A person's height reduces by about 1% during the day, due to loss of fluid from weight bearing. Lying down takes the pressure off, allowing the fluid to return. Spinal movements help this fluid exchange, while static posture reduces it. If this leads to insufficient nutrients coming to the disc, it can start to degenerate.

All of the vertebrae, except for the coccyx, have a hole for the spinal cord, which is formed by an **arch** that loops backwards like a horseshoe from the vertebral body. When the vertebrae stack up one on the other, the arches form the **spinal canal** (also called the **vertebral canal**), within which the meninges continue down from the brain to form a protective wrapping around the spinal cord and its accompanying blood vessels.

On each side of the arch, there is a small upper and lower notch. The notches of consecutive vertebrae together form a rounded hole for the passage of nerves from the spinal cord and for blood vessels. This hole is known as the **intervertebral foramen**.

The nerve roots emerging from the spine are labelled in relation to the vertebrae. The cervical nerves are numbered C1–C8. C1 is the nerve emerging between the cranium and the top cervical vertebra. Nerve C2 exits above the second cervical vertebra and this numbering continues down to nerve C8 that exits above the first thoracic vertebra.

The other spinal nerves take their label from the vertebrae immediately above their exit from the spinal cord – T1–T12, L1–L5, and S1–S5. S1–S4 emerge from holes within the sacrum, and S5 from between the sacrum and the coccyx. There is one coccygeal nerve (Co).

Normally the nerve takes up between one third and a half of the foramen, which alters in size as the vertebrae move. If the bones move to their limits and become stuck there, they or the associated soft tissue can put pressure on the nerve that affects its functioning. Chiropractic and osteopathy are designed to address this situation.

Just behind the intervertebral foramina on each side of the arch are two projections, one pointing upwards and one downwards. These four articular processes form gliding joints where they meet with corresponding projections from the vertebrae above and below, each vertebrae thus having two superior and two inferior articular processes. Collectively, these processes form two secondary columns of support, a minor aid to the main weight bearing column formed by the vertebral bodies. They allow small movements between consecutive vertebrae. Their main role is to limit the movements without rigidifying the spine, so as to prevent damage to the spinal cord.

Towards the back of the arch, three projecting 'fingers' of bone form a rough cross. The central one is called the **spinous process** (meaning 'the projection of the spine'). This back most projection of each vertebra is the part that we feel when we are touching the spine. The two side projections from the back part of the arch are the **transverse processes**. These three processes are present in all vertebrae from C2 to L5, but vary in their proportions and the directions in which they incline throughout the spine.

They serve as anchor sites for the network of ligaments and small muscles that connect the processes of consecutive vertebrae and thus orchestrate the fine-tuning of spinal posture and movements. Some connect matching processes, e.g. spinous process to spinous process. Others run diagonally across the 'gutter' formed on each side of the spine by the spinous and transverse processes to join different processes of consecutive or close vertebrae. The larger postural muscles and those that connect to the scapula and the arm also attach to the processes.

The ligaments between the vertebrae also help to stabilise the spine and to limit the range of movements that could otherwise damage the spinal cord. Two large ligaments extend from the occiput to the sacrum to hold the vertebral bodies and discs in their stack. One runs up the front of the vertebral bodies (anterior longitudinal ligament) and the other is on the back surface of the bodies, i.e. the front of the vertebral canal (the posterior longitudinal ligament).

The ligamentum flavum runs up the inner surface of the back of the arch, i.e. the back of the vertebral canal.

The supraspinous ligament, which joins the backs of the spinous processes, and becomes the nuchal ligament in the neck, regulates the range of flexion. There are also short ligaments between the processes of adjacent vertebrae, the interspinous ligaments between spinous processes and the intertransversarii between transverse processes.

When the vertebrae of the **sacrum** grow together into a single flattened, roughly triangular bone, they leave a tubular opening down the middle for the spinal cord and four holes on both the left and right sides for the exit of the spinal nerves. The spinous processes form a single uneven back-projecting ridge from top to bottom.

Special Features of Cervical Vertebrae

All of the cervical vertebrae have a small vertical hole through each transverse process that allows the passage of an artery on each side which feeds to the brain. This arrangement protects the blood vessels that could otherwise only be covered by soft tissue, thus backing up the role of the carotid artery that is in the front of the neck. However, cervical injuries or bone growths can affect the blood supply in the cervical artery, producing intermittent dizziness or nerve problems.

Apart from C1, all the cervical vertebrae have a forked spinous process, for the attachment of the strong sheet of ligament at the back of the neck. This is the **nuchal ligament**, which helps to support the head, and limits the amount that it can drop forward onto the chest, such as happens when a person is tired. It is a smaller version of the very strong ligament that holds the head up in four legged animals.

The bottom cervical vertebra (C7) is also called **vertebra prominens** because its spinous process sticks back considerably further than that of the other neck vertebrae. This is a useful landmark, which is relatively easy to identify by touching it while moving your neck forward and back. You will then feel this vertebra moving. However, if you are touching the next vertebra down (T1) it will hardly shift with this neck movement.

The lower end of the nuchal ligament attaches strongly to the prominent spinous process of C7. The back of the ligament runs directly up to the occiput, forming a strong rope-like back edge, from which it spreads forward like a sail to attach to the other cervical vertebrae.

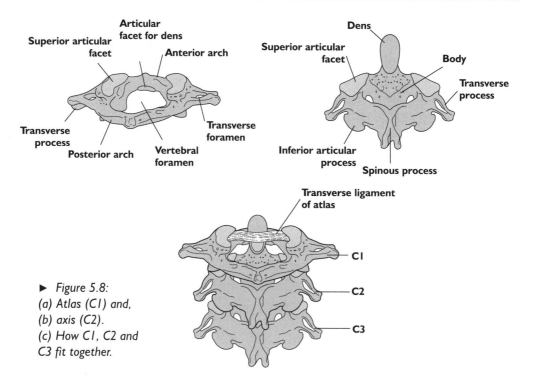

▶ Figure 5.8:
(a) Atlas (C1) and,
(b) axis (C2).
(c) How C1, C2 and
C3 fit together.

The top two cervical vertebrae have a special relationship to the head, and special names. C1, the **atlas**, supports the skull. The name refers to Atlas, the classical Greek hero who carried the world on his shoulders. Unlike the other vertebrae, the atlas doesn't have a body or a spinous process. It is a wide 'pinched' oval-shaped of bone, with widely stretching transverse processes that extend considerably further to each side than those of the other cervical vertebrae. The top of the atlas has two flattened dips on which rest the two knobbly 'rockers' of the skull, the occipital condyles, on which the head can make small rocking movements to nod 'yes'.

C2, the next cervical vertebra, is called the **axis**. It has the features common to all the other cervical vertebrae, plus a unique addition, a tooth-like projection, called the dens or odontoid process. This sticks up from the body of the axis, nestling just inside the centre front of the atlas. A ligament passes behind it, holding the atlas against it, which can then be rotated with the skull around this pivot, in a small movement of turning the head 'no'.

There are no discs between the cranium and the atlas, or between the atlas and the axis. However, strong ligaments and muscles control the movements, preventing damage to the brainstem and giving greater stability than a disc would.

Appendicular Skeleton

The bones of the upper and lower limbs have many similarities, the main differences being due to their different functioning. The shoulder girdles and arms have more ability to reach and take hold, while the pelvis and legs play the main role in supporting the body weight and in locomotion.

Our upper and lower limbs are not as alike as those of monkeys and apes, who use their front and back legs more interchangeably for both gripping and locomotion. However, we humans *can* use our arms for briefly supporting our weight in climbing, and some people *can* walk on their hands; and people born with no arms alert the rest of us to some of the potential dexterity of the feet. Therefore, our limbs have more similarities than those of creatures such as bats, birds or kangaroos where the functions of the upper and lower limbs are very different.

In both the upper and lower limbs, there are bones that bridge between the axial skeleton and the limb. This is the collarbone and the shoulder blade in the shoulder girdle, and the bones of the pelvis for the leg. The shoulder blade can move around over the ribs to give a big range of arm movements; in contrast the pelvis has minimal movement.

There are equivalent bones in each limb. The bones in the leg are bigger and stronger than those in the arm and the equivalent joints of the leg are more firmly strengthened by ligaments and less mobile because of the need for stability in weight bearing. The pattern for the bones of each limb is:

1. One bone in the upper part of the limb (the upper arm and the thigh);
2. Two bones in the lower part (the forearm and the lower leg) with a strong membrane between them, holding them together along their length;
3. A group of bones at the back of the hand and foot – eight in the hand and seven in the foot;
4. Five bones across the palm and the arch of the foot;
5. Five fingers (including the thumb) and five toes with three bony sections in each one, except for the thumb and big toe which each have two bones.

Bear in mind the specific ways in which the terms for movements are used at the shoulder joint and the hip joint:

1. Flexion is taking the limb forward; in the case of the arm, this terminology is used to describe the whole range of movement in this direction continuing up to the vertical;
2. Extension is the reverse of flexion – returning the limb down to the side of the body, and taking it backwards;
3. Abduction is taking the limb out to the side, including sweeping the arm up through 180° to the vertical;
4. Adduction is the reverse of abduction, returning the limb to the side of the body and also continuing to sweep it across either the front or back of the body;
5. Circumduction is taking the limb around through a cone shape that incorporates the previous four directions;
6. Rotation is turning the whole limb as a single unit around its own axis, like the action of screwing and unscrewing a bolt.

Also remember that the anatomical term for the back of the hand and the back (= top) of the foot is the dorsum or dorsal surface. The term for the front of the hand is the palm or palmar surface and for the sole of the foot is the plantar surface (the surface that you 'plant' down as you walk).

Upper Limb

The **shoulder girdle** is comprised of the collarbone or clavicle, and the shoulder blade or scapula. The upper arm bone is attached to the scapula. The only bony connection of

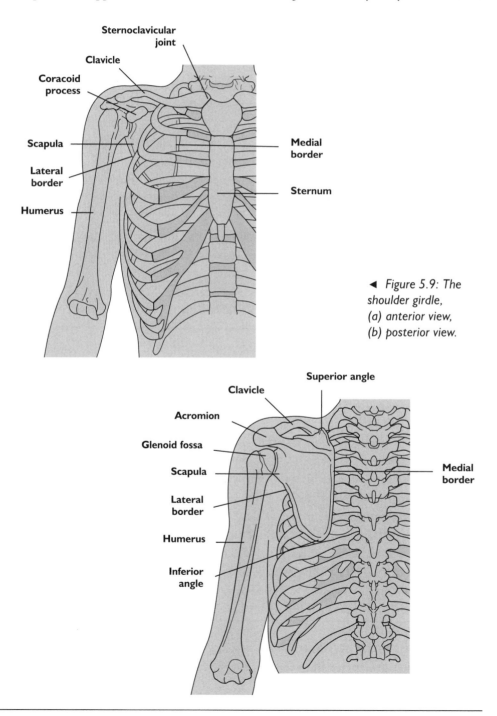

◄ Figure 5.9: The shoulder girdle, (a) anterior view, (b) posterior view.

the arm to the axial skeleton is through the joint between the collarbone and the top of the breastbone, the **sternoclavicular joint**, which has a small range of movement.

The **clavicle** is 'S' shaped. It acts mainly as a strut for the scapula, pivoting on the sternoclavicular joint. The joint between the clavicle and the scapula that forms the point of the shoulder also has only a very small range of movement.

The greatest mobility here is in the **scapula** which is moved and then held in place by muscles, providing a mobile 'platform' for the wide range of actions of which the arm is capable. The clavicle has a few muscles that attach to it, but the scapula is shaped for muscle attachments over most of its surface, because it needs many muscles to move it through the large range that it covers, to stabilise it, and then to move the arm.

It is a roughly triangular bone, fairly thin with a reasonably smooth under surface, which curves slightly to follow the shape of the ribs, which it slides over. At the top, it has a small 'finger' of bone sticking forward under the clavicle – the coracoid process ('crow's beak'). This serves as an important point of attachment for a small chest muscle and the main muscles of the front of the arm.

Towards the top of the back, there is a ridge, the **spine of the scapula**, running slightly diagonally upwards from the medial edge. It becomes more prominent and therefore easier to feel as it crosses the back of the scapula. At the outer end, it flattens out to form the point of the shoulder, the **acromion**, which is strongly attached to the lateral end of the clavicle.

The bottom point of the scapula, that sticks out like a little wing when the arm is taken behind the back, is called the **inferior angle**. The **superior angle** is the top medial corner (which cannot be palpated as it is covered by the trapezius muscle). The socket into which the humerus fits is called the **glenoid fossa**.

The scapula can be raised (elevated) or lowered (depressed), taken back towards the spine (retracted) or around the side of the ribs (protracted), tilted forward at the top, rotated (with the point of the shoulder lifting – upwards rotation – or lowering – downwards rotation), or combinations of these movements.

The **upper arm** bone is called the **humerus**. It is the classic cartoon bone shape, having a long shaft with a bulge at each end. The top end is called the **head of the humerus**. At the lower end, it has flattened bulges to each side, the **medial** and **lateral epicondyles**, to which a large number of the forearm muscles attach. Between them lies the **trochlea**, around which the upper end of the ulna rotates in flexion and extension of the forearm and next to it a small bulge that accommodates the proximal end of the radius.

The head of the humerus forms a joint with the scapula just below the joint between the acromion and the clavicle, which protects it a little. This is a ball and socket joint – a 'universal joint' that can move in any direction, like the rear-view mirror of a car.

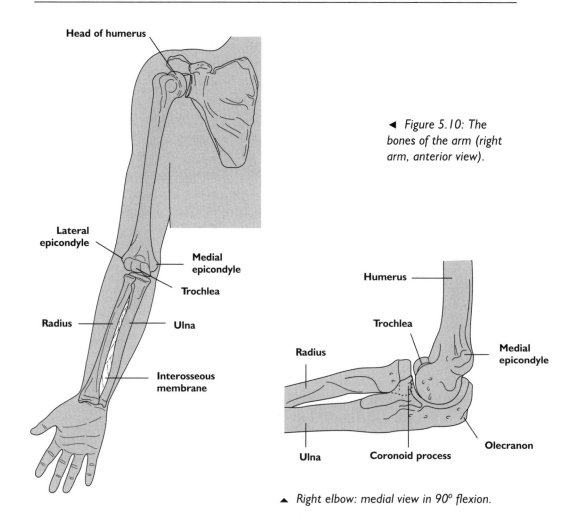

◄ *Figure 5.10: The bones of the arm (right arm, anterior view).*

▲ *Right elbow: medial view in 90° flexion.*

The joint surface of the head of the humerus is nearly half a sphere, but the **glenoid fossa of the scapula** into which it fits is quite shallow. A fibrocartilage ring at the rim of this socket slightly deepens and stabilises the gleno-humeral joint. In order to allow the arm to move through a large range of movements, there are not many ligaments holding the joint. Instead, it is mainly stabilised by muscles that can respond to the task in different arm positions. However, this does make it more vulnerable to dislocation than many other joints.

There are two long bones in the **forearm**, the ulna on the little finger side and the radius on the thumb side. Remember that, in reference to the anatomical position, the ulna is on the medial side of the forearm and the radius on the lateral side. They are parallel in the anatomical position, but the radius crosses over the ulna when it moves.

The **ulna** is largest at the proximal end, where it forms the elbow joint with the humerus; this is a hinge joint. It tapers towards the wrist, forming a very small part of the joint there. At the proximal end of the ulna, the point of the elbow on the posterior side is called the **olecranon** or **olecronon process**. At the front there is another projection, the **coranoid process** and between them the **trochlea notch**. The two projections grip the trochlea of the humerus like a spanner and slide around it as the forearm is bent and straightened.

The radius is smaller at the top end, which is flat where it butts against the distal humerus. It is larger at the distal end where it forms the wrist joint with the bones of the wrist. The radius and ulna have a very strong membrane between them throughout their length – the **interosseous membrane**. This keeps the bones from pulling apart, but allows the radius to rotate around the ulna, turning the hand with it as it does so. The actions of the radius and hand turning are **pronation** (turning the palms down) and **supination** (turning the hands up – often remembered by the image of holding the hands out for a bowl of 's(o)up') (*see* figure 4.6).

The lower ends of the radius and ulna form the wrist with the bones of the base of the **hand**. The eight **carpal bones** are like small, slightly distorted bony cubes, arranged roughly in two rows of four bones each. They are only capable of small gliding movements, so they are able to transmit the power of arm movements fairly undiluted through to the rest of the hand. The wrist is primarily an ellipsoid joint formed between the distal end of the radius and the proximal row of carpal bones. Flexion and extension are the primary movements at the wrist joint (bending the hand forward and backwards respectively), although there can also be side bending – abduction and adduction.

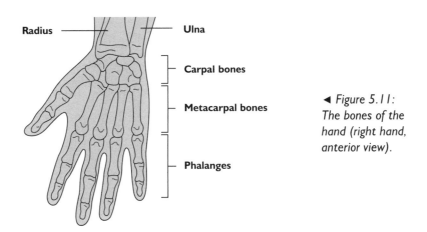

Radius — Ulna

Carpal bones

Metacarpal bones

Phalanges

◄ *Figure 5.11: The bones of the hand (right hand, anterior view).*

From the carpals at the base of the hand, four **metacarpal bones** spread across the palm to form the base of each finger and one forms the base of the thumb. Their distal ends are the knuckles at the edge of the palm and the first joint of the thumb. Their independent actions are restricted by the ligaments between them, and the webbing between the thumb and index finger, but they have enough movement to enable a person to spread his fingers apart, or to wrap his hands around an object (or massage a client's arm)!

Beyond the edge of the hand, there are three **phalanges** in each finger and two in the thumb, enabling them to be curled up or straightened – flexion and extension. The joint at the base of the thumb, which is a saddle joint, allows the thumb to move in four directions for gripping, but not to rotate, which would be a problem.

Lower Limb

The **pelvis** is a 'basin' formed by the sacrum and the two hipbones and the many

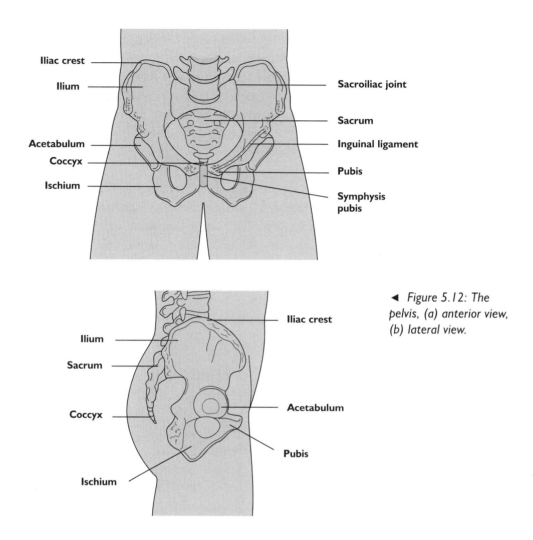

◄ *Figure 5.12: The pelvis, (a) anterior view, (b) lateral view.*

ligaments that join them. Ideally it has very little internal movement, but is moved as a unit by muscles of the lower trunk and of the thigh.

The 'hip' bones are known technically as the **innominate bones** (literally the 'no name' bones) or more commonly as the pelvic bones. Because so much of the pelvis is covered by muscle, it is not obvious that the three bony parts that one can feel are joined together. At birth, each pelvic bone is actually made up of three separate bones that begin to grow together very early in life; they need to be fused enough for weight bearing before we learn to stand up.

In adulthood, the innominate bones are two bones, one on each side, joined at the front by cartilage, called the **symphysis pubis**. At the front of the top part of each bone is the **ilium**, which can be felt as the 'hip' bone that sticks forward just above the outside end of the groin. The top edge of the bone, the **crest of the ilium**, can be palpated around towards the back. How far around this is possible is determined by a person's build. Try not to confuse this ilium bone with the ileum, the second half of the small intestine, which is a confusing similarly named structure in close proximity.

Under the lower part of each buttock is a sitting bone – the **ischium**. At the front of the groin, the two **pubic bones** join together at the symphysis pubis. The fusion between the three parts of the bone is at the socket of the hip joint – the **acetabulum**. This socket can be difficult to visualise as it lies about halfway between the front and back surfaces of the body, behind the line of the groin.

The top front projection of the ilium, the **anterior superior iliac spine** (ASIS for short) is often referred to as the hipbone. It has a number of thigh muscles attaching to it. Running along the line of the groin from each ASIS to the medial part of each pubic bone is the inguinal ligament, which covers and protects muscles, nerves and blood vessels which cross over in front of the bone from the trunk to the thigh.

The pelvic bones can be difficult to make sense of, so try feeling what you can on yourself while looking at pictures that give you images from a number of angles. You are trying to build up an image of the pelvic girdle as a 'funnel' with a large opening at the bottom, formed by the two innominate bones and the sacrum. On average, the pelvis slopes more sharply inwards towards the lower end in men, and is wider with more vertical sides in women to allow for childbirth.

The sacrum at the back is strongly fixed to the ilium at the **sacroiliac joint**. This is normally, of necessity, a very stable joint, held together by some of the strongest ligaments in the body, and only capable of a small gliding movement. This is a significant joint in the transfer of the body's weight from the trunk to the legs, or of the power of locomotion from the legs up to the trunk, so the stability is crucial. The hip joint between the pelvis and thigh bone transfers these same forces between the pelvis and the legs.

In the later stages of pregnancy, the ligaments soften up in this area to give flexibility in the pelvis for the birth process. Sometimes, after childbirth, they do not tighten up again and the joint remains less stable and often a source of pain. This can also happen after injuries that stretch the ligaments. Most other joints in the body have muscles which can take over some of the stabilising role from weakened ligaments, but there are none which cross the sacroiliac joint, so this instability can become an ongoing problem.

The thighbone, the **femur**, is generally the longest and strongest bone in the body. It is well clothed in muscles and can only be palpated in two places where it is close to the surface – at the top outside edge of the thigh and where it forms the top of the knee joint. It is shaped like a letter 'L' upside down, with the medial end of the short section forming the joint with the pelvis and the long shaft running the length of the thigh to the knee.

The round **head**, which is over half a sphere, fits deeply into the acetabulum of the pelvis to form the hip joint. This is a ball and socket joint stabilised by a very strong wrapping of ligaments between the pelvis and the femur. This ensures the stability of this weight bearing joint, while allowing the range of movement necessary for such activities as stepping, turning, running, dancing, jumping, climbing and swimming.

From the head of the femur, a short section called the **neck of the femur** extends outwards and slightly downwards to the side of the thigh, ending in a large 'bump'. This is the **greater trochanter**, which can be felt on the side of the thigh, 10–15cms below the crest of the ilium. Many of the muscles that regulate movements and balance between the pelvis and the femur attach to the great trochanter, and a few to its small neighbour, the lesser trochanter, which lies on the inside of the bend between the neck and shaft of the femur.

Two common problems can arise in this area. The head of the femur can become worn as a result of injuries or of conditions such as osteoarthritis. In serious cases, this may need an operation to replace the hip with an artificial joint of metal or plastic. A 'broken hip' caused by a fall, especially in old people, is in fact a fracture of the neck of the femur. This may require a metal screw or plate to rejoin the bones or sometimes the replacement of the whole neck and head.

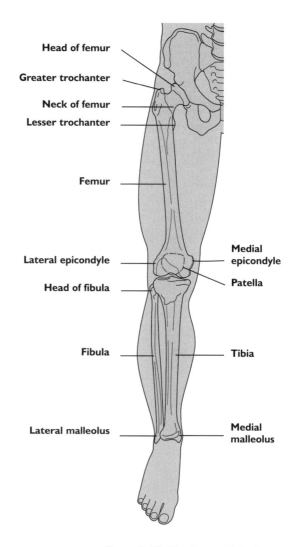

▲ *Figure 5.13: The bones of the leg (right leg, anterior view).*

The shaft extends down from the bend, curving slightly. At the distal end, it widens out into two condyles that form the top of the knee joint. The bottom of the femur and the top of the shinbone together make up the **knee joint**, which primarily allows flexion and extension. The kneecap or **patella** fits snugly into the notch at the front of the femur. It is not attached to the other bones, but develops inside the tendon of the large quadriceps muscle that crosses the front of this joint, helping to hold the tendon in place.

In addition to strong ligaments surrounding the joint to stabilise it, there are two ligaments which cross one another at the centre between the bones – the **cruciate ligaments**. They are attached to the femur in the notch between the condyles, and to the central ridge of the top surface of the shinbone.

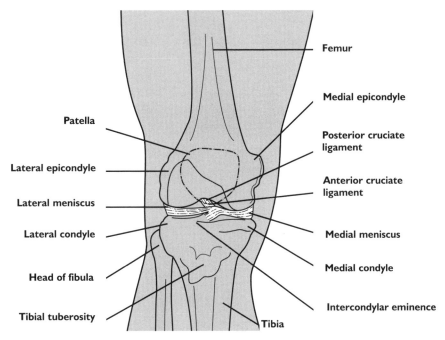

Femur

Medial epicondyle

Posterior cruciate ligament

Patella

Anterior cruciate ligament

Lateral epicondyle

Lateral meniscus

Medial meniscus

Lateral condyle

Medial condyle

Head of fibula

Intercondylar eminence

Tibial tuberosity

Tibia

▲ *Figure 5.14: The knee joint (right knee, anterior view).*

To give further stability to this important joint, there are two wedges of cartilage called **menisci** on this surface, one on either side of the ridge (*see* page 77). The two lower leg bones are held together by a strong interosseous membrane but, unlike the forearm bones, there is very little movement between them.

The shinbone, the **tibia**, is thick and strong and is the main weight bearer. At the top, it spreads out to form the lower side of the knee joint. The top surface is a flat shelf, with a central ridge (the intercondylar eminence – running from front to back) that engages the notch between the condyles of the femur, helping to keep the femur on track as the knee bends. The bulges on either side of this ridge are known as the tibial condyles.

A little below the knee, there is a bulge in the front of the shin, the tibial tuberosity, to which the powerful quadriceps muscle of the thigh attaches. The bottom end of the tibia sits on the top bone of the foot and bulges to the medial side of it, making up the inside anklebone.

The other bone of the lower leg, the **fibula**, is much thinner and carries very little of the weight. Its name is the Latin word for '*pin*'; it acts as a bracing bone for the tibia, like the pin of a brooch. The head can be palpated as a little bony bulge just under the lateral condyle of the tibia. The lower end forms the outside anklebone. Note that a useful way of remembering the names of these two bones is to consider that the **t**ibia is the '**t**ough' one, and the **f**ibula is the '**f**eeble' one.

The distal ends of the tibia and fibula sit on the top bone of the foot, the **talus**, and wrap snuggly around each side of it to form the **anklebones**, in a close fit that is supported by strong ligaments.

These ligaments are over-stretched when the ankle is sprained. This is one of the most common sporting injuries, caused when the foot is twisted onto the outside edge with the full weight of the body on it. The joint can be unstable for quite some time after this, as the ligaments heal slowly. During this time, muscles take over the work of supporting the joint.

The joint bends upwards and downwards. These movements at the ankle are described respectively as dorsiflexion and plantar flexion. Dorsiflexion means to bend up the dorsum of the foot (the 'back' is the top of the foot); and plantar flexion to bend down the plantar surface (the sole).

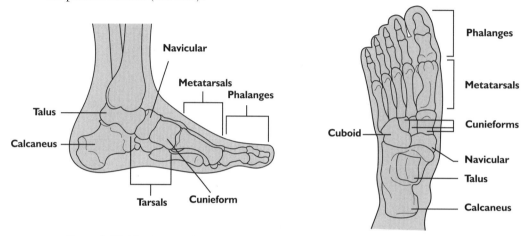

◄ *Figure 5.15: The bones of the left foot (medial view and superior view).*

The **foot** is primarily shaped for weight bearing, but also allows a little movement. It is very evident when walking in the country that the foot needs flexibility to adapt to uneven ground, while still allowing a person to maintain upright posture. Even when walking on flat surfaces, there needs to be a little springiness in the foot to minimise jarring at each step.

The back half of the foot is made up of seven **tarsal bones**. As befits their weight bearing role, they are significantly larger than the equivalent carpal bones of the hand. They too allow small gliding movements between themselves, which permit **eversion** and **inversion** of the foot, turning the sole outwards and inwards. The talus sits above the others, transferring the bodyweight from the lower leg forward towards the toes and backwards to the heel bone – the **calcaneus** – which projects some distance behind it.

The other five tarsal bones form the central part of the main arch under the foot. The navicular bone connects from the front of the talus to the three cuneiform bones that form the medial part of the arch. The cuboid bone lies next to the lateral cuneiform on the outer edge, between the calcaneus and the lateral two metatarsals. Slightly elastic ligaments, layers of muscle between the heel and toes on the underside of the foot, and muscles in the lower leg, keep the arch springy.

From the front part of the arch, there are five **metatarsal bones** spread across the width of the foot, which extend to the front of the fleshy part of the foot. Like their counterparts in the hand, they can be spread further apart (abduction) or brought together (adduction).

The toes each contain three **phalanges** (the same name as for the bones of the fingers), except for the big toes which each have only two phalanges. They can be curled under (flexion) or bent up (extension).

Review of the Bones of the Skeleton

There are 206 bones in the human body.

Skull

Cranium: 8 cranial bones, 14 facial bones including the mandible (lower jaw) and 3 tiny ossicles in each ear.
Hyoid bone – horseshoe shaped bone at base of mouth, top of neck.

Spine

Cervical vertebrae: 7.
Thoracic vertebrae: 12.
Lumbar vertebrae: 5.
Sacrum: 1 (5 fused vertebrae).
Coccyx: 1 (commonly 3–4 fused vertebrae).

Ribs

12 pairs.

Shoulder Girdle

Clavicle – collarbone: bony connection for whole shoulder girdle and arm via sternoclavicular joint.
Scapula – shoulder blade: joins clavicle at point of shoulder.

Arm

Humerus – upper arm bone: connected to scapula.
Ulna – bone on little finger side, from point of elbow (olecranon) to wrist.
Radius – bone on thumb side: turns hand by rotating forearm around ulna.

Hand

Carpals: 8 – two rows of 4 each, base of hand.
Metacarpals: 5 – four in palm, one forms base of thumb to side of palm.
Phalanges: 14 finger bones – 2 in thumb, 3 in each finger.

Pelvis

Innominate bone: two, each made of three fused bones – ilium, ishium and pubis (together with sacrum make up the pelvis).

Leg

Femur – thigh bone.
Patella – kneecap: a bone in quadriceps tendon.
Tibia – shin: large bone of lower leg.
Fibula – bracing bone of lower leg, on lateral side.

Foot

Tarsals: 7 – ankle and heel to mid foot (including tarsus and calcaneus).
Metatarsals: 5 – arch to ball of foot.
Phalanges – toe bones: 14 – 2 in big toe, 3 in other toes.

Surface Features of Bones – Terminology

Much of the surface area of bones is relatively smooth. The end of a bone, where it joins with another bone, appears absolutely smooth. The other smooth areas, where large muscles often attach to the bone over a wide area, are pierced by many small holes for the passage of blood vessels and nerves into and out of the bone, such as on the shoulder blades and the pelvic bones.

Tendons, which attach long muscles to bones, usually do so at roughened areas that often form bumps; the larger the muscle attaching, the larger the bulge in the bone. Bony projections can also serve as attachments for ligaments – the 'ropes' which hold bones together. As you study the bones, you will come across many words for the projections and depressions that cover their surfaces and for the holes through them. There are a few general words used regularly, and a large number of terms that describe only one or two particular bone parts.

Projections

Condyle ('knuckle'): polished joint surface, usually rounded, that articulates with another bone, e.g. the distal ends of the femur and humerus; on the occipital bone to articulate with the atlas.
Epicondyle: small projection related to a condyle, e.g. the lateral and medial epicondyles of humerus and femur.
Head: the large round end of a bone, e.g. head of the humerus and femur.
Neck: a narrowed part closely related to an expanded end, e.g. the neck of the femur.
Process: a projection or outgrowth of bone, e.g the transverse and spinous processes of the vertebrae; the coracoid process of the scapula; the mastoid process of the occiput behind the ear.

Protuberance: a general name for a palpable bulge or swelling.

Spine: a sharp projection or projecting ridge, e.g. the spine of the scapula; the spinous processes of the vertebrae.

Tubercle/tuberosity: small and large bumps respectively, e.g. the tubercles at the head of the humerus; the ischial tuberosity.

Trochanter: two bumps on the femur just below the neck, i.e. the greater trochanter and lesser trochanter.

Crest: a prominent ridge or border of bone, e.g. the iliac crest at the top of the hipbone.

Depressions

Fossa: a furrow or shallow depression (the supraspinous and infraspinous fossae at the back of the scapula – above and below the scapula spine; the iliac fossa – on the inside of the hip).

Sinus: a chamber within a bone usually filled with air (most of which are in the head).

Recess and **cavity** are other common words.

Holes

Foramen (**pl**. foramina): an opening or small hole for the passage of nerves or blood vessels (foramen magnum – the 'great hole' in the occiput through which the spinal cord leaves the cranium; the intervertebral foramina – between the vertebrae, through which the nerves leave the spinal chord).

Chapter 6 Physiology of Bones

The bones of the body provide a solid framework for the other tissues of the body, maintaining the body's shape and, via the action of muscles, allowing movement. Some bones surround and protect vulnerable structures, such as the brain, heart and lungs. They act as a storehouse for minerals, particularly calcium, which is important in the functioning of nerves, muscles and blood. Blood cell formation also happens in certain bones.

Key Words

Salts	Periosteum
Matrix	Hyaline / articular cartilage
Collagen fibres	Bones – long, short, flat, irregular, sesamoid
Compact bone	Ossification
Spongy bone	Calcification
Marrow cavity	

Make-up of Bones

Many people have an image of bone that has come from seeing skeletons in museums or laboratories. However, this is only the mineral salts that remain after death, when the living part of the bone has leached away. The word skeleton in fact comes from a Greek word meaning '*dried up*'.

These remains are about two thirds, by weight, of a living bone – the **salts**, mainly calcium phosphate and calcium carbonate, which give bone its hardness and rigidity, in a similar way to adding a hardener to a putty mix.

Bone is a type of connective tissue. The organic part of the bone, the living part that has gone from the display skeleton, has many blood vessels and nerves to feed it. This fibrous **matrix** is a thick gelatinous material containing combined protein and sugar molecules, with **collagen fibres**, a protein, woven like tough threads through it. The matrix is secreted by the growing bone cells, which it then surrounds and incorporates. Small amounts of bone salts are deposited in or removed from this gel, depending on other body processes and needs.

These three components, matrix, fibres and salts, are essential for the combined qualities of bones, balancing strength with lightness. Bones need to be strong to give a framework for the soft tissues of the body. The rubber-like connective tissue of the matrix resists squashing well, but would not have the necessary rigidity without the mineral salts. The mineral salts give the bones strength to support the weight that is placed on them, both the weight of the body and that of objects that we carry.

Higher mineral content is useful in the tiny bones in our ears. Their consequent hardness increases their ability to resonate, and they are protected from damage by the softer surrounding structures. However, a large bone that was made primarily of these minerals would be like unprotected glass, strong but not resilient enough and too easily breakable.

The fibres allow the bones to resist shearing when they are pulled or twisted by the workloads placed on them by muscles, both in everyday tasks, and in more demanding activities. If these fibres all ran in the same direction, the bone would be strong in that direction but weak in all others, like wood that is hard to break across the grain but easy to break along it. Therefore, the collagen fibres run in different directions in successive layers of bone, although there are more in the directions that require more tensile strength (resistance to being stretched).

Classification of Bones

Different groups of bones play different roles in the body. They are usually grouped in five categories:

1. **Long bones** are the classic bone shape seen in cartoons, with a long central shaft that is hollow – the diaphysis – and a bulge or head at each end – the epiphysis. These bones act as levers, capable of achieving large and fast movements with a relatively small muscle pull. All the limb bones are of this type, including the bones in the hands and feet, except for the carpals and tarsals. The central shaft acts rather like bamboo or scaffolding. It is a strong tube of compact bone that is neither as heavy nor as inflexible as a solid cylinder would be. Although they sometimes have a thin inner lining of spongy bone, the shafts of long bones are the only internal area in any bones – except for the sinus cavities in the cranium – that are not filled with a honeycomb-like network of spongy bone tissue.

2. **Short bones** are the squat, roughly cube-shaped bones found at the base of the hand (carpals) and at the back half of the foot (tarsals), where strength and solidity are needed. Small gliding movements are possible within these groups of bones, and between them and the adjacent metacarpals or metatarsals. Bigger movements occur at the wrist and ankle, where they meet the bones of the lower arm or lower leg.

3. **Flat bones** are thin, and have a smooth surface that is usually slightly curved. These bones function either to protect vital softer tissues (the sternum, the ribs and the bones of the cranium), or to provide a big surface for muscle attachments (the scapula), or both (the pelvic bones). The scapula is classed as a flat bone in spite of the ridge and projections at the top. These bones have a thin layer of spongy bone sandwiched in between compact bone – like the corrugated layer between the two flat layers of the walls of a cardboard box.

4. **Irregular bones** are those that do not fit into the other categories. Examples are the vertebrae, all of the facial bones, and the tiny bones of the inner ear. The bones of the head are so shaped in order to accommodate the brain, blood vessels and nerves and the needs of the eyes, ears, nose and mouth. Many of the bulges on all

bones are for muscle attachments via tendons, or sometimes for ligaments. The 'irregular' projections towards the back of the vertebrae, called the transverse and spinous processes, are indicative of a need for many areas for attachments, in this case the network of short ligaments and muscles that run up and down the spinal column, making connections between the vertebrae.

5. **Sesamoid bones** are usually very tiny bones, like a sesame seed in size and shape. They are not attached to other bones, but form in a tendon where it bends at an angle across a joint. They help to reduce friction and brace the tendon as it crosses the joint. They are most common in the hands and feet, where they do not always completely ossify. The only one of any size is the kneecap (patella) which grows inside the quadriceps tendon. It stabilises the tendon from being pulled out of place by the pull of the medial or lateral sections of the quadriceps muscle. The patella is so well-shaped for the job that it is very hard to dislodge from its snug position in the notch at the front of the distal end of the femur.

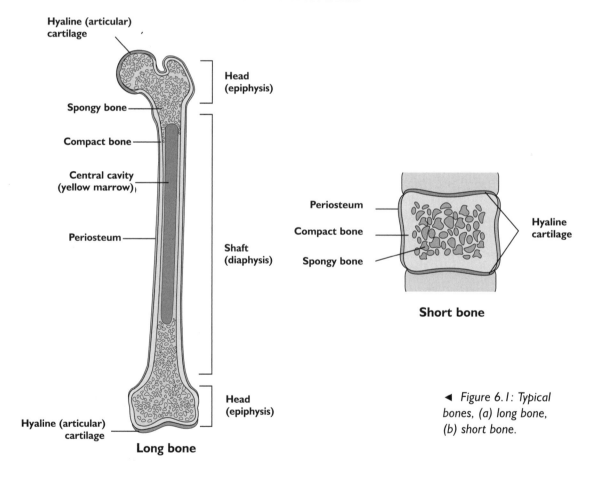

◀ Figure 6.1: Typical bones, (a) long bone, (b) short bone.

Bone Structure

The living skeleton is made of various types of connective tissue – bone, cartilage and periosteum, the covering material. These tissues are described in the section that follows. For types of cartilage (*see* page 75).

In looking at the cross section of a bone, you can see two types of bone tissue, which can thicken or become denser where necessary for extra strength. The remaining internal spaces of the bone contain two types of marrow, which have important roles in the living bone.

Compact bone looks dense and solid, and makes up the outside wall of every bone. Large blood vessels and nerves pass through it to the underlying spongy bone and the marrow within the bone. Some of the holes for the passage of these blood vessels are visible to the naked eye, particularly towards the ends of long bones. You can look for these in old animal bones that you might find on a country hillside.

The compact bone actually has a network of tiny canals containing blood vessels that carry materials for its own maintenance and repair. The main canals, which are visible under a microscope, run along the long axis of the bone, with smaller linking canals crossing between them. The bone is layered around the larger canals, with successive sheets having fibres running in different directions for maximum strength.

Spongy bone ('cancellous bone') looks and feels like a dried-out sponge. It is strong but the spaces make it light and flexible. Spongy bone is always covered and therefore protected by compact bone.

In the long bones, spongy bone is found in the heads of the bone; in some it also extends down the inside of the shaft. In all other bones, it forms the central mass of bone within a compact bone lining. This latticework of bone is much lighter than solid bone would be, and more resilient to pressure – like the steel framework of a multistorey building. It has its own blood circulation, fed by vessels passing through the compact bone covering.

In foetal life and at birth, there is red marrow throughout the skeleton. In adults, only the spaces around the spongy bone in the vertebrae, the sternum, the ribs, the pelvis, the skull and the upper ends of the femur and humerus are filled with red bone marrow. The precursors of all blood cells are formed in this marrow, and all of the red blood cells and some white blood cells and platelets are grown to maturity.

Long bones contain a long hollow space in the shaft, called a **marrow cavity**, surrounded by compact bone and sometimes by a thin layer of spongy bone. The red marrow which fills this space at birth is gradually replaced, beginning about age five. By adulthood, this is filled with yellow marrow, consisting of fat cells for fat storage. If the body needs, some of the yellow marrow areas can be harnessed back into blood cell production.

Blood vessels enter the bone at many points to supply the compact bone, the spongy bone and bone marrow. They are more numerous in the areas of the red bone marrow. Lymph vessels are most abundant in the periosteum.

Tiny nerves pass into the bone with the blood vessels. They are mostly motor nerves that control the blood vessels, but there are also sensory nerves that can monitor damage to the bone.

Bone Coverings

Periosteum, a thick gristle, covers most of the outside of a living bone, wrapping around it in tight layers like clingfilm. This protects the bone, especially as it grows, and holds in place the nutrient blood vessels, lymphatics and nerves that feed the bone. The tendons from muscles and the ligaments normally knit into the perisoteum, not directly into the bone itself.

The cells that form and repair bones (osteoblasts) are found in the periosteum. In someone in reasonable health, broken bones will only fail to mend if the perisoteum is very severely damaged or torn right away from the bone.

The only bony surfaces not covered by periosteum are the joint surfaces, where the bone articulates with another bone. The smooth surface is covered by **hyaline** ('glassy') **cartilage**, which is a slightly compressible fibrous cartilage with a glassy surface appearance. Its role is to cushion the ends of the bones, stopping the hard bony surfaces from rubbing together. This cartilage is also known as **articular cartilage**.

Bone Growth

Ossification is the name given to the formation of bone, which can happen in one of two ways.

Most bones are formed from an initial small mould or template of hyaline cartilage, which is then gradually replaced by bone. A few bones, such as the skull bones and clavicles, are formed directly from membrane.

Ossification is a cooperative process. Initially bone-producing cells (osteoblasts) lay down solid bone and then bone-removing cells (osteoclasts) sculpt it. The osteoblasts remain within the developing bone matrix, becoming the osteocytes – the mature bone cells.

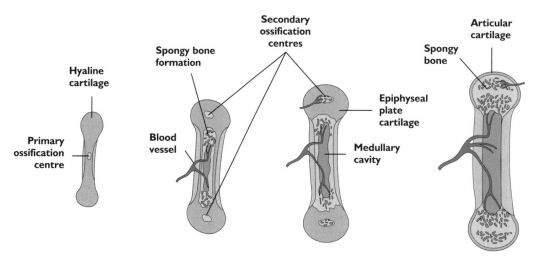

▲ *Figure 6.2: Bone growth.*

This process of bone remodelling helps the developing bone to keep pace with the growing body. It keeps the compact lining at the right thickness in a growing bone and creates the marrow cavities and the 'honeycomb' spaces in spongy bone. This process commences during foetal life and is normally completed in most bones in adolescence, but continues in small pockets of some bones into the mid-twenties.

Long bones start to ossify at the centre of the shaft first, growing out in each direction to replace the cartilage. After birth the ends of the long bone also begin to ossify. Between the ossified areas there remains a layer of cartilage – the epiphyseal plates – where the bone continues to grow in length until the growing surfaces join.

On average, the bones reach their full length in women a few years younger than in men, hence the shorter average height of women. Even when the bone has stopped growing in length, there is still further ossification of the remaining cartilage areas, which can continue in some bones into one's mid-twenties.

Short bones have a single growth plate between just two areas of ossification. Many other bones grow from a greater number of centres. For example, most vertebrae grow from seven centres of ossification, and the shoulder blade usually has seven or eight – one for each bony bulge.

In some cranial bones, a sinus can develop. This is an air-filled cavity in the bone that can grow throughout life, giving more prominent ridges and brows as people age.

Bone Changes and Repair

Throughout life, bone is continually being remodelled by both osteoblasts and osteoclasts. The development, repair and changes in bone tissue are controlled by hormones,

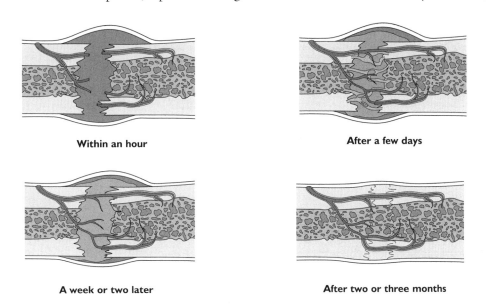

Within an hour

After a few days

A week or two later

After two or three months

▲ *Figure 6.3: Bone repair.*

and affected by genetic inheritance, diet and activity. Sometimes this process can get out of balance, with too much bone being laid down (e.g. ankylosis in which joints fuse together), or too much being taken away (osteoporosis).

When a bone has been broken and then set, it undergoes **calcification** – the laying down of new bone to repair the damage. The break is firstly splinted by a mass of fibrocartilage, which is later replaced by bone. Initially, an excess of bone will be laid down, which can be felt as a bump on the injured bone area. Over a few months, this is then gradually reduced to what is appropriate so that a broken bone, properly set, will return to virtually as good as new. Calcification can also be an attempt to fuse bones together to replace torn ligaments around a joint in order to stabilise it – most commonly in the spine.

Bone is Living Tissue

There are constant small physiological processes at work in living bones. As described above, they are a storage area for minerals and fats – brought via the circulatory system and released back into it when needed. They are also the site for the formation of blood cells. In addition to these processes, the structure of the bones can change too. Throughout life, the density and to a small extent the size and shape of bones can change in response to natural processes and our activities. Genetic factors play a part, such as one's build and metabolism.

Life processes such as puberty, pregnancy, menopause and ageing, all affect bones. Bone changes are governed by hormones so that any hormonal changes may influence them. After menopause, for example, women have an increased risk of developing osteoporosis (brittle bones), which many people try to reduce through exercise and the use of hormone replacement therapy. As one ages, bones tend to gradually dry out, increasing the proportion of calcium salts and making them more brittle and thus more vulnerable to injury. During pregnancy, calcium may be leached from the mother's bones to provide it for the growing foetus if there is not enough arriving in the diet.

Lifestyle changes can also have their effect, especially changes of work or leisure activities – such as taking up exercise, changing one's diet, moving from an active to a sedentary job, or when patterns of activity change as a consequence of having children or through retirement.

Activity and exercise are essential for bones. They respond to being used – to the pull of muscles and the effects of gravity. Both exercise and heavy work strengthen bone tissue and may lead to a fractional enlargement of the bone; lack of exercise will lead to a thinning. Children need activity to help develop their bones. Older people need exercise, no matter how little, to help maintain their bones.

Traumas and accidents change weight bearing patterns, producing responses in bones, as does putting on or taking off weight.

Joints – Arthrology

Joints – 'articulations' – are formed where two, or occasionally more, bones meet. There are three main classifications of joints: fibrous, cartilaginous and synovial.

In massage, we are particularly concerned with the latter two, especially the last one. Learning about joints helps us to understand their potential for movement, and the role played by the muscles in moving and stabilising them (*see* Chapters 7 and 8). Massage practitioners can bring this understanding to guide their work on specific muscles and the passive movements and stretches that will be of most use in helping to mobilise particular joints and simultaneously enhance the stretching and relaxation of chosen muscles.

Key Words

Articulation	Capsule
Fibrous joint	Synovial membrane
Suture	Ligament
Cartilaginous joint	Types of synovial joints – hinge, gliding,
Intervertebral disc	ball and socket, saddle, ellipsoid, pivot
Synovial joint	Menisci
Articular cartilage	Bursa
Synovial fluid	

In **fibrous joints**, the bones form a connection with fibrous tissue between them. The most distinctive fibrous joints in the body are the **sutures** (sewing lines) formed between the bones of the skull. The bones dovetail together like adjacent pieces of a jigsaw as they grow, with a small layer of fibrous tissue between them, which is a continuation of their periosteums. These are also known technically as 'immovable joints' although very small movements are actually possible.

Unlike most other bones in the body, they are formed directly from the tissue and not via cartilage, hence the surviving tissue between them. These bones have softer areas between them at birth – the fontanelles – which have not yet ossified, to allow the head to accommodate to the birth canal.

There are other fibrous joints that have larger amounts of fibrous tissue between them. These are the connections between the lower end of the tibia and fibula, and similarly between the lower end of the radius and ulna. In both cases, the bones are joined by interosseous membrane, a sheet of fibrous tissue that joins each set of bones through most of their length, holding them together. There is little movement between the tibia and fibula, but much more is possible between the forearm bones. The teeth in their sockets are also considered to be fibrous joints.

Cartilaginous joints are also called 'slightly movable'. Some cartilaginous joints consist merely of hyaline cartilage, which only allows a small amount of movement – such as the costal cartilage between the ribs and sternum, and the growing plate of cartilage between the ossified areas of the bones in a growing child.

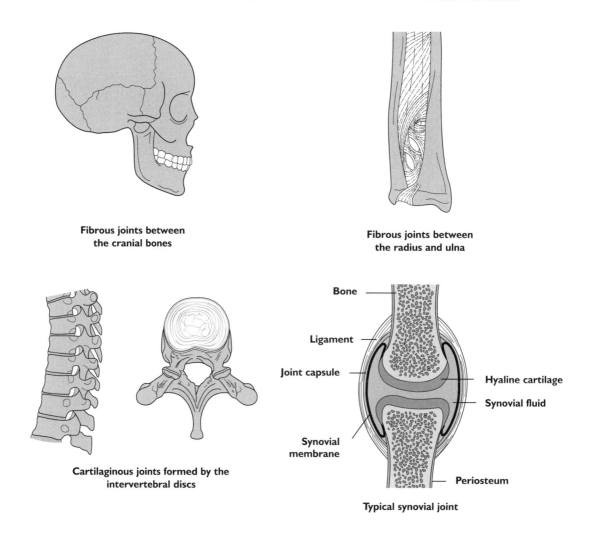

Fibrous joints between
the cranial bones

Fibrous joints between
the radius and ulna

Cartilaginous joints formed by the
intervertebral discs

Bone

Ligament

Joint capsule

Synovial
membrane

Hyaline cartilage

Synovial fluid

Periosteum

Typical synovial joint

▲ *Figure 6.4: Types of joints, (a and b) fibrous, (c) cartilaginous, (d) synovial.*

The symphysis pubis, the connection between the two pubic bones, consists of fibrocartilage. It also has limited movement, except in late pregnancy when the surrounding ligaments soften up to give flexibility in the pelvis for giving birth.

In the cartilaginous joints formed between each **intervertebral disc** and its adjacent vertebrae, there is a more elaborate structure and more mobility. The articulating surfaces of the bones are covered by hyaline cartilage, there is fibrocartilage in the discs between the bones, and the joint is supported by some ligaments.

The discs are formed from tough flexible fibrocartilage called the anulus fibrosis, with a soft jelly-like core called the nucleus pulposus. The cartilage is in circular layers, with fibres running in different directions in consecutive layers to maintain strength and integrity in all the possible movements of the spine. The discs lie between the bodies of consecutive vertebrae, cushioning the spine as it bends. Each disc is firmly fixed to the upper and lower bony surfaces, so that pressure can squeeze one area without dislodging the whole disc – like sitting on the corner of a water bed. The bones are connected by ligaments, which do not completely surround the joint or form a capsule as they do in the synovial joints.

It is worth briefly reviewing the three types of cartilage, because of the role two of them play in joints. All cartilage is a type of connective tissue, with cells imbedded in a gel that contains fibres of collagen, making it rather like bone without the salts – less hard and more flexible and resilient. It provides a solid but flexible support for the skeleton.

Most cartilage has no direct blood circulation. It is dependent for maintenance on nutrients arriving in the fluids that bathe it, so it doesn't regenerate well after injury. Damaged cartilage is often replaced by fibrous tissue (scar tissue). As it ages, cartilage may thin out and has a tendency to calcify.

Hyaline cartilage is the most common type. It is the cartilage of the foetal skeleton and the growing part of children's bones. It remains in adulthood in a few areas, e.g. in the voice box in the throat, and the thick costal cartilage between the ribs and the sternum. This costal cartilage is the only cartilage in the body that has blood circulation. Where it remains at the ends of the bones, forming a thin but tough lining for joint surfaces, it is called articular cartilage.

Fibrocartilage contains a large amount of collagen, making it strong but more compressible. It makes up 'shock absorbers' in some joints, such as the intervertebral discs and the menisci that pad the knee. Elastic cartilage doesn't occur in joints. It is softer and more rubbery, and forms the external ear and the epiglottis.

Most of the joints of the body are **synovial joints**, also called freely movable. They and the discs of the spine are of most concern in massage, because they form the connections between the bones that the skeletal muscles control and move.

In synovial joints the articulating surfaces of the adjacent bones are shaped to fit neatly together, allowing and also limiting the range of movement. This range is also determined by the arrangement of the surrounding ligaments and muscles. The joint surface of the ends of the bones is lined by a protective layer of specialised hyaline cartilage called **articular cartilage** (cartilage 'of the joint'). It is slightly compressible and elastic, and has a hard-wearing surface.

Movements between the bones are facilitated by **synovial fluid**, which looks like egg white (hence the name: *syn-ovial* - 'egg-like'). This fluid, which is contained in a fibrous **capsule** that stretches between the two bones, acts as a lubricant and also carries nutrients to the articular cartilage.

The fluid is secreted by the **synovial membrane**, which lines the inside of the capsule. The membrane covers the whole inner surface, except for where the cartilage covers the articulating surfaces of the bones. It also covers any tendons or ligaments that are partly or completely within the capsule. In the shoulder joint, for example, some tendons enter the joint capsule, and inside the knee joint there are internal bracing ligaments. **Ligaments**, the tough inelastic ropes of fibrous gristle which tie the bone ends together, form the outer wall of the capsule. They thus surround and protect the joint, which is further strengthened by muscles, whose tendons also cross the joint.

A brief reminder about the terminology – a tendon attaches a muscle to bone, or occasionally to another muscle or to fascia; a ligament binds bone to bone.

Where a joint, such as the hip joint needs great stability, the ligaments are thick and strong and are firmly knitted together around the whole joint. Where more flexibility is needed, such as in the shoulder joint, they are thinner and sparser to allow more movement, and their role is supplemented by muscles.

As muscles pull on a bone causing it to move, the ligaments and the capsule begin to concertina together on the side of the joint that is shortening, while those on the opposite side of the joint are stretched. When these latter ligaments are fully stretched, the brain usually acts to limit further movement in this direction, to avoid any damage to the ligaments or other structures of the joint.

Sometimes a movement is too fast for the brain to monitor and restrict, e.g. in throwing or kicking too hard, or when the weight of the body forces a joint too far, e.g. in twisting one's ankle. In these situations, which happen most commonly in sports or dance performance, the ligaments are overstretched (sprained).

Types of Synovial Joints

Synovial joints are classified into six groups, according to their structure and the range of movements that they permit.

Hinge joints move in one plane only, allowing flexion and extension. Examples are the elbow, the ankle and the joints within the fingers and toes. The knee is commonly referred to as a hinge joint, although it also has a small range of rotatory movements. The muscle tendons are at the front and back of the joint and pull in each direction (e.g. biceps and triceps).

In **gliding joints**, the adjoining bone surfaces are fairly flat, and one bone slides on the other. The connections between adjacent carpal bones and between the tarsal bones are of this type. Their small movements can be initiated by muscles that cross the joint (e.g. the wrist) without attaching to the carpal bones, as well as those that directly move the bones.

Ball and socket joints are the most mobile, giving movements in all directions – flexion, extension, abduction, adduction, circumduction and rotation. The two joints of this type are the hip and the shoulder joint. The shoulder has a very shallow 'socket' – the glenoid fossa of the scapula – to allow the greater range of movement possible here. The muscles cross this type of joint on all sides – to move the limb in all directions and to stabilise the joint as the limb is moved.

A **saddle joint** is a modified ball and socket joint. The socket has a saddle-like ridge in it, and the ball has a corresponding indentation. The main example is the base of the thumb. This arrangement gives a more restricted and correspondingly more stable joint than the ball and socket joint, which is important for the thumb. It does not permit rotation, but does allow flexion, extension, abduction, adduction and circumduction. The thumb has muscles on all sides to move it through these ranges.

An **ellipsoid joint** (sometimes called condyloid) is also a modified ball and socket joint, the ball being oval-shaped, like an egg lying on its side, and the socket like a sideways egg cup designed to support the 'egg' in this position. It allows flexion, extension, abduction and adduction.

The connection between the radius and the carpal bones is an ellipsoid joint. The movements of this joint combine with gliding movements between the carpal bones to give a range of circumduction of the hand. There are muscles on four sides of the wrist to co-ordinate its movements.

In contrast, the **pivot joint** merely allows rotation. At the top of the spine, the atlas rotates around the axis in this way when one shakes the head ('no') controlled by the complex of muscles between the neck and the head. Muscles in the arm move the proximal end of the radius around the ulna.

Structures Related to Synovial Joints

A few synovial joints contain pads of fibrocartilage, called **menisci**, which help stabilise the joint. In the knee, there are two menisci (singular meniscus), half-moon 'wedges' shaped like segments of an orange, one on each side.

Damage to the cartilage of the knee generally means a tear in one of these menisci, not the articular cartilage, usually from twisting injuries and most commonly sustained in sport. This can result in reduced range of movement and may lead to osteoarthitis in the joint. It is treated using an arthroscope to penetrate the joint and guide, via a monitor, the cutting of the damaged tissue.

In the sternoclavicular joint, there is an articular disc that completely separates the bones. In the temporomandibular joint, the cartilage pad is sometimes a complete disc and sometimes only partial.

Sesamoid bones, found in some tendons as they cross the joints, have been described in the section on the classification of bones. The patella is the only sizeable one in the human body. A **bursa** ('sack') is a small 'pad', internally lined by membrane and filled with synovial fluid. It cushions tendons that would otherwise rub on a bone or another muscle, particularly near joints. There are a number around the knee joint, the shoulder and the elbow.

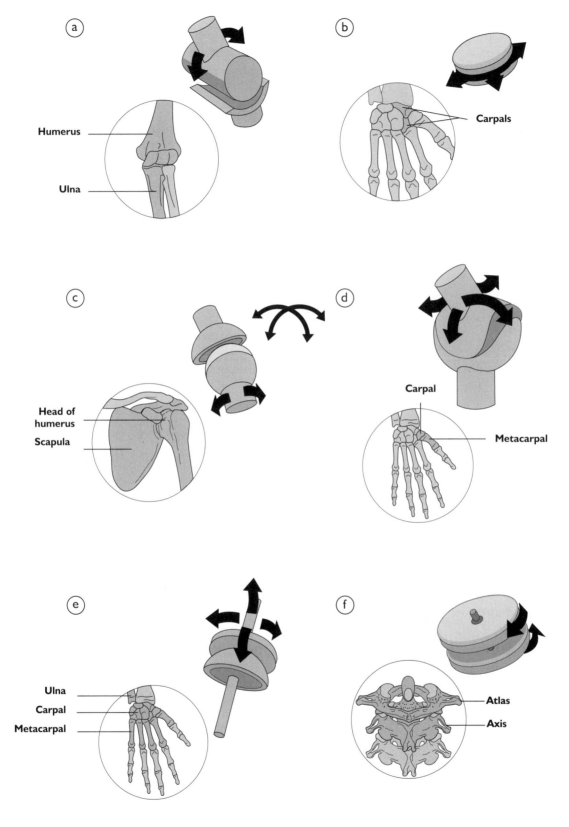

▲ Figure 6.5: Types of synovial joints, (a) hinge, (b) gliding, (c) ball and socket, (d) saddle, (e) ellipsoid, (f) pivot.

Blood and Nerve Supply to Synovial Joints

Most of the structures of the joint have no direct blood circulation. The significant circulation is to the synovial membrane on the inner surface of the capsule.

This membrane secretes the lubricating fluid in response to demand, so an unused joint tends to dry out and takes time to become re-lubricated when called into action again. This is one of many reasons why continuing exercise is important in old age. Lack of synovial fluid can cause problems. When there is less lubrication for the joint, it will become stiffer and movement will cause more wear, rather like not having enough oil in a car engine.

The articular cartilage has no direct circulation. It depends on the synovial fluid to bring nutrients from the blood vessels of the synovial membrane and to carry away wastes. This is satisfactory for the routine maintenance of the cartilage, although damaged cartilage is quite slow to heal. A reduction of fluid will lead to a decreased supply of nutrients and can cause thinning or breaking down of the cartilage.

Ligaments also have poor blood circulation, so they too are slow to heal when damaged. If the joint needs support over this healing time, for example in a weight bearing joint such as the ankle, or a well-used joint such as the shoulder joint, related muscles will tighten up to take over some of the role. Even after the ligaments have healed, the muscles can become habituated to protecting the joint and thus remain tight – something for massage practitioners to look for.

Sensory nerves from the capsule, the membrane and some ligaments, monitor position, movement, stresses on the joint, and pain. Many of these nerves branch from nerves that supply the muscles that move the joint, so they can initiate reflex responses in those muscles, such as postural balance reflexes in the lower leg.

Disorders of the Skeletal System and its Articulations

These can be due either to injuries, or to diseases that upset normal bone processes.

Key Words

Fractures
Sprain
Bursitis
Spinal curvature
Kyphosis
Lordosis
Scoliosis
Herniated or 'slipped' disc

Osteoarthritis
Rheumatoid arthritis
Ankylosing spondylitis
Osteoporosis
Osteomalacia
Rickets
Paget's disease

Injuries

Fractures are breaks in bones, varying from a hairline crack to complete breaks with bony parts penetrating the skin. They can happen throughout life, but are more common in youth due to injuries sustained in the physical activities of this age group or in old age when bones are thinner and weaker. In between those ages, fractures most often come from sports injuries or vehicle accidents.

They are painful and involve some reduction of movement at the nearest joint. If they are well splinted, many can heal within two months, although it takes longer in big bones or for older people.

Fractures fall into three major groups:

1. Partial fractures in which the bone is not completely broken;
2. Simple fractures where there is a clean break that does not damage surrounding tissues or the skin;
3. Compound fractures, where the broken ends protrude through soft tissues and the skin.

There are many further classifications. In comminuted fractures, the bone splinters at the break; in impacted fractures, the broken bones ends have been pushed into one another. A greenstick fracture occurs in children whose bones are not completely ossified. There is bending and partial fracture of the bone, similar to the breaking of a green twig.

Recommendations for massage:

1. A fracture is a local contra-indication to massage. The rest of the body can be massaged normally, assuming no other complications.
2. Gentle massage of muscles adjacent to the fracture may be attempted once the bone is well set.
3. It is also useful to massage the other areas of the body that have been overused to compensate for this restriction.
4. Broken bone can take months to heal, especially in large or weight bearing bones, or in older people. Massage can be helpful in the later stages of this process to stimulate muscles and to reduce their stiffness.

Sprain refers to damage to ligaments, when they are forced past their normal range of movement. The most common sprain is a twisted ankle, followed by injuries to the ligaments of the sacroiliac joint and the fingers and knees (especially in sport). The damage can be chronic or acute, and can range from a few torn fibres, to a complete tear.

Note that a sprain refers to damage to ligaments. Strains involve the stretching or tearing of muscle fibres, which is less serious on two counts. Firstly, muscles have better circulation and will therefore heal faster, and secondly, damage to a ligament is more likely to also involve damage to the joint itself.

Sprained ligaments swell up and are painful. Due to being stretched, they may become flabby, which can result in an unstable joint. Ligaments have poor blood circulation, so when damaged they are slow to heal. Muscles surrounding a sprain will tend to tighten to protect the joint, and even after the ligaments have healed, the muscles may stay tight and overworking. This is something for massage practitioners to watch out for.

A sprain in which there is tissue tearing, may give rise to considerable scar tissue, leading to the likelihood of further injury, unless it is treated by a professional trained to deal with sports injuries – a sports masseur or trainer, or a physiotherapist.

Recommendations for massage:

- Do **NOT** attempt to massage acute injuries unless you are trained to do so.
- After the acute stage has subsided, draining strokes can be helpful to disperse swelling. General massage can help reduce the consequent muscle stiffness and reawaken the joint through gentle movements.
- When a joint is sprained, the surrounding muscles attempt to take over the job of the damaged ligaments, and may become very tense. Even after the ligaments have healed, the muscles may have become habituated to this role. Massage of these muscles is beneficial.

Bursitis is the inflammation of a bursa through pressure, friction or injury, leading to pain that is aggravated by movement. Prolonged kneeling can lead to Housemaid's knee. The other more common problem sites are the shoulder joint (sub-acromial bursitis) and the base of the big toe (bunions).

Recommendations for massage:

- When the condition is acute, massage is contra-indicated locally.
- In the non-acute phases, massage of the surrounding muscles and passive movements within a comfortable range are useful.
- Massage on other body areas that are being overused in compensation is also helpful.

Spinal curvature – The spine has natural curves for resilience – a convex curve between the shoulders and concave curves in the neck and lower back. We all have small postural imbalances, but they become problematic when these curves become exaggerated, and rigidify into unbalanced positions. This can occur for a number of reasons; inherited factors, accidents, or poor posture over a long time.

A pronounced curve in the upper spine is a **kyphosis**, commonly called a hunchback, and a curve in the lower back is a **lordosis**, or swayback. Cervical lordosis is an excessive curve in the neck. A pronounced curve to the side is a **scoliosis**. These are rarely 'pure' curves, as they often also involve rotations and occur in combinations.

Recommendations for massage:

1. Unless there is a pathological component that precludes massage, it can be used to reduce muscular tension, which may be part of the cause and will certainly be a consequence.
2. Massage may not change the posture, but it will usually help to regain some mobility.
3. When working with clients with pronounced spinal curvatures, use cushions or pillows to ensure they have adequate support.

Herniated or **'slipped' disc** – As one ages, the fibres of the intervertebral discs can become worn and tear under pressure, especially if there is excessive or sudden strain on the spine. A 'slipped disc' then occurs when part of the central pulp becomes displaced, bulging out to one side, and putting pressure on the spinal cord and/or the nerve roots as they emerge from the spine.

This can appear to happen very suddenly without any obvious cause, although the affected disc may have been degenerating for some time. Since the cartilage has no nerve supply, there are no warning signals. The lumbar spine is most likely to be affected, with severe back pain and tenderness, and pain may be referred down the legs as well. Doctors usually recommend bed rest and painkillers. In extreme cases surgery is considered, either to remove the pulp of the disc or to fuse the vertebrae together.

People sometimes refer to any sharp back pain as a slipped disc, but an actual slipped disc is very painful and debilitating. If the trauma in the close spinal muscles is on one side only, this is more likely to be a trapped nerve, which massage may ease. If the trauma is on both sides of the spine, it is more likely to be a slipped disc in which case refer the client to a good osteopath, chiropractor or physiotherapist.

Recommendations for massage:

1. Soothing massage on other areas of the body, such as the head, may help calm the person in acute stages (if they are amenable to any touch at all).
2. Gentle massage, sensitively applied, may help relieve pain from associated muscle spasms, when the most acute stage has subsided.

Arthritis and Rheumatism

These terms are often used interchangeably in everyday language to refer to pain connected with movement. Arthritis means inflammation of joints – with pain, stiffness and loss of movement – whilst rheumatism usually refers to aches or pains that come from muscles, tendons or ligaments, as well as from joints. Arthritis is commonly a secondary condition arising from other diseases. There are many varieties of arthritis; this section looks at three of the most common forms.

Osteoarthritis is a very common condition, affecting almost everyone over the age of 60 to some extent, but to varying degrees. For the majority of people, this may be experienced merely as stiff joints. For some, the symptoms can include pain, stiffness and swelling and can lead to reduced movement as the condition worsens. It usually develops slowly, although when the condition is more advanced, it may include inflammation.

It is caused by wear and tear of the hyaline cartilage, and is made worse by previous injury or excessive pressure on the joint in overweight people. As the cartilage thins with age, cracks appear and penetrate to the bone underneath, and bony growths can also develop. Weight bearing joints such as the hip and the knee are most often affected, and also the fingers (which may not be painful) and the spine.

Recommendations for massage:

- Massage can be beneficial in providing some pain relief, and gentle mobilisation of the joints may prevent further deterioration, provided more care is taken around any painful joints.
- Local massage is contra-indicated in the acute phases.

Rheumatoid arthritis is an auto-immune disease, in which the immune system attacks the body's own tissues. This chronic disease can cause inflammation of many parts of the body. The skin, lungs, eyes and internal organs may all be affected as well as the joints, and sometimes also muscles, tendons and blood vessels. The onset is usually between 30–50 years. It is not necessarily constant but can regularly flare up and then die down.

The joints most affected are usually the hands and feet, often on both sides of the body at once, and sometimes the neck. Inside the joint, the synovial membrane becomes inflamed, the fluid builds up and the joint swells. If it progresses, which only happens in a proportion of people, the cartilage and then the bone is affected until, over time, the joint may be deformed and/or fused together.

Recommendations for massage:

- Massage is contra-indicated in acute stages.
- At other times, general massage may help reduce stress – a factor in the flaring up of the disease.
- Gentle massage of the tissues around the joints may help relieve pain. Careful movements of joints can be used to increase mobility.
- Stretches or manipulations of the spine are contra-indicated, particularly in the cervical region, because this could disturb or break bony fusions that may have developed between the vertebrae.

Ankylosing spondylitis, a spinal inflammation, is a type of arthritis that leads to stiff and sometimes fused joints, often slightly flexed. It is an inherited auto-immune disease that mostly affects men in their mid-teens to mid-thirties.

Mostly commonly it starts as lower back pain and stiffness, especially around the sacrum. It may stay here, although sometimes it progresses up the spine, and occasionally affects joints outside the spine. It can flare up at times, and there may also be inflammation of the lungs, heart, eyes and other organs.

Recommendations for massage:

- In acute phases, massage is contra-indicated in areas of pain and inflammation.
- At other times, work under a doctor's supervision. Massage may give pain relief, and, in the early stages, help maintain some mobility.
- Do not put pressure on muscles near the spine, as they may be involved in protective splinting of the vulnerable areas.

Other Disorders

Osteoporosis ('brittle bones') is fairly common in elderly people, particularly women after menopause. The onset is usually around 60 years, and in the early stages, a person may not know that she has it. There is a loss of bone density, particularly of calcium and collagen, and the bones become soft and crumbly, and liable to break easily on sudden impact, especially the wrist and hip. There may be chronic back pain and, in the advanced stages, the vertebrae may collapse.

Recommendations for massage:

1. Do not massage over known osteoporotic areas.
2. Massage should be gentle, with no stretches, joint manipulations or use of percussive strokes. The main intention is to help the client relax.
3. Negotiate comfortable positions and use of supports with the person. Take particular care in getting the client on and off the table.
4. Be cautious when massaging an older person, particularly women, as they may unknowingly have a tendency to osteoporosis. Feel your way carefully as you increase the pressure of the massage.

Osteomalacia is a softening of the bones. Vitamin D, which is present in a balanced diet, and also produced in the body through exposure to sunlight, is necessary for strong bone formation. If it is absent, the bones soften and swell. **Rickets** is the childhood variety of osteomalacia.

Recommendations for massage – Gentle massage for the relief of symptoms should only be done under a doctor's supervision.

Paget's disease is a fairly rare disease where bone is replaced by fibrous tissue that then becomes hard and brittle, with much pain. Bones most likely to be affected are the skull, spine and leg bones.

Recommendations for massage – Gentle massage for the relief of symptoms should only be done under a doctor's supervision.

Chapter 7 Physiology of Muscles

Muscle tissue has the special ability to contract and relax, or to be passively stretched. Wherever there is movement in the human body, it is produced by the action of muscles, whether it is the large visible movements of the body parts or the movement of material through the tubes of the body by the muscles that line them.

Key Words

Structure	Function
Smooth / involuntary muscle	Levers
Cardiac muscle	Isometric contractions
Skeletal / voluntary muscle	Isotonic contractions
Belly	Concentric contractions
Tendon	Eccentric contractions
Aponeurosis	Antagonistic muscles / antagonists
Fascia	Agonist / prime mover
Myofibrils	Synergists
Actin	Fixators
Myosin	Muscle tone
Fast / white fibres	Muscle tension
Slow / red fibres	Muscle spindles
Intermediate fibres	Golgi tendon organs
Attachments	Proprioceptors
Origin	Motor end plate
Insertion	Motor unit
Parallel fibres	Stretch reflex
Convergent fibres	Glucose
Pennate muscles	Adenosine triphosphate (ATP)
Circular muscles	Adenosine diphosphate (ADP)
	Lactic acid
	Anaerobic respiration
	Oxygen debt
	Aerobic respiration

The muscular system includes three types of muscle tissue: the smooth muscles which line the organs and the ducts of the body; the cardiac muscle which is the tissue of the walls of the heart, and; the skeletal muscles which mainly attach to and move bones.

Smooth muscle (also called **involuntary** or **visceral** muscle) is found in the walls of internal organs (hence the name 'visceral'), blood vessels, the digestive tract, respiratory passages and the urinary and genital ducts.

The tiny filaments in smooth muscle fibres are similar to those in skeletal muscles (*see* below), but are arranged differently. They appear smooth under a microscope, compared to the striations of skeletal muscle tissue.

Smooth muscle usually consists of two lining sheets which work in complementary ways; one is circular, wrapping around the tube or organ, and the other stretches along the length. This type of tissue responds evenly to a stimulus, more slowly than skeletal muscle but does not fatigue easily, so that it can work continuously when needed. The contractions are slow and sustained, and may produce great force, such as when a woman is in labour.

Smooth muscle is part of automatic body functioning (hence the name 'involuntary'). Much of its functioning is controlled by its own 'pacemaker' cells, whose signals can be modified by hormones and the autonomic nervous system. If the nerves are damaged, smooth muscle therefore continues to operate at a steady pace, but is unable to adjust to varying body needs.

In some places in the body, smooth muscle is intermixed with voluntary muscle, e.g. the diaphragm, eyelids, and parts of the digestive tract.

Cardiac muscle is the tissue of the walls of the heart. It rhythmically contracts and relaxes, and fortunately is difficult to fatigue. Cardiac tissue has striations that are visible under a microscope, but they are not as marked as those of skeletal muscles.

Like smooth muscle, cardiac muscle is involuntary and has an internal pacemaker (the sinoatrial node) which initiates its regular contractions. As activity changes, this signal is normally modified by instructions from the autonomic nervous system (*see* Chapter 9). The heart will continue to beat without a nerve signal, keeping a person alive, but it is then unable to adapt to changing body needs.

If cardiac tissue is damaged, it is not able to regenerate but is replaced by fibrous scar tissue that cannot contract. This reduces the heart's effectiveness.

Skeletal muscle (also called **voluntary** or **striated** muscle) is the type of muscle we are concerned with in massage. In fact, when we speak loosely of 'muscles' in massage, and throughout the rest of this book, unless otherwise indicated, we are referring only to skeletal muscles. These muscles are under voluntary control, although we can and do tighten them without knowing it, leading to habitual tensions.

Generally, skeletal muscles are attached to bones at either end, and by contracting or shortening, they move one bone closer to the other. They thus give the body the power of movement, as well as being involved in the skilful manipulation of tools and instruments, communication through speech and gesture, and aspects of breathing and digestion that can be consciously controlled such as chewing, swallowing, urinating, and defecating.

Some skeletal muscles do not move bones. Apart from those that move the jaw, the remainder of the facial muscles move the skin or other muscles. Some muscles control body openings, such as the mouth, the eyes, the bladder and the anus.

Skeletal muscles are the 'meat' of the body, accounting for about 40% of its weight. Under the microscope, their fibres appear striated (striped). These fibres are larger than those of smooth muscle and have better circulation. This is to maintain the supply of the materials they need to carry out their tasks. They are controlled by the voluntary nervous system although some, such as the diaphragm, also have smooth muscle fibres mixed in.

They respond to stimulation more quickly than smooth muscles, but tire more rapidly and are less able to be stretched than the smooth muscle of the digestive tract and blood vessels.

Skeletal muscle is capable of limited self-repair if it is damaged, unless large regions are affected, in which case the muscle tissue is replaced by scar tissue. This is fibrous connective tissue, which is stiffer and cannot contract, reducing the muscle's effectiveness. If the nerve feeding the muscle is irreparably damaged, the fibres will wither and ultimately be replaced by connective tissue.

Properties of Skeletal Muscles

Muscles create movement. As a skeletal muscle shortens, it pulls one bone towards another. Through the collective actions of our muscles, we are able to maintain posture, do physical tasks, exercise and play sport, undertake leisure activities and express ourselves both through creative activities, such as playing an instrument or doing handiwork, and through our gestures and body language.

Muscles assist in joint support. In most joints of the body, there is a balance between the ligaments that hold the joint and the muscles that help stabilise but also move it. The knee and the hip joints, for example, have strong ligaments, but also depend for stability on the muscles whose tendons cross them. In the shoulder joint, there are only a few ligaments, so muscles are responsible for most of the stability.

Muscles protect against trauma. They take over the work of stabilising a joint in which the ligaments have been injured or weakened, such as a twisted ankle. This can also occur in the spine, where a ligament has been overstretched and the consequent instability of the vertebrae could lead to damage to the spinal cord. These protective tensions can become habitual, remaining in place long after an injury has healed. In this situation, massage can be very useful in coaxing the muscles to release.

However, if you know or suspect that the muscles are still serving a protective function, be cautious about doing heavy massage on them. Encourage the muscles to release but don't try to force your way through the tensions.

Muscles are interlinked with many other body systems. They contribute to the functioning of many systems, but are also dependent on them. Their actions are initiated, monitored and coordinated by the nervous system. The skin protects the skeletal muscles and helps dissipate the heat produced by their activity.

Sugars from digestion and oxygen from respiration, which are the materials that muscles use for working, are brought via the circulatory system. It also carries away the waste products of muscle metabolism to be excreted via the lungs and the kidneys. Because skeletal muscles use so much energy, they need good circulation to keep them well supplied with these energy materials. In turn they aid the circulation. When muscles are active, they squeeze the blood vessels that pass through them. If they are alternately contracting and relaxing, the *muscles pump blood and lymph* towards the heart as they contract.

However, if they remain contracted for a long time, blood circulation is restricted. Because there are less nutrients coming in and the wastes are not being completely cleared, the muscle gets sluggish, hard and less responsive.

Muscles produce heat. The chemical processes in the body only work within a small temperature range, so they need a fairly constant source of heat. All of the cells of the body use sugars to produce the energy that powers their functioning, and heat is a major outcome of this process. The muscle cells use the same process to create energy for body activity, and produce over a third of the body's heat. Doing physical activity warms us. When we feel cold, we involuntarily start to shiver, which is our body's way of activating muscles to create heat.

Muscle Structure

Any one muscle consists of many bundles of fibres. These bundles are capable of some independent movement. The fibres, and therefore the whole muscle, can only actively contract to pull on bones and move them; they cannot push.

Relaxation does not change the length of a muscle, but while the muscle is relaxed, it may be passively stretched. A muscle cannot stretch or lengthen on its own and it can only be stretched by the action of reciprocal muscles or by the pull of gravity on it.

The fleshy part of a muscle – the 'meat' where the fibres are – is called the **belly** of the muscle. This is the working part of the muscle. At rest, it is relatively soft to the touch. It moves a bone by contracting – swelling a little and becoming tighter in the process. The relative hardness of the muscle indicates how hard it is working.

Muscle hardness can also indicate that the muscle remains working when it is no longer needed for immediate activity. This is the process by which we accumulate long-term tension.

The strong, relatively inelastic parts at each end of a muscle are **tendons**, which attach the muscle to a bone by knitting very strongly into the periosteum. In the sausage shaped muscles, tendons feel stringy and cord-like and attach to the periosteum in quite a small area. When the muscle contracts, they are pulled taut like a rope, and can be so hard that they may be mistaken for bones by a novice. Some muscles have more than one tendon at one end. A number of the forearm muscles, for example, each have tendons to all four fingers.

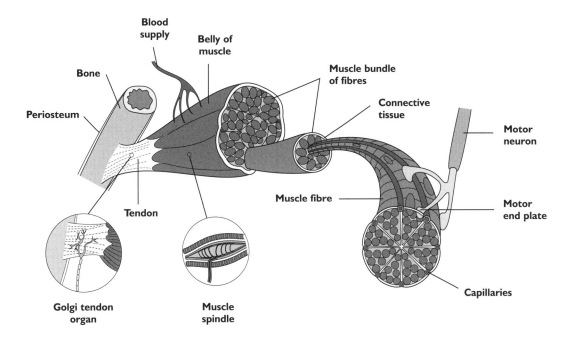

▲ *Figure 7.1: A skeletal muscle.*

Tears are most common in the soft muscle belly. They are much rarer where the tendon attaches to the bone; this injury is almost always caused by a sudden, very forceful pull on the muscle. This type of injury is most common in the Achilles tendon that attaches the strong calf muscles to the heel bone.

Wide, flat muscles have a flattened 'sheet' of tendon called an **aponeurosis**, by which they are attached to the bone along a long narrow line, similar to the lashing between a sail and the ship's mast. This is the case, for example, where the chest muscle (pectoralis major) attaches along the edge of the sternum and the underside of the clavicle.

The aponeurosis may divide into slips that attach to a series of bones, particularly along the spine. The trapezius muscle, which covers the back of the neck, the shoulders and the upper back, has individual slips to all the thoracic vertebrae, as well as attaching to the occiput and the nuchal ligament.

Reference to a 'muscle' normally includes the tendons or aponeuroses. A muscle, including the tendons, is surrounded by a sheath of **fascia** which is a wrapping of strong gristle. In bodywork, the terms fascia and connective tissue (CT) are generally used interchangeably to describe the sheaths that surround and give shape to the soft structures of the body – muscles, organs, tubes and skin – and hold them in place, in relation to the bones and each other.

Bear in mind however, that in precise anatomical terms, connective tissue is the term that describes all of the tissues of the body except muscles, nerves and lining tissue (*see* Chapter 3).

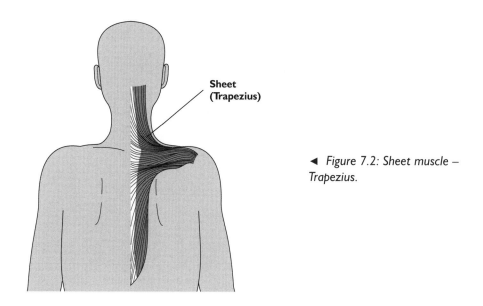

Sheet (Trapezius)

◄ *Figure 7.2: Sheet muscle – Trapezius.*

In a healthy state, especially when we are young, the muscle sheath remains soft and pliable. As a muscle contracts, the connective tissue sheath also shortens; as the muscle relaxes or is stretched, the fascia also adjusts.

However, if a muscle remains tense and contracted for a long period, the fascia becomes harder, stiffer and less responsive, initiating a vicious cycle whereby the muscles are less able to respond. Myofascial release is a style of bodywork that works on fascial adhesions just below the skin. Deeper fascial adhesions around muscles are addressed by deep tissue massage, of which the best known is probably Rolfing. This comprehensive sequence of deep tissue work, which is designed to align the body segments, was developed by Ida Rolf (1896–1979), an American woman with a background in the biochemistry of connective tissue.

Muscle Fibres

Muscles have very little intercellular tissue. They consist almost entirely of muscle fibres held together by fibrous connective tissue and penetrated by numerous tiny blood vessels and nerves. These long, slender fibres are the muscle cells. Even small muscles contain thousands of them. They vary in size – in the longest muscles they can be up to 30cms (1 foot) long, while others are microscopic.

Each muscle fibre has an individual wrapping sheath of fine connective tissue ('endomysium'), making it like a very long, thin sausage. These are further wrapped together in bundles ('fasciculi' covered by 'perimysium'), which are then gathered to form the muscle belly with its own sheath – the fascia ('epimysium'). The tendon or aponeurosis is usually made up of the continuation of the endomysium and perimysium wrapping material.

Each muscle fibre is made up of even thinner fibres called **myofibrils**. These consist of long strands of microfilaments, made of two different types of protein strands called

actin and **myosin**. It is the arrangement of actin and myosin filaments in skeletal muscle fibres, which gives the striated or striped appearance when viewed under a microscope. They slide along one another during muscle contraction causing the fibre as a whole to shorten.

Most skeletal muscles are made of a combination of three types of fibres:

1. **Fast (white) fibres** have fast, strong reactions but tire quickly, so they are well adapted for rapid movements and short bursts of activity, such as a sprint. They mainly use the energy stored in the muscle as a sugar called glucose, which can be transferred into manual energy without oxygen.

2. **Slow (red) fibres** have greater endurance, but do not produce as much strength, so they are suited to slower movements, the continual demands of posture and sustained activities, such as running a marathon or riding long cycle races. Their energy comes from the breaking down of glucose by oxygen and they depend on a continuing supply of glucose for endurance. The oxygen and the extra glucose are brought in the blood, so they have a good circulation. The red colour comes from both the circulation and from the presence of a red pigmented protein that stores the oxygen.

If you eat chicken meat, you'll have observed the differences between the 'red meat' and 'white meat'. The leg muscles are much darker because chickens stand all day, while the breast muscles that flap the wings and are only used for short intermittent periods, are much lighter.

3. **Intermediate fibres** have some properties of both fast and slow fibres. They have better blood circulation and more endurance than fast fibres, but less than slow fibres so they are pale by comparison.

Red, white and intermediate fibres are found in the same muscle, with different compositions, for different muscles. There are great variations in the number of red and white fibres that different people have throughout their bodies. It is possible to change the characteristics of some fibres through physical conditioning, particularly changing fast and slow fibres towards intermediate – by using fast fibres for endurance activities, or slow fibres for greater movement.

Each person is born with a set number of muscle fibres, which cannot be increased. An increase in the size of a muscle is due to exercise that increases the size of the individual fibres, and they will shrink again with disuse. Men are more able to enlarge their muscles through exercise than women due to the effects of male hormones.

Attachments

A muscle attaches to a bone via the tendon or aponeurosis knitting into the periosteum around the bone. Tendons, aponeuroses and perisoteum are very similar types of dense connective tissue so the connection is actually a blending together of fibrous material, rather than an abrupt junction. Muscle **attachments** are known by the terms of **origin** and **insertion**.

Generally, the end of the muscle closest to the centre of the body is referred to as the origin, and that furthest away, as the insertion. For example, biceps, the muscle of the upper arm that bends the elbow, is said to originate on the scapula and insert into the radius.

Origins are often shorter and broader, and attach over a larger area, while insertions are commonly longer, and the fibres are more densely concentrated, attaching to a smaller bone area. The insertion is more often where the work is done.

Where a muscle divides into more than one attachment at one end (e.g. biceps = 'two-headed'; triceps = 'three-headed') or has a long line of attachment at one end, e.g. deltoid, there will generally be a number of actions possible. This will depend on which sections are activated by separate nerve signals, and the counter-balancing actions of complementary muscles.

In the strict anatomical definition, origin refers to the end of the muscle that is attached to the bone that remains stationary, while the insertion is the attachment to the bone that moves.

This usually amounts to the same thing as the common definition used above. However, the strict terminology is relative to a particular movement, and can therefore change.

When a person bends his arm towards his body, the two definitions coincide. However, if the strict definition was applied when our person was pulling himself up while climbing, i.e. moving his trunk while keeping his forearm stationary, the origin of biceps would be considered to be on the forearm for this movement and the insertions on the scapula.

You can therefore appreciate how these two definitions can sometimes be at odds and cause great confusion. In this book, we will follow the usual convention, that the origin is closest to the centre of the body and the insertion is the further attachment.

Muscle Shapes

The way that the bundles of fibres lie next to one another in the muscle determines its cross sectional shape.

Spindle-shaped muscles, such as the brachialis, have a long, fleshy central bulge and narrow, round tendons at each end. Sheet-like muscles have an aponeurotic connection to the bones at one or both ends. The trapezius, for example, has an aponeurosis at each end.

Muscles are a variation of one or another type, or combine aspects of both. Pectoralis major, for example, which is small and round in cross section where it attaches to the humerus and crosses the front of the armpit, spreads sheet-like across the front of the chest. The possible actions of a muscle, including the strength and direction of its pull, are determined by its 'geometry'. This relates to:

- The size and shape of its cross section;
- The angle between the muscle fibres and the pull of the tendon;
- The overall length of the muscle and the length of the individual fibres;
- The relative distances away from the joint of the bony attachments, and;
- Whether it is straight or bends or twists.

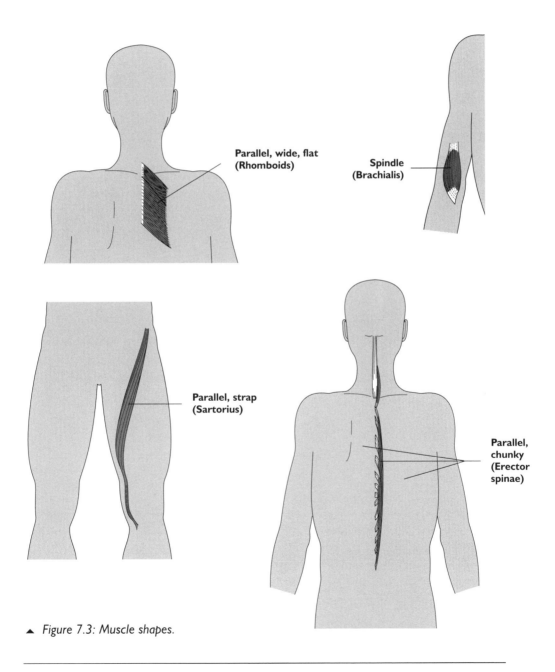

▲ *Figure 7.3: Muscle shapes.*

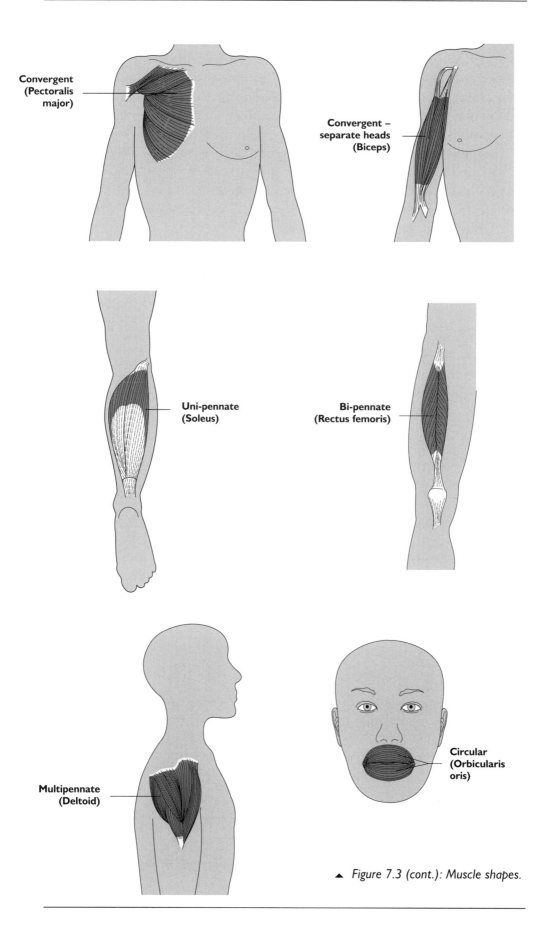

Convergent
(Pectoralis
major)

Convergent –
separate heads
(Biceps)

Uni-pennate
(Soleus)

Bi-pennate
(Rectus femoris)

Multipennate
(Deltoid)

Circular
(Orbicularis
oris)

▲ *Figure 7.3 (cont.): Muscle shapes.*

Common muscle fibre arrangements include:

1. Muscles with **parallel fibres**, which can contract together over a long distance, pulling in a direct line, tend to work only in one direction. These can vary from short, flat muscles to spindle-shaped muscles to long straps. Their actions are not as strong as the convergent fibres or the pennate arrangement. The thinner 'strap' muscles with this arrangement are involved in large, rapid movements. The long sartorius of the thigh is of this type. The thicker muscles, such as the long postural muscles of the back and the abdomen, deliver a more constant strength.

2. **Convergent muscles**, in which the fibres coverage towards a single insertion point for maximum concentration of the contraction. The direction of movement is determined by which sections of the muscle are activated. The muscle may be a triangular sheet, such as the pectoralis major that crosses the front of the shoulder joint from the chest, or made up of separate muscle bellies converging to a single tendon, such as the biceps muscle. These muscles often cross joints that have a large range of possible movements, such as the pectoralis major and the latissimus dorsi that cross the shoulder joint. They provide a strong but steady pull, fine-tuning the angle of movement, and thus balancing movement with continuing stability in the joint. There is an overlap with the next grouping, the pennates, and many authorities incorporate them into one group under the pennate title. The gluteals that cross the hip joint can be classed with either group.

3. **Pennate muscles** ('like a feather or quill'), in which the fibres lie at an angle to the tendon and therefore also to the direction of pull. They have lots of short fibres, so the muscle pull is short but strong. Many of the muscles of the forearm that flex and extend the wrist and fingers, and some of the muscles at the back of the upper and lower leg, are of this type. They can be:

- Uni-pennate. Diagonal muscle fibres attach to one side of the tendon only, e.g. the soleus which lies under the bulky mass of the outer calf muscle;
- Bi-pennate. The fibres converge onto a central tendon from both sides, e.g. rectus femoris at the front of the thigh, or;
- Multipennate. The muscle has several tendons of origin, e.g. the deltoid at the top of the arm.

4. **Circular muscles**, which surround orifices and close openings when active, such as the mouth, the urinary sphincter and the anus.

Each time we use a muscle, we tend to initially call the same section into play, gradually building up tension in that area. The muscle fibres shorten along their length, so tension often accumulates in lines in the longer muscles, particularly in those with parallel fibres such as the deep postural muscles of the back. With massage experience, you will develop the ability to discern these lines of tension and identify the muscle layer in which they lie.

In the muscles with shorter fibres, including the pennates and many with convergent fibres, tension is often in knots rather than in definable lines.

Muscle Actions

Muscles contract to create a movement, to oppose or reduce a movement, or to stabilise a joint. They can shorten to about two thirds of their resting length. Skeletal muscles are involved in the sustained work of posture, the intermittent demands of movement, or both.

Short muscles, such as the network of muscles alongside the spine, are responsible for small, precise adjustments of posture. Long muscles, such as those in the leg, are used more for large movements.

Leverage

Muscle pulls are usually at an angle to the bone to be moved. The power and range of a muscle pull is affected by the distance between the joint, the point of attachment of the muscle and the weight to be moved (which can be just the weight of body parts or supplemented by a load that a person is carrying).

The closer to a joint that a muscle inserts on a bone that it moves, the bigger the range of movement that it can produce at the far end of that bone, but the greater the force that it needs to do this. This balance between force and range of movement is rather like seating a heavy child close to the centre of a seesaw, so that a lighter child on the far end can balance the heavier child but moves through a larger distance. However in the body, unlike a seesaw, the muscle attachment and therefore its pull, is usually *between* the joint and the far end of the bone that is moved.

Levers

In physics, a **lever** is defined as a bar that is pivoted on a balance point called a fulcrum, in order to move a load, when an effort is applied to the lever. In the body, the lever is a bone and the fulcrum is the joint upon which it acts. The effort is supplied by the muscles, and the load is the weight of the body parts moved (and any extra objects that one is carrying). There are three 'orders' of levers, depending on the relative positions of the load, the fulcrum and the weight being moved.

In a first order lever, the fulcrum is between the load and the effort, as in a seesaw. The head, which is balanced on the top of the spine, is pulled down by the muscles of the back of the neck.

In the second order lever, the load is between the fulcrum and the effort, as in a wheelbarrow. This type of lever action is used to stand on tiptoe, with the calf muscles lifting the weight of the body.

In the third order lever, the effort is between the weight and the fulcrum. This is the way most of the muscles pull on the bones of the body, for example, the biceps muscle raising the forearm and hand.

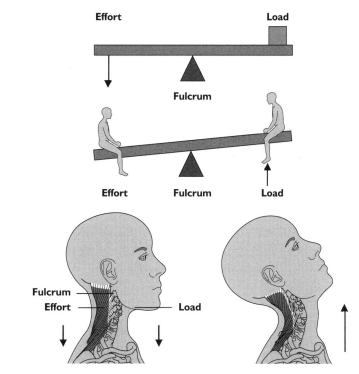

First order lever

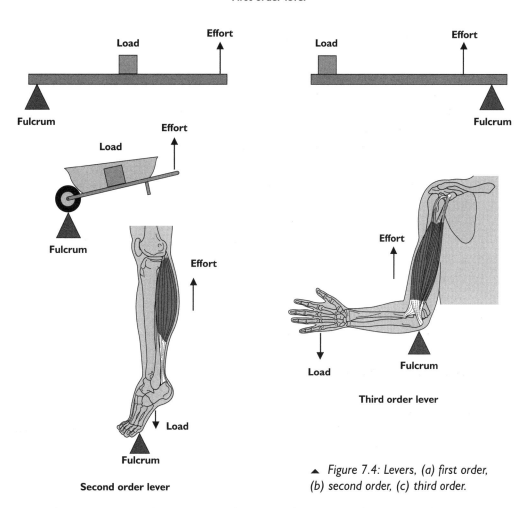

Second order lever

Third order lever

▲ *Figure 7.4: Levers, (a) first order, (b) second order, (c) third order.*

Types of Muscular Work

Muscles respond in different ways to the demands placed on them. If they are moving a small weight, they can contract quickly, but if the weight is heavier, they will work more strongly but more slowly to move it. They thus work at their fastest when moving the lightest load, and generate the greatest power when attempting to move a stationary object. These characteristics are used in gym workouts, body building and sports training to develop specific muscle strengths, stamina or speed of response. Note that when a muscle is working, it is described as 'contracting' even when an external resistance prevents it from shortening, or actually stretches it.

In an **isometric contraction**, the muscle works without movement happening ('*iso*' means same and '*metric*' means length). This is how the postural muscles work. In the gym, this trait is used to develop static strength in muscles by attempting to pull or push against static equipment.

In an **isotonic contraction**, the muscle force is considered to be constant ('*tonic*' means same tone or tension), but the muscle length changes. In the gym this type of contraction is used to develop more dynamic strength. There are two types of isotonic contraction:

1. **Concentric contractions** ('towards the centre') occur when the muscle shortens to move the attachments closer, such as a biceps curl in which the biceps bends up the forearm. This is not as strong as the isometric contraction.
2. **Eccentric contractions** ('away from the centre') occur when a muscle is stretched as it tries to resist a force pulling the bones of attachment away from each other, such as tensing your biceps as someone stronger pulls your forearm straight. These contractions generate even greater force than the isometric contraction.

These types of work occur all the time in everyday life. If you are standing up, the muscle at the front of your thigh that straightens your knee, the quadriceps muscle, keeps you upright by preventing your knee from bending – isometric contraction. If you slowly sit down, this muscle is stretched, while it controls the rate at which your knee bends to lower your body – eccentric contraction. If you then stand up, the muscle works concentrically to straighten the knee again.

During many actions, both isometric and isotonic actions occur simultaneously. For example, when kicking a ball, one leg is stable while the other executes the kick.

Muscle Coordination

Although muscles are usually described as doing a particular action, they do not act alone. Any movement is the result of cooperation between a large number of muscles, which is coordinated in the cerebellum in the brain, for smooth efficient actions. Each muscle can also perform varied roles in different movements.

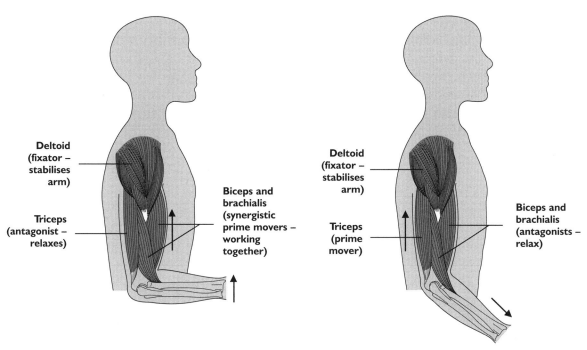

▲ *Figure 7.5: Muscle co-ordination.*

Antagonistic muscles are two muscles or sets of muscles, which pull in opposite directions to each other, hence the name. This terminology can give a misleading image. They don't actually work against one another but work in a reciprocal, complementary way, with one relaxing to allow the other to contract. This reciprocal relationship is coordinated in the brain.

The main activating muscle for an action is known as the **agonist** or **prime mover**. A muscle that is relaxing and being stretched by the action of the prime mover is called an **antagonist**.

These terms are used in relation to a specific action. The roles, and therefore the terminology, are relative to one another and changeable. Biceps is the agonist in flexion of the elbow joint and triceps, at the back of the upper arm, is the antagonist. In relation to straightening the elbow, the roles are reversed.

They can have a more complex interrelationship too. The antagonist may come into play towards the end of a fast movement to brake it before damage is caused to muscles, ligaments or the joint. For example, if the biceps is bending your arm very quickly, the triceps is activated to stop your hand from hitting your shoulder.

In eccentric movements, such as straightening your arm to lower a heavy load, the movement is controlled by the biceps, whilst the triceps remains relaxed. And they may work simultaneously to stabilise a joint.

Muscles usually act in antagonistic groups, rather than just paired antagonists. In hinge joints such as the elbow, the knee or the fingers, the antagonists will be on opposite sides of the joint, one muscle or group to bend the joint and the other to straighten it.

Muscles on the same side of the joint that work together to do the same movement are called **synergists** ('working together'). In flexing of the elbow, biceps actually works synergistically with the brachialis muscle, which lies underneath it.

Sometimes, there is a prime mover that initiates the movement and other muscles that play a small synergistic supporting part. Triceps is the main extensor of the elbow; its action is supported by anconeus, a small muscle that crosses the back of the elbow joint.

Around joints with a more varied range of movement, or the scapula that moves over the back and the side of the ribs, there is a more complex arrangement of muscle balances.

Around the hip joint for example, which has four ranges of movement, there are paired groups of antagonists; muscles at the front flex the leg, and muscles at the back extend it, muscles on the medial surface adduct it, while muscles on the lateral edge abduct it. As well as working in these paired arrangements, the muscle groups are involved to varying degrees in rotation of the leg, and in movements of the leg that blend these 'pure' axes of movement, such as flexion combined with abduction.

This collaboration between the muscles could be likened a little to steering a horse via four reins. The usual two to turn its head to the left or right, one attached to the top of its head to pull its head up, and another low down on its neck to pull the lower neck backwards.

A further group of muscles is involved in many movements. **Fixators** are muscles that stabilise a bone to give a steady base from which the agonist works. For biceps and triceps to flex and extend the elbow joint, muscles around the shoulder and upper back control the position of the arm.

Muscle Tone and Tension

In any muscle, even when it is at rest, there is some minimal stimulation, rather like keeping a car engine quietly ticking over so that it is always ready for action. While this is too small to actually contract the muscle, it gives a resting **muscle tone**.

The resting tone varies throughout a person's body. It is generally higher in the postural muscles. It will also be higher in the muscles that the person uses most regularly. In fact, with experience, you'll begin to use this as an indicator of how the person 'inhabits' and uses his body.

Top body builders work to develop the ability to move their muscles from low tone (fairly relaxed) to high tone (alert and rippling) very quickly without tension. In such a person, in fact in anyone who uses their body actively, you will be able to feel some tone – an 'aliveness' – in their muscles even when they are quite relaxed. Conversely, low tone will be felt in the muscles of an inactive person as a softness or deadness with no sense of energy in it.

In the terminology of the sports world, a muscle with 'high tone' has a strong, dynamic feel to the touch, indicating a condition of active use and 'aliveness' while a flaccid, unused muscle has 'low tone'. This is not the same as tension; a muscle that is held tightly is said to lose some of its tone as it becomes more rigid and less dynamic.

Muscle tension is different to tone. It arises when a person is tightening muscles beyond the needs of the present situation. Much of this occurs unconsciously, through a slow but gradual accumulation over time. A person does a task, but does not relax completely afterwards; he is stressed and consequently tenses up, holding that tension until it becomes an unconscious part of himself. Initially, tight muscles are sore, but over time, they become less sensitive so the person is unaware of the process of accumulating tension.

If muscles are constantly tight, they are working and consuming energy for no good effect. This is tiring, and one's actions are restricted because the muscles have so little potential for movement.

A person's build and activities will influence the way that tension and tone occur. People with soft muscles, especially women, will generally have a lower resting tone even if they are quite active, while it will be higher in those of a sinewy build. People with large builds commonly have a more even tone and distribution of tension throughout the body.

In all of these groups, there can often be a great variation in tone throughout the body, between the areas where muscles are regularly used and those not exercised. There will also be similar variations in chronic tension patterns. The stresses that a person is presently managing will affect these qualities, and so will a person's attitude to life.

Higher air temperatures reduce muscle tone and relax the muscles and cold induces muscles to tighten. This fact highlights the importance of keeping massage recipients warm so that their muscles are as relaxed as possible when you work on them, making it easier to have an effect.

Nerves and Muscles

The nervous system is an essential part of muscular functioning. Muscles have both motor (activating) nerves and sensory (sensing) nerves via which muscular activity is initiated, monitored and coordinated.

Sensory Nerves

The sensory nerves allow a person to sense what is happening with the muscles. Within each muscle there is a scattering of **muscle spindles** – special muscle fibres with wrappings of sensory nerves contained in a spindle-shaped capsule (*see* figure 7.1).

These nerves monitor changes in the length of the fibres and whether they are being stretched. There are similar nerves that monitor tension in specific collagen fibres in tendons called **Golgi tendon organs**. There are more of these in the limb muscles than in the trunk.

There are also a few Golgi endings in the ligaments that surround the joints, and many more stretch monitoring receptors in the capsular lining. These are most common in the postural joints, such as the hip and knee. Receptors in the skin also register stretching of the skin at the extremes of joint movement.

These monitors collectively inform the central nervous system about the positions, movements and tensions of the body – of the muscles, the tendons, the ligaments and the joint capsules. Some of the impulses from these sensory nerves initiate reflex actions in motor nerves that protect the body from harm (*see* below).

They are aided in monitoring the body by specialised sensory nerves in the balance organ in the middle ear, which monitors the orientation and movement of the head. The eyes also contribute to the brain's awareness of bodily position and movement.

All of these receptors are collectively called **proprioceptors** (literally, 'one's own sensors'). The brain relies on the information that it receives from them for both the unconscious regulation of posture, muscle tone, coordination and movement, and for conscious awareness and control of the body's position and movements.

All bodily learning and control, comes via the feedback that we receive through the proprioceptors. This includes the basic learning that we all go through in discovering how to walk and talk; the special skills involved in sports, recreational or work activities; and the awareness of one's tensions and how to relax that comes via massage or through learning relaxation procedures.

If you remain still for a period of time with no discernible changes in muscles (apart from quiet breathing), your sense of your body begins to diminish. This is a feature of many meditation practices. It is also why we can be disorientated on waking suddenly from deep sleep.

Motor Nerves

All of the time that we are alive the tone of a muscle is maintained by tiny motor nerve impulses. These only disappear under an anaesthetic which causes a muscle to go flaccid, or when the nerve is cut which, if serious enough, will lead to the muscle withering.

As we stand, move and do tasks, motor nerves activate muscles by stimulating the release of a neurotransmitter where the nerve fibre terminates on an individual muscle fibre called the **motor end plate**.

A **motor unit** is the neuromuscular junction formed by a single motor nerve cell and the muscle fibres that its branches activate. The fibres that each nerve can activate are spread throughout a section of the muscle and interspersed with fibres innervated by other motor nerves. This arrangement ensures an even response throughout the muscle, and allows the fibres of one motor unit to relax and undergo their necessary recovery time, while adjacent fibres take over.

The number of motor units that feed a muscle will determine the possible complexity of its actions. The tongue and the muscles of the eyes have a large number of motor units, some of which serve as few as 10–12 muscle fibres. This offers great precision of movement. The facial muscles and the muscles of the forearm that serve the hands also contain many motor units.

In contrast, the muscles of the buttocks and thigh have considerably fewer motor units, each of which activates thousands of muscle fibres, providing a simple and powerful movement in response to a single message from the brain.

Sensory and Motor Interplay

Coordination of the motor and sensory nerves is crucial in voluntary muscles, so that we can feel what we are doing and thus use our bodies effectively.

In addition to this conscious monitoring, some of the sensory impulses stimulate reflex responses in motor nerves to maintain muscle tone and the body's postural balance, reflexes that coordinate antagonistic muscles, and other reflexes.

One of these mechanisms is the **stretch reflex**, which causes a muscle to contract when it has been overstretched in order to protect itself from possible damage. The most widely known stretch reflex is the knee jerk response; when the patellar ligament is tapped with a rubber mallet, the quadriceps causes the leg to extend (*see* reflex arcs in Chapter 9).

These reflexes are responses to sudden changes in a muscle's length or tension. However, if tension accumulates slowly, or a person tightens up through injury, the brain can become accustomed to a level of tightness and assume it to be the 'natural' resting level of the muscle, hence the slow unconscious build up of tension in muscles.

In addition to massage directly encouraging relaxation in muscles, it can also be important in bringing these unconscious tensions into the client's awareness, so that he can begin to do something about reducing them.

Muscle Energy – Aerobic and Anaerobic Metabolism

All of the cells of the body use glucose and oxygen to create energy for functioning and to maintain their internal temperature. The muscle cells additionally use this process to create energy for contraction.

Glucose is a product of the breakdown of carbohydrates (starches and sugar foods) in the food we eat. Some glucose from digestion is carried by the blood to the muscle cells and stored there, in readiness for immediate use; however, the muscle cells can only store a limited amount. Much of the glucose from digestion is initially stored in the liver as glycogen, and released into the bloodstream for transport to the muscles during activity, being then reduced to glucose for use.

Excess calories from protein foods, fats or additional carbohydrates are converted to body fat stores. This can be released as fatty acids into the bloodstream to provide an additional source of energy for muscle contraction if needed.

Energy provided by the breaking down of glucose cannot be used directly by the cells. Instead, it is stored as chemical energy in **adenosine triphosphate (ATP)**, a chemical that is manufactured in the cell from glucose or fatty acids. This substance is sometimes referred to as the 'energy currency' of the body because it contains the energy required to power the cellular functions of the body including muscle contraction.

The bonds between the phosphate parts of ATP are sometimes likened to a coiled spring, primed with energy that is awaiting release. These bonds can easily be broken by the cell's mitochondria, yielding **ADP (adenosine diphosphate)**, a free-floating phosphate and considerable energy for the cell to use.

The ADP and the phosphate are then joined to reform ATP by the breaking down of further glucose.

Anaerobic Tissue Respiration

When there is no oxygen present, the muscle cells can manufacture some ATP from glucose. This method produces **lactic acid**, which has a tendency to build up in the muscles and irritate the nerve endings, contributing to the sensations of stiffness and soreness often experienced after engaging in more intensive exercise than usual. The manufacture of ATP without oxygen is known as **anaerobic** ('without air') **respiration**.

Glucose > ATP + Lactic Acid + Energy

The white / fast fibres of muscles function mostly anaerobically which enables them to contract rapidly and powerfully for action, but they fatigue quickly because their ATP supply is quickly depleted.

The lactic acid is removed from the muscle and transported to the liver by the bloodstream. The liver can reconvert lactic acid to glucose when sufficient oxygen becomes available.

The oxygen required to replenish depleted ATP reserves in the muscle cells and to reconvert lactic acid to glucose in the liver, is called the **oxygen debt**. After strenuous activity, we puff and pant to take in more oxygen, and continue to generate heat.

Aerobic Tissue Respiration

When the muscle cells are receiving sufficient oxygen from the bloodstream, they can burn glucose or fatty acids to produce plenty of ATP for energy – about five times as much as the anaerobic process. The glucose is broken down beyond the lactic acid stage to carbon dioxide and water, which are readily passed from the muscle cells to the bloodstream. This process is known as **aerobic** ('with air') **respiration**.

Glucose or Fatty Acids + Oxygen > ATP + Water + Carbon Dioxide + Energy

The red / slow fibres of muscles function mostly aerobically, using the continual input of glucose and oxygen to continually manufacture ATP efficiently, allowing them to sustain their activity.

If the body has used its stores of glucose, it will then call upon stored fats for energy. If these too are all used (e.g. in starvation or in eating disorders such as anorexia nervosa), the body can then begin to use proteins to maintain internal energy (i.e. the body begins to eat itself).

Blood Circulation in Muscles

When muscles are active, the body responds to muscle activity by increasing the heart and breathing rates, and dilating (expanding) the blood vessels that pass through the muscles, bringing increased oxygen and glucose, and removing the waste products more quickly. At the same time, the activity of the muscles squeezes their internal blood and lymph vessels, pumping the fluids through and thus increasing the flow back to the heart.

Even when one is not particularly active, minute involuntary activations of muscles squeeze the blood slowly back towards the heart, and are essential to the maintenance of the circulation in the lower limbs. Regular exercise is thus an essential part of maintaining both circulatory and muscular health.

Blood also brings materials from the digestion for muscle maintenance and repair. The waste products of muscle activity are carried away, the carbon dioxide going to the lungs and the water being used in other body processes. Used proteins from the cells in the form of urea are carried away in the blood and lymph vessels and excreted via the urinary system.

This all works well when muscles contract and then relax. If however, muscles are chronically tight, this interferes with the blood flow through the muscle and thus with the muscle's functioning; it doesn't receive a full supply of nutrients and the wastes build up. This discomfort can initiate a vicious cycle, causing the muscle to tense up more. Over time habitual tension leads to hardening of the fibres and a reduction of functioning – sometimes with chronic pain, sometimes with just stiffness and deadness of feeling.

General Massage Considerations

This section briefly summarises some of the massage points already covered and looks at some further implications.

Muscle tension indicates that the muscle is working even when the person is relaxing. It can develop as a result of particular activities, protective reactions after trauma that have become habitual, attitudes to life, or via a slow and often unconscious accumulation in response to the demands of life.

If muscles are constantly tight, blood circulation is restricted and they do not function as well as when they are relaxed. They are working and consuming energy for no good effect, which is tiring. It is harder to be active because the muscles have so little potential for movement. Initially, tight muscles are sore, but over time, they usually become less sensitive. General massage techniques will work well in these conditions, supplemented by deeper work if you are trained to apply it.

Tension often accumulates in lines in the long muscles of the limbs and the wide muscles of the trunk, which can be addressed most effectively by using techniques that knead the muscle and stretch it in various ways, and also pressure strokes. In shorter muscles, such as the network of muscles alongside the spine, where there are commonly knots of tension, pressure strokes may be most useful as it is harder to move the muscles around.

What Does Massage do for Muscles?

Even a friendly touch on the skin may be calming for some people, encouraging them to relax and this may encourage some muscle relaxation (*see* Chapter 9).

As we age, we tend to accumulate tensions in our muscles and they, along with many other body tissues, tend to dry out. Massage is one of the ways of halting and reversing this sequence. Massage can help muscles to soften generally and can be applied to specific adhesions to reduce or release them. Softening will help the muscle's own blood flow. Kneading and sliding pressure strokes can actively pump blood, lymph and other fluids through the muscle.

When a muscle becomes tight, the fascia around it will also shorten and stiffen. These adhesions can be addressed by myofascial and deep tissue techniques.

However, if you think that muscle tightness is protecting a weakness or an injury, be cautious in your approach, or refer the client to a person trained in dealing with such injuries.

Some bodywork systems use the reciprocal inhibition of antagonistic muscles to promote release in tight muscles and/or rebalance between them. If a muscle is tense, tightening the antagonistic muscle will encourage it to let go. While a chronically tight muscle may need relaxation, the antagonist may need to be stimulated.

A number of approaches also make use of other reflexes. For example, in Proprioceptive Neuromuscular Facilitation (PNF) a muscle is taken to its comfortable limit and then contracted against a resistance that prevents movement; it can then often be stretched further by the practitioner.

Massage, either through techniques applied directly to the muscles or via passive movements that stretch the muscles, increases the potential for flexibility.

Initially a massage practitioner wants to be able to work effectively on muscles, but after a time, many practitioners want to search out and address the deeper causes and habits that contribute to muscular tension. A person's tensions and postural habits develop gradually from his activities, injuries and accidents, and are also shaped by the person's attitude to life and his feelings and beliefs. Massage, in addition to the physical effects described above, can help to increase the client's awareness of his tensions, allowing him to consider ways of reducing these tensions and changing physical and attitudinal habits that encourage the accumulation of tension.

Disorders of the Muscular System

Key Words

Cramp	Carpal Tunnel Syndrome
Muscle spasm	Frozen shoulder
Fibrosis	Deltoid bursitis
Fibrositis / fibromyalgia / muscular rheumatism	Housemaid's knee
Sports injuries	Tennis elbow
Strain	Ankle tendon injuries
Tendinitis	Muscular dystrophy
Repetitive Strain Injury (RSI)	Myasthenia gravis

Disorders of muscles, tendons and ligaments fall into two categories. The majority are caused by trauma or overuse, and are very common, can be painful, can limit mobility, and range from minor temporary stiffness or strains to the chronic and incapacitating repetitive strain injuries. This group of disorders also includes the increasingly common sports injuries. A much smaller category of muscular disorders are caused by disease processes. These are rare and serious.

Wherever pain is experienced in the body, the surrounding tissues tend to stiffen up in order to protect the damaged area. This may reduce blood flow and the circulation of nutrients to and waste matter away from the tissues. Over time, the connective tissues may lose their elasticity.

So gentle massage of the areas around the pain or inflammation is certainly beneficial, as well as massage of the other limb or other areas of the body which may be working harder than usual to compensate for the loss of function.

Common Muscular Tensions

It is fine to massage an overused or *overworked muscle*, being sensitive to the appropriate pressure for the recipient, so long as you are satisfied that there is no actual injury. If you are not sure, refer your client to a sympathetic medical person for their opinion.

Postural habits and rigidities, which we all carry to some degree, restrict muscles and so they tighten up. Massage is helpful and, although it will not cure the problem, it will reduce this accumulating muscle tension and rigidity, and highlight the need to do something about it.

The physical consequence of *mental tension and life's constant demands and stresses* on a person, whatever the cause, is the tightening up of muscles that can lead to habitual tensions, often unconsciously maintained. Massage has an important role to play in helping to stop and reverse this process. In emotional distress, there can be considerable physical tension; a friendly soothing quality of touch should be foremost, if massage is at all acceptable to the client.

When done without an adequate warm-up beforehand or cool-down afterwards, muscles can remain tense after exercise or *vigorous physical activity*. Massage has a straightforward role here.

Common Muscular Problems

Cramp is an involuntary contraction of a muscle, usually accompanied by pain, which occurs mostly in the calf muscles and sometimes in the forearm muscles. It is commonly caused by lack of oxygen to a muscle, either through overworking the muscle or because of chronic tension in the muscle that is impeding the blood supply. It can also be due to, or aggravated by, a lack of calcium or magnesium or, in hot climates, of salt.

Recommendations for massage:

1. In the immediate situation, stretch the muscle to relieve the cramp. Be wary of doing massage until it has calmed down.
2. When the cramp has reduced, massage can help the muscle to relax.
3. In the long-term, regular massage and stretching exercises should reduce the likelihood of further episodes, and can reduce long-term spasms.
4. If the condition regularly reoccurs in spite of this, the client should look at nutritional factors that may be contributing.

Muscles can have longer-term involuntary **muscle spasms** that ache rather than give a sharp pain. These too can be symptoms of muscle overuse, in which case treat them in the same way as for cramp.

However, such spasms also commonly occur when muscles tighten to protect injuries or to reduce movement in painful joints. If the client's history indicates that this could be the case, don't apply pressure, and be careful when doing passive movements.

Strictly speaking, **fibrosis** refers to inflammation in the muscle with accompanying soreness or pain, which may lead to the formation of scar tissue. One cause is chronic muscular tension, which benefits from massage. However, if it is due to other factors, apply massage appropriately according to the cause.

Fibrositis, fibromyositis and **muscular rheumatism** are all terms for a condition that involves chronic muscle pain, tenderness and sleep disorder. Careful massage that does not irritate is fine.

Unless you have specific training in dealing with **sports injuries**, you should not massage injuries or suspected injuries. If this area does interest you, there are many training courses available. An excellent book covering both prevention and recovery from sports injuries is '*Sports Injuries: A Self-help Guide*' by Vivian Grisigono (John Murray, London, 1984).

Strain (pulled muscle) is damage to muscle tissue that occurs when a muscle is subjected to excessive or violent sudden force, either when it is contracting or when it is being stretched. It can range from a mild condition where a few muscle fibres are torn and there is a little bleeding, to the situation in which much of the muscle tissue and the surrounding sheath are torn, and there is considerable bleeding. In the most serious strains, there is complete rupture of the muscle. This is very serious, causes extreme pain and requires hospital treatment.

When muscle tissue is damaged, scarring occurs as part of the healing process. Scar tissue and adhesions in the connective tissue of the muscle limit mobility.

Recommendations for massage:

1. Treatment of acute strains resulting from injury is a specialised skill. Unless you have specific training in sports injury massage, you should not massage the area affected in any of these conditions.
2. Never massage over areas of bruising, which is an indicator of internal muscle injury with internal bleeding or fluid seepage, which massage would aggravate.
3. Massage of mild strains may be beneficial after 48 hours, to improve circulation to the area. If you are not certain of the appropriateness of massage, consult with a sports trainer or physiotherapist.
4. After a strain, the muscle will repair itself by forming scars. It may also remain tight even if the area no longer needs protection. Massage of chronic scars and the residual holding patterns is very beneficial.

Tendinitis is the result of a strain that can occur in a tendon, often at the junction with the muscle or with the persiosteum. This gives rise to inflammation, pain and stiffness. As the tendon recovers, scar tissue will be formed, which is less stretchable than the original material and susceptible to re-injury. Massage should not be done in the acute stage, but is helpful when this has passed.

Musculoskeletal Problems Arising From Overuse

These all require a similar massage approach that is covered at the end of this section.

Repetitive Strain Injury (RSI) refers to any overuse condition, such as strain, tendinitis or fibrositis, in any part of the body. It is a term that has only recently been given recognised status, as a result of legal cases claiming compensation for injuries received in an occupational setting.

Carpal Tunnel Syndrome is the most common type of repetitive strain injury. It can occur as a result of occupational injury, such as prolonged typing, but it can also be one of the complications of pregnancy.

The tendons from the muscles of the forearm that flex the fingers pass under a band of fibrous tissue on the front of the wrist – the carpal tunnel. Overuse or regular awkward use of these muscles can inflame the tissue and cause the tendons to swell, putting pressure on the nerves and blood vessels that also pass through here. The result can be weakness and numbness or tingling in the hands.

Frozen shoulder. The socket of the shoulder joint is shallow, to allow for a large range of movement. Stability is provided by the muscles and the ligaments that surround the joint. Damage to them causes pain and instinctive restriction when movement is attempted, and is called a frozen shoulder. Inflammation may occur in any muscle or tendon separately; then only the movement initiated by that muscle will be affected.

Deltoid bursitis. Beneath the deltoid muscle is a bursa that can become inflamed. This is common in tennis players and gymnasts.

Housemaid's knee refers to inflammation of any of the bursae in the knee joint.

Tennis elbow is tendinitis of the muscles of the back of the forearm at their insertion and is caused by excessive hammering or sawing type movements, or a tense, awkward grip on a tennis racquet.

Ankle tendon injuries. The Achilles tendon is susceptible to strains. At the insertion with the calcaneus is a bursa that can become inflamed. Both of these problems can occur in runners who wear inadequate footwear.

Recommendations for massage:

1. Don't massage directly on areas of painful inflammation.
2. Massage of surrounding muscles may help relieve pain, and prevent immobilisation if a joint is involved.
3. Many overuse conditions take a very long time to clear up.

Diseases of the Muscles

Muscular dystrophy is a group of diseases that are inherited, and cause progressive weakening and degeneration of the skeletal muscle.

Myasthenia gravis is a disease of the immune system that affects nerve impulses to the muscles, resulting in muscle weakness and fatigue. The limb muscles and those to do with speech, swallowing and chewing are most affected.

Recommendations for massage:

1. In both of these conditions, gentle massage may help to relieve pain or muscle spasm.
2. If there is loss of feeling, be very careful when moving limbs.
3. In myasthenia gravis, medication may reduce immune system functioning, so take care not to expose the client to infection.

Chapter 8 Main Skeletal Muscles

There are over 600 named muscles in the body. This chapter describes the main skeletal / voluntary muscles of direct interest to massage practitioners. It covers the names of the muscles, their positions and functioning, and a little of their complex interactions with other muscles.

Apart from two muscles in the head which cross the centreline of the body all the muscles covered are mirrored on each side of the body. Please note that, when referring to the number of muscles in a group, e.g. three hamstrings and five adductors in the thigh, this is the number on one side of the body only.

The Naming of Muscles

It is useful to begin by looking at the derivations of muscle names. The anatomical names are usually descriptive of particular aspects of the muscle:

Shape

Trapezius	kite-shaped
Rhomboid	diamond
Quadratus	square
Teres	round (in cross section)
Rectus	straight
Deltoid	triangular
Serratus	serrated, like the edge of a sawblade

Size

Major / minor	bigger / smaller
Maximus / medius / minimis	biggest / middle size / smallest
Longus / brevis	long / short
Latissimus	broadest
Longissimus	longest
Magnus	big
Vastus	immense(vast)

Position

Anterior / posterior	in front / behind
Superior / supra-	above
Inferior / infra-	below
Medialis / lateralis	towards the centreline / side of the body
Interosseus	between bones

Oculi	of the eye
Oris	of the mouth
Capitis	of the head
Cervicis	of the neck
Nuchal	of the back of the neck
Brachii	of the upper arm
Radialis / ulnaris	on radial / ulna side of the forearm
Carpi	of the carpal bones = wrist
Digitorum	of the fingers / toes
Pollicis / hallucis	of the thumb / big toe
Pectoralis	of the chest
Costal	of the ribs
Abdominis	of the abdomen
Dorsi	of the back / back of the hand / top of the foot
Femoris	of the femur = thigh
Tibialis	of the shin / lower leg

Number of Heads

Biceps / triceps / quadriceps	two / three / four

('ceps' meaning head – as in 'cap', 'captain' and 'capital')

Direction of Fibres

Oblique	slanting
Transversus	across

Depth

Superficialis / profundus	superficial / deep

Places of Attachment

Brachioradialis	upper arm – radius
Coracobrachialis	coracoid process (scapula) – upper arm
Sternocleidomastoid	sternum and clavicle – mastoid process (occiput)

Action

Flexor / extensor	bending / straightening
Abductor / adduction	taking away from / towards the side of the body
Levator / depressor	raising / lowering
Supinator / pronator	turns forearm to turn hand up / down
Erector	maintains uprightness

Note that the names that describe a muscle in this last way can be misleading; they denote the *main* but not the *only* action of the muscle. For example, flexor carpi radialis flexes the wrist, but it also works with the radial extensors to abduct the hand.

The terms are often combined in muscle names:

Levator scapulae	raises the scapula
Extensor digitorum	bends the fingers back
Erector spinae	holds the spine upright
Flexor digitorum profundus	deep flexor of the fingers
Flexor carpi radialis	flexor of the fingers on the radial side (of the forearm)

Some names are similar to one another. The differences in their names are designed to distinguish them. Examples are gluteus maximus / gluteus medius / gluteus minimus (biggest / middle / smallest of the buttock) and biceps brachii / biceps femoris (the two-headed muscle of the arm / of the thigh). If there is a 'major' muscle, there will usually be a 'minor', if one is called 'anterior', there is usually a 'posterior', etc.

Identifying Muscles

The best way to understand the description of the muscles in this chapter is to palpate them, i.e. locate them by feel. Try this with a partner, ideally someone who knows the muscles and can guide you. Once you have a sense of what you're trying to feel, you can usefully explore many of the muscles on your own body as well, which will give you a feeling of how to approach palpation.

Then try this on as many fellow students, colleagues and friends as you can, so that you learn to identify muscles on people with a variety of builds and muscle tones. You'll find it easiest on those with sinewy bodies, where the muscles and the tensions in them are most distinct. Individual muscles are generally harder to distinguish on those with large builds, unless they are highly active people. Although they are more readily identifiable on those with a small build and soft muscles, you have to take care not to press too much.

Initially, in attempting to locate muscles, most people try too hard, tensing their hands, which interferes with their ability to feel – in the same way that most of us try too hard when we are first learning massage strokes. Place your hands on the area that you are feeling, relax them and give yourself time. It often helps to defocus or close your eyes.

Start with a sense of curiosity. When investigating any new territory, it can at first be disorientating and perhaps frustrating as well as exciting and fun. Persevere and you will learn to locate specific muscles. If you cannot initially locate what you are searching for but you discover other discernible features, explore these. It all aids the development of your touch.

You will find surface muscles far easier to identify than the underlying ones. You may only gain an impression of the deeper muscles by having your partner use them while you press through the superficial ones.

Although this book follows the common convention of describing the muscles from the head down, it's easiest to begin palpating the long sausage-shaped muscles of the upper arm or the thigh. These are generally easier to feel than the muscles of the trunk, many of which are flat sheets and often thin, particularly those wrapping around the surface. The biceps, at the front of the upper arm, is a good place to start, as it is easy to feel the muscle belly working and also to distinguish the tendon.

When you come to the trunk, try initially palpating muscles whose fibres condense together to cross to the limbs or neck – at the armpit, hip or shoulder. The upper part of trapezius is a good place to begin, and an important one for massage practitioners to know, as virtually everyone is tight here and most people want massage on their shoulders. Pectoralis major is also relatively discernible where it forms the front of the armpit. Incidentally, it is quite difficult to feel the aponeuroses by which sheets of muscles attach to the bones.

As you investigate muscles in action, bear in mind the interplay between them, so that you are not bamboozled by feeling a muscle working when it 'shouldn't' be. Describing muscles as doing one or a few limited actions is a useful simplification, but remember that some other muscles (antagonists) have to relax to allow them to work, some other muscles help the action (synergists) and yet others hold bones in place (fixators) to allow them to act. For those who are interested, the factors involved in this coordination of muscles are discussed in more detail at the end of this chapter, in the review of muscle actions.

Investigate the muscle initially while it is relaxed. Have your partner sitting or lying as comfortably as possible. If you are feeling muscles in the arm, have their arm resting on a supporting surface so that the muscles do not need to work. Feel across the muscle as well as along it, and see if you can stretch it.

Then keep your hand still on the muscle and get your partner to work it. Start by having them use the muscle so that you can identify the belly as it hardens and the tendon as it is pulled taut. With biceps, for example, this involves slowly bending up the forearm. If your partner then alternately contracts and then relaxes the muscle slowly enough, you will be able to get a clearer sense of where the muscle is and also how it works.

In the larger, thicker muscles, you will often feel strands of tightness even when the muscle is relaxed. This shows there is chronic tension in some of its fibres. The direction of the tension indicates the direction of the fibres, allowing you to identify which muscle it is in, particularly when you are palpating areas where there are layers of muscle, such as between the shoulder blades or along the top of the shoulders.

Sometimes, it can be useful to offer a resistance to your partner's movement, forcing them to work the muscle more strongly so that you can more clearly distinguish it. In the case of biceps, this would be by pressing down on their lower forearm to slow down the movement or stop it completely (being careful not to cause damage by using excessive force). This is especially helpful when you are feeling through surface muscles to try and gain some sense of the deeper ones working.

Muscles and Massage

As you gain experience in identifying muscles on people of different builds, you will find that you can also begin to identify tension in the muscles. Over time this will allow you to assess the level of tension in an individual's muscles, comparing it to your developing experience of the common distribution of tension throughout the body for someone of similar age and build.

When you have explored the bodies of a range of people, you will start to sense the effect of repetitive or constant job or leisure activities. Massaging people of varied ages will help you develop a feeling for the slow accumulation of tension over time that comes from postural habits, sedentary lifestyles, and/or responses to injuries. You'll begin to gain a sense of how each person uses their body.

This developing feeling can extend beyond merely sensing how your client's physical activities and postural habits affect his or her body. You may also start to gain an appreciation of how their attitude to life affects their body, i.e. how they live in their body. A worrier, for example, may develop a fixed frown or be constantly fidgeting and be unable to relax. Be wary, of course, of glibly reading meaning into every tension you encounter in your client's body. And make sure that you listen to their thoughts and feelings about their tensions, rather than making rigid assumptions.

Therefore, as you massage, it is worth keeping in mind that massage may do more than just encourage the recipient to release some of the tension they have developed through activities and physical habits. As they let go of some physical tension, they may also let go a little of some of the attitudes that contribute to the tensions, even if it is only for the duration of the massage session. In the case of the worrier, for example, their forehead may smooth out and they may feel more relaxed and less concerned than usual. This is one of the reasons why people can feel a little dazed after a massage; they are not quite 'themselves', i.e. the way that they are used to being.

In the rest of this chapter, the description of factors that commonly contribute to muscle tension focuses primarily on activities, work situations and postural habits. Attitudinal habits are referred to in the section that describes the muscles of the face, as this is the area of the body where they are most obvious and are often the major cause of tension.

Where there are references to massage strokes or to exercises given to clients, these are general suggestions about what would be appropriate for the average person. It is assumed that readers will adapt these to suit the recipients, being guided by their build, injuries, sensitivities, muscle tone and their responses.

Head

The muscles of the head that can easily be massaged are thin, flat muscles, either wide sheets of muscle or short straps. Apart from the jaw muscles, most have only small attachments to bones and pull instead on other soft tissues.

The scalp muscle covers the top of the head, spanning from the forehead to the occiput. Facial expressions come primarily from the actions of the small straps of muscle that pull and stretch the three oval muscles of the face, one around each eye and one around the mouth. The muscle around each eye only has two associated muscles, but there are many going to the mouth to help shape vocal sounds and expressions. In addition, there are small muscles that knit the eyebrows and wrinkle the nose.

There are two large chewing muscles on the outside of the mouth that are important in massage. The base of the mouth is also formed by muscles, which can be massaged just behind the mandible.

Although the face is a small area of the body, there are a large number of motor and sensory nerves to this area, controlling and monitoring the range of expression that we use for communication. Thus, a significant part of our brain is concerned with this area. We often hold much tension here, and a good face and scalp massage can have a beneficial releasing effect that is disproportionate to the area covered.

Because of the importance of the face in communication, tensions here will often be related to responses to events or attitudes to life, especially those around the mouth and jaw and to a lesser extent the eyes.

Scalp

Occipitofrontalis: The muscle of the top of the scalp (also known as the *epicranius*) consists of three parts:

1. A short muscle at the back attached to the occipital bone (*occipitalis*);
2. The short *frontalis* muscle at the front attached to the muscles above the eyes, and;
3. A long aponeurosis joining them (the *galea aponeurotica*).

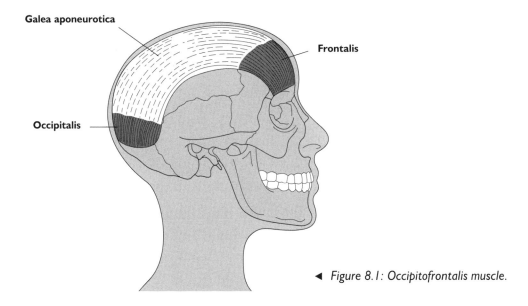

Galea aponeurotica

Frontalis

Occipitalis

◀ *Figure 8.1: Occipitofrontalis muscle.*

Its potential movements are small, acting via these short muscles fibres at each end either to pull the scalp forward or backward, or to raise the eyebrows. When you massage over the top of the scalp, you can usually get some movement in this muscle, although in some people it seems to be held fast. At the front, it overlaps with the muscles at the top of the nose, and those just above the eyes. This is one of the few muscles that straddle the centreline of the body.

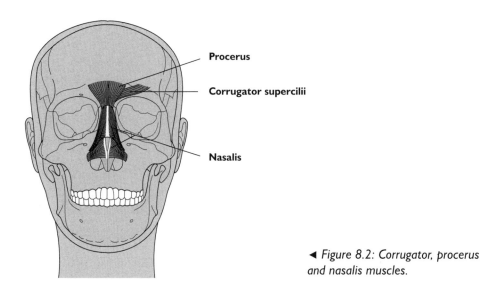

◄ *Figure 8.2: Corrugator, procerus and nasalis muscles.*

Facial Expression

The nasal muscles: *Corrugator (corrugator supercilii)* and *procerus* are two small muscles that join to the occipitofrontalis just above the bridge of the nose. They draw the eyebrows down and together, in expressions of frowning or puzzlement. *Nasalis* covers the lower half of each side of the nose, widening or narrowing the openings of the nostrils.

Sensitively performed, massage across the forehead and around the bridge of the nose can give the recipient a feeling of opening out in this area and, for a while, can relieve the pressure of a frown or sinus congestion.

Around the eyes: Each *orbicularis oculi* muscle ('orb-shaped of the eye') is attached to the bones around the eye socket in a few small places and has just two short 'straps' of muscle that move it. Much of its movement comes from its own sphincter-like activity – squeezing in on itself in parts, e.g. in winking, closing the eyelid, or squeezing the tear ducts. These muscles should not be worked on directly, but they relax when the surrounding muscles are softened through massage.

The mouth: In contrast to the eye muscles, the *orbicularis oris* ('orb-shaped of the mouth') is not attached at all to bones. It is held in place, stretched and moved (in vocalising, sucking or for expression) by a number of strap muscles that attach at their outer ends to the bones of the skull. Some called *levators* lift the upper lip or the corner of the

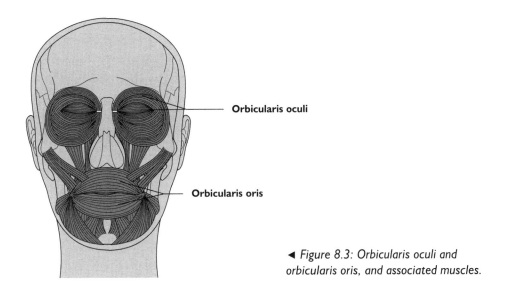

◄ *Figure 8.3: Orbicularis oculi and orbicularis oris, and associated muscles.*

mouth, e.g. in smiling. Some called *depressors* pull down on the lips or the corners, e.g. in an expression of sadness, and orbicularis oris itself can tighten or purse the lips, allowing us the range of expressions of which we are capable.

Singing teachers and theatre voice coaches often comment on the mouth tension that they encounter in their students, and it seems common for many of us to hold our lips stiffly much of the time. Massage can again play a role here in releasing, at least for a short time, habitual expressions and tensions.

Platysma, which covers the lower face muscles and then continues down the front of the neck, is described more fully in the section on the neck.

The cheek: *Buccinator* is a thin, square muscle that stretches between the mandible, the maxilla and the orbicularis oris to form the inner lining of the cheeks. It moves the food between the teeth in chewing. It also compresses the cheeks when they have been stretched, so it is important in blowing; its name comes from the Latin word for a trumpeter/bugler.

Chewing Muscles (Muscles of Mastication)

There are two muscles on the inside of the mouth at the back (the pterygoids) that masseurs ordinarily do not work on, but the two larger ones on the outside are important for massage practitioners.

Masseter is a relatively short but strong muscle running between the corner of the mandible (jawbone) and the cheekbone (the zygomatic arch of the temporal and zygomatic bones). It is easy to palpate at the back of the cheeks when it is contracted.

Temporalis runs from the top of the mandible, behind the cheekbone, to the side of the head, where it attaches to the side of the skull above and round the ear, behind the edge

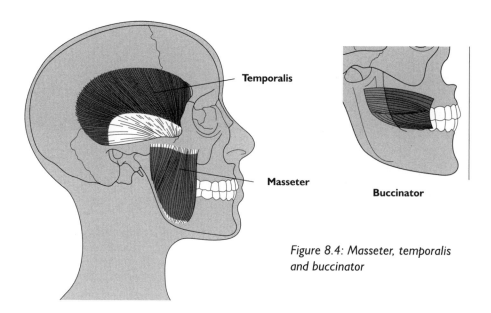

Figure 8.4: Masseter, temporalis and buccinator

of the temple. You can often usefully work with pressure on this muscle, but you also need to exercise care, as it can be quite sensitive at times of great stress, when the accumulated tension can lead to headaches spreading from the temples and around the side of the head.

These muscles, which are so essential to masticating food and are also involved in speech and singing, need to be strong for the amount of work they do. They can also become jaw-clenching muscles when chronically tight. We tense them when we put on a 'social face', (e.g. a polite smile when we don't feel like it) push ourselves hard (when we 'grit our teeth') or hold back from expressing feelings ('bite back our words'). Many people hold considerable tension in the jaw muscles, which shows itself as unconscious grinding of the teeth at night, waking with an aching jaw or headaches.

Base of the Mouth

Suprahyoids ('superior to = above the hyoid') are a group of flat muscles which form the base of the mouth, spanning between the hyoid bone and lower edge of the mandible and the skull.

Below the hyoid bone, the *infrahyoids* form a covering over the windpipe and its associated structures at the front of the neck, stretching to the top of the sternum (and one to the scapula). Together, the suprahyoids and infrahyoids hold the hyoid in place and can move it when swallowing, talking or singing (similar to the wires on a suspension bridge that lift it to allow the passage of boats). They also give stability for the tongue, itself a compound muscle involved in speech and moving food around in the mouth.

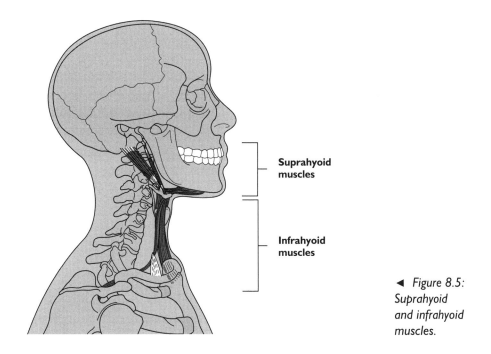

◄ Figure 8.5: Suprahyoid and infrahyoid muscles.

Review of the Muscles of the Head

Scalp: occipitofrontalis.
Eyes: orbicularis oculi, corrugator.
Mouth: orbicularis oris, levators and depressors of the lips.
Nasal: procerus, nasalis.
Cheek: buccinator.
Chewing: masseter, temporalis.
Covering lower face and neck: platysma.
Moving the hyoid (swallowing etc.): suprahyoids, infrahyoids.

Muscles of the Neck

The main muscles of the front, sides and back of the neck control the position and movements of the neck and the head.

In the lower part of the front, the *sternocleidomastoid* muscles cover the infrahyoids. At the side of the neck are the *scalenes* that act as side 'guy-ropes', stabilising the side to side balance the neck.

At the back, *trapezius*, which forms the outer layer, and its associated underlying muscle, *levator scapulae*, raise the shoulders, and are involved with other muscles in moving the scapula.

Under trapezius, the *splenii* muscles in turn cover the top section of the deep postural muscles of the back, the *erector spinae*, and the small, deep layer that forms the network of fine-tuning muscles between adjacent vertebrae.

Just under the base of the skull are the very small *sub-occipital* muscles that control the small nodding and turning movements of the head.

All of these muscles, by their actions of balancing and stabilising the neck, respond to movements from within the head, such as chewing or will stiffen with lack of neck or head movement. Suboccipital tension can often be related to eye tension, and can be a step in the build up of headaches; headaches can also be related to jaw tension. Tension in the neck, especially in the lower cervical region, can be a consequence of tension in the back and shoulders. And of course tension in all these areas can be due to injuries and/or part of postural habits.

Front of the Neck

The *infrahyoids*, described on page 120, form the front of the neck below the hyoid bone. The *sternocleidomastoid* (SCM) covers the lower parts of the infrahyoids.

The main part of the SCM extends between the top of the sternum and the mastoid process of the occiput, just behind the ears. A short fork at the lower end goes to the clavicle – the 'cleido' part – not as easily visible when the muscle is relaxed, but able to be felt, and usually seen, in action. This gives the sternocleidomastoid a secondary leverage point for the movements of the head that it controls in coordination with other neck muscles – especially the scalenes, splenii, levator scapulae and the upper trapezius.

Depending on the actions of these other muscles, one SCM can act to turn the head to the side – the right SCM turning the head to the left and vice versa; it is easy to see on the exposed side of the neck in this action. The SCM also helps in bending the neck strongly to one side (lateral flexion).

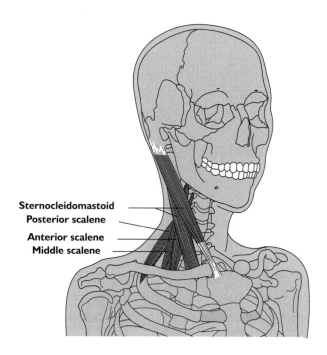

Sternocleidomastoid
Posterior scalene
Anterior scalene
Middle scalene

◄ *Figure 8.6: Sternocleidomastoid and the scalene muscles.*

If both sides are working, it is a major flexor of the neck, tilting the head towards the chest, but it can also play a part in extension (tilting the head backwards). It is sometimes called upon to play a part in forceful inspiration, raising the sternum and clavicle at the front to increase the ribcage area.

When massaging this muscle, do strokes which stretch it lengthways or that lift it away from the underlying tissues. Avoid applying pressure that could affect the structures that it covers, particularly the windpipe, which lies between the 'V' shape formed by the two SCM's, and the carotid artery that carries the main blood supply to the head.

Platysma covers the SCM and the infrahyoids. It is a thin sheet of muscle that stretches from the muscles on the lower side of the lip to those covering the upper chest. It can pull the outer corner of the mouth down in an expression of aversion or wrinkle the skin of the neck. It is the same muscle that a horse will twitch to flick flies off its neck.

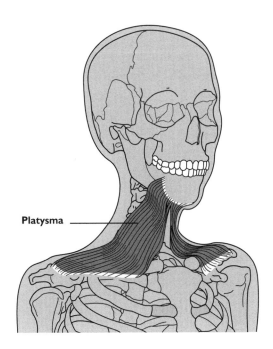

Platysma

◄ *Figure 8.7: Platysma.*

Side of the Neck

The *scalenes* are three muscles (anterior, medius and posterior), deep in each side of the neck. They run from the transverse processes of most of the cervical vertebrae (C2–C7) to the first and second ribs. The lower parts can be palpated at the side of the neck, in the angle formed between the back of the sternocleidomastoid and the front of trapezius.

These are the side 'guy-ropes' for the neck, holding the neck and head upright or working more strongly on one side to tilt the neck and head to that side. They can also be involved in forceful inhalation by lifting the ribs.

They are tight in most people, especially those who spend a lot of time at a computer, or working at a bench.

Back of the Neck

The outer layer of the back of the neck is formed by the upper part of the two *trapezius* muscles, which are involved in stabilising the neck or conversely in raising the shoulders, either on one side only or both together.

The name refers to the collective shape of the two muscles, which together form a trapezoid – a kite shape. The trapezius muscles are attached along the centreline of the neck and the trunk – to the occiput, the nuchal ligament in the cervical area and all of the thoracic vertebrae to T12. They stretch to the shoulder girdle, attaching to the outer third of the clavicle and the whole top edge of the spine of the scapula.

The upper section runs between the outer part of the shoulder girdle and the cervical spine. The structure of the rest of the muscle and its role in movements of the scapula is covered in detail in the next section on the muscles of the shoulder and the arm.

If the shoulders are held still by other muscles, one side of the upper trapezius can either act with the same side SCM to turn the head to the opposite side, or with the scalenes to side bend the neck (pulling the head down on this same side). The head and neck can be bent backwards by the simultaneous action of the upper part of both trapezius muscles.

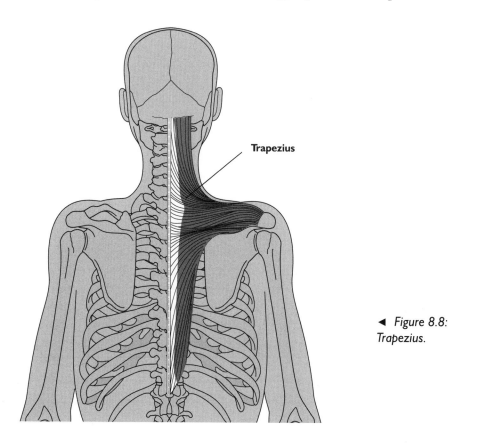

Trapezius

◄ *Figure 8.8: Trapezius.*

The *levator scapulae* ('the elevator – the raiser of the scapula') also lifts the shoulders and side bends the neck. It is a small rounded 'strap' of muscle that lies just underneath each trapezius. It runs between the top inside corner of the scapula (the superior angle) and the upper half of the neck (the transverse processes of C1–C4).

It is hard to distinguish on people with large builds but, on those with a small or sinewy build, the lower end in the shoulders is relatively easy to palpate. By pressing through trapezius just above the superior angle of the scapula, it can be felt like a small 'strap' (often sensitive to pressure) which runs diagonally up towards the mid-cervical spine. If the lower (scapular) end is sensitive, there is often a corresponding sensitivity in the mid-neck area (the lowest point of attachment of the cervical end of the muscle).

Both trapezius and levator scapulae are involved in any action of lifting the shoulders, acting like two guiding 'reins' to control the direction of the lift. If the trapezius does most of the work, the outer point of the shoulder is lifted more, rising towards the ear, (upward rotation – anticlockwise rotation of the right scapula). If levator scapulae is more active, the point of the shoulder drops down and the inferior angle moves towards the spine (downward rotation).

This part of the shoulders is the most common area of tension in the body, and the area people most often want to have massaged. It holds tension for two reasons. Firstly, when one feels stressed, this is the most common area to tense up – 'shoulders rising about one's ears'.

Additionally, these two muscles, as well as lifting the shoulders, come into play to brace the shoulder girdle whenever one lifts, pushes or pulls something. In fact they do this whenever the arms and hands are being used, even when the arms are held in place for small hand or finger actions, such as typing. Thus, for example, if one is doing a lot of computer work, the cumulative effect over time can be a hardening in the tissue of the upper trapezius and the levator scapulae – gradually building up considerable tension in this area, especially if one is also under stress.

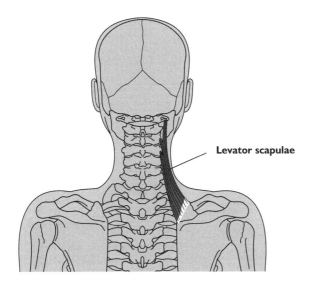

Levator scapulae

◀ *Figure 8.9:*
Levator scapulae.

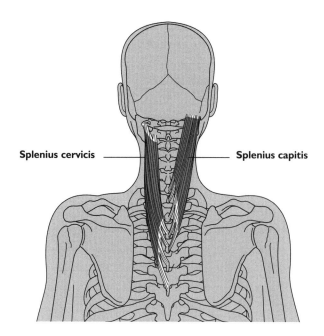

◄ *Figure 8.10:*
Splenius capitis and
splenius cervicis.

The *'bandage' muscles* make up the next layer of muscle in the neck under trapezius. *Splenius capitis* ('bandage, of the head' – indicating that it attaches to the skull) spans from the upper thoracic and lower cervical vertebrae to the occiput, with the upper end of levator scapulae passing under it. Just under it is the *splenius cervicis* ('bandage, of the neck'), running from upper thoracic vertebrae to the upper two or three cervical vertebrae.

These two muscles help maintain the uprightness of the neck and head and can help rotate the head. Splenius capitis, working only on one side, can also be involved in side bending the neck. They 'bandage' the deeper postural muscles of the neck – the top section of the erector spinae group and of the small para-vertebrals (*see* page 128).

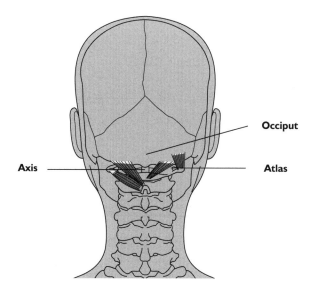

◄ *Figure 8.11: The*
sub-occipital muscles.

Sub-occipitals: Under the base of the skull are four short muscles on each side that link between the occiput, the atlas (C1) and the axis (C2). They control tiny 'nodding' and 'shaking' movements of the head, 'yes' and 'no'. They are involved in fine-tuning movements of the head, especially in response to concentrated use of the eyes, e.g. while reading.

To appreciate this role, place your fingers or thumbs under the back of your skull. You will probably be able to sense the sub-occipital muscles moving under the overlying muscles as you slowly move your eyes in a range of directions while keeping your head still.

They can therefore become quite tight and sensitive to massage when one is doing considerable computer work, thus holding the head in a fixed position for extended periods.

Review of the Muscles Involved in Movements of the Neck

Flexion: sternocleidomastoid, anterior scalene.
Extension: erector spinae group, para-vertebrals, splenius capitis and cervicis.
Lateral flexion: scalenes, splenius capitis and cervicis, sternocleidomastoid.
Rotation: para-vertebrals, splenius capitis and cervicis, sternocleidomastoid, scalenes.
Movements at the top of the neck – rock, tilt and rotate head: sub-occipitals.

Upper Back and Shoulders

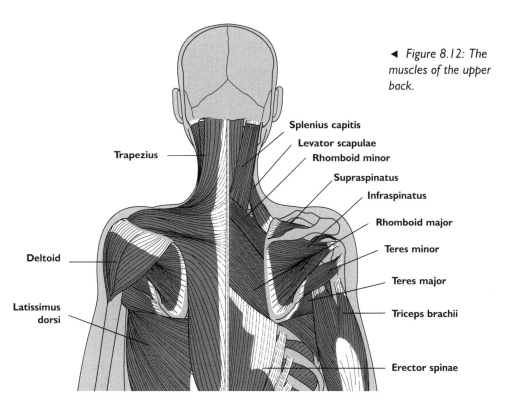

◀ *Figure 8.12: The muscles of the upper back.*

Splenius capitis
Levator scapulae
Rhomboid minor
Supraspinatus
Infraspinatus
Rhomboid major
Teres minor
Teres major
Triceps brachii
Erector spinae
Trapezius
Deltoid
Latissimus dorsi

The muscles of the upper back and shoulders belong to two groups; the postural muscles of the back and, overlaying those, the muscles involved in movements of the shoulder girdle and upper limb.

Postural Muscles of the Back (the 'Para-vertebrals')

There are two deep groups of postural muscles that stretch from the sacrum up to the base of the skull, the *erector spinae* group and the smaller 'gutter' muscles, which are described in detail in the section on the trunk (*see* page 148).

They are covered in the upper back and neck by the muscles involved in the movements of the shoulder girdle and arm. Between these two groups of muscles in the neck, there are also layers of muscles (the *splenii, see* page 126) which control the movements of the neck and head.

The erector spinae / sacrospinalis are the large postural muscle group which maintain the uprightness of the spine, straighten it up from forward bending or hyperextend it. This group is made up of overlapping groups of muscles, which attach to each vertebra and the back of each rib. They spread widely out from the spine in the lower and mid back. They are commonly known either as the *erector spinae* group ('keeping the spine upright') or *sacrospinalis* ('from the sacrum, of the spine').

The *para-vertebrals* are a network of tiny muscles which fill the 'gutter' formed by the spinous and transverse processes of the vertebrae. They fine-tune the posture and the movements of the spine.

Muscles Involved in Movements of the Shoulders and Arms

The shoulders are formed by the bones of the shoulder girdle (clavicle and scapula) and the muscles that connect them to the upper trunk and the neck. The shoulder blades are moved and then stabilised to form a 'platform' for the action of the arms throughout a range of positions. These movements are pivotted around the sterno-clavicular joint.

Most of the time, we use our hands in front of the trunk, and our muscles are designed for this. There are stronger muscles to bring the arms to the front of the body than to take them behind. And the muscles of the arm itself are consistently larger and more numerous on the front surface for bending the arm in front of the body and gripping objects. These muscles are therefore generally more used, and more in need of massage. The main activities that require us to move our hands out of this common range are sports and exercise procedures, dancing, and some gardening and DIY activities.

The muscles involved in movements of the shoulders and arm are easiest to understand by considering them in functional groupings: the muscles of 'scapular stabilisation'; the 'prime movers' of the arm; the 'rotator cuff'; and the upper arm muscles that help hold the humerus against the scapula. While this division is useful for the purposes of study, bear in mind that movements of the shoulder girdle and arm involve a complex interplay between all of these muscles – moving the scapula to give a mobile but stable 'platform' for the movements of the humerus in the shoulder joint.

The Muscles of Scapular Stabilisation

Trapezius, levator scapulae, the *rhomboids, serratus anterior,* and *pectoralis minor* are the muscles that hold the scapula in place and move it around over the back and side of the ribs. They work as coordinated controllers of the scapula, constantly changing their synchronised roles as agonists, antagonists and synergists in a much more complex way than the simple agonist / antagonist relationship of muscles such as biceps and triceps. Even when they are not actively moving the scapula, they are often acting to stabilise it for the other muscles and to give a platform for arm movements.

The upper part of trapezius works with the underlying levator scapulae, in lifting the shoulders. The rhomboids can also help lift the scapula, but their main action is to work with the middle section of trapezius to draw the shoulder blade back towards the spine (retraction).

Serratus anterior pulls the shoulder blades forward, from the back of the ribs around towards the side (protraction). It works with trapezius to rotate the scapula upwards (when the inferior angle twists out to the side). Downward rotation of the scapula (when the inferior angle twists in towards the spine) is a joint action of the rhomboids and levator scapulae.

Pectoralis minor can tilt the top of the scapula forward (hunching the shoulders over the chest), but its main role is to stabilise it.

Trapezius ('kite-shaped') is the superficial muscle covering most of the upper back apart from the scapula (*see* figure 8.8). It attaches centrally to the occiput, the nuchal ligament, the seventh cervical and all of the thoracic vertebrae.

From this attachment to the central 'pole' of the back, trapezius stretches to the shoulder girdle, attaching to the outer third of the clavicle and the whole of the spine of the scapula. It thus moves the shoulder, particularly the scapula. The whole of trapezius can brace the scapula for strong arm movements (e.g. lying face down with one's arms outstretched to the side and lifting them), but more commonly only one of its three sections is active as each part can initiate different movements of the scapula.

The *upper section of trapezius* acts with *levator scapulae* to lift the shoulders, especially when people are stressed, or hunch their shoulders against the cold, or to stabilise the neck (*see* page 124). However, it is more consistently involved in bracing the shoulders. This is either to keep the shoulders up when lifting or carrying objects, or most often to stabilise the shoulders for any arm or hand activities, e.g. working at computer key-boards, driving, household tasks, DIY, sports activities and playing musical instruments. This is therefore a much used area, and is a favourite area for receiving massage.

The *middle section of trapezius* works with the rhomboids, to square the shoulders back, and the *lower section* takes the scapula back and downwards.

Levator scapulae ('lifter of the scapula') lies underneath trapezius (*see* figure 8.9). It runs from the inside top corner of the scapula (the superior angle) up to the upper half of the neck – the top four cervical vertebrae. In people with small to medium builds, it can be palpated as a thin 'rope' under the upper trapezius, which can be sensitive. In people with larger builds, it is not as distinct. It works with the upper trapezius to lift the shoulders, stabilise the neck when both sides are working or to rotate or side bend the neck when only one side is working.

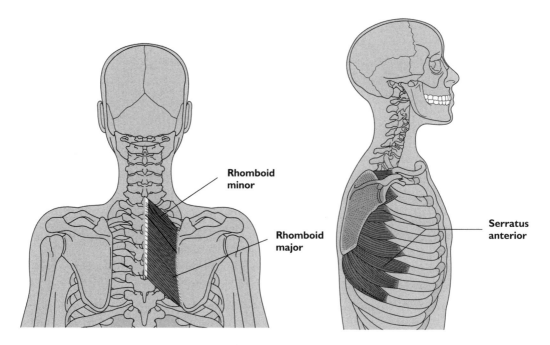

▲ *Figure 8.13: The rhomboids.*   ▲ *Figure 8.14: Serratus anterior.*

The *rhomboids* ('diamond-shaped'), under trapezius, run diagonally upwards from the medial edge of the scapula to the lower cervical and upper thoracic vertebrae. These two muscles (*major* and *minor*) have the same innervation and work as one. They work mainly with the *middle section of trapezius* that runs slightly downward from the medial end of the scapular spine to the mid-thoracic vertebrae. Together they draw the scapula backward towards the spine – retraction, e.g. in the squaring back of the shoulders of a military posture. They can also aid levator scapulae in lifting the shoulders and in downward rotation of the scapula (clockwise rotation of the right scapula).

Serratus anterior ('serrated, of the front' – like a saw blade, each slip of the serratus attaching to a rib) originates on the vertebral edge of the scapula, and passes between the scapula and the ribs to attach to the side of the ribs below the armpit. It can only be palpated at the side of the ribs below the back of the armpit, by sliding your fingers under the edge of the latissimus dorsi. Its primary action is to draw the shoulder blade forward towards the side of the ribs – protraction – e.g. in pushing, punching, or press-ups.

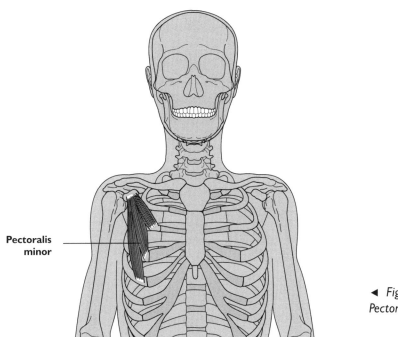

Pectoralis minor

◀ *Figure 8.15: Pectoralis minor.*

The *lower section of trapezius* works with serratus anterior to depress the shoulder, pulling the scapula down the back. It can combine with the rest of trapezius to stabilise the scapula when pulling strongly backwards (e.g. when opening a stiff door).

Pectoralis minor ('small, of the chest') is a narrow, triangular muscle, spanning from the coracoid process at the front of the scapula – palpable just below the clavicle above the armpit – straight down to the second or third to fifth ribs. It is covered by the pectoralis major muscle (the main muscle of the chest) so it is hard to palpate if that is tight.

It can tilt the top of the shoulder blade forward, so it will be quite tight in those who consistently hunch their shoulders forward over the top of the chest. Its main action is to assist the other scapular muscles or to act as a stabilising balance for them.

Prime Movers of the Arm

Two muscles, *pectoralis major* and *latissimus dorsi*, run directly to the humerus from the axial skeleton; they move the arm in relation to the trunk. They are wide and flat across the trunk, narrowing to strong, bulky 'straps' across the armpit towards their attachments on the upper humerus. A third muscle, the *deltoid*, forms the bulgy roundness of the top of the arm; it initiates movements of the humerus from the shoulder girdle.

These muscles work in coordination with the scapular stabilisers (described above) and the rotator cuff (*see* page 134) to activate the largest and strongest movements of the arms. The pectoralis and the deltoid can be quite tight in manual workers and body builders, and respond well to massage. The latissimus dorsi is most effectively massaged at the back of the armpit.

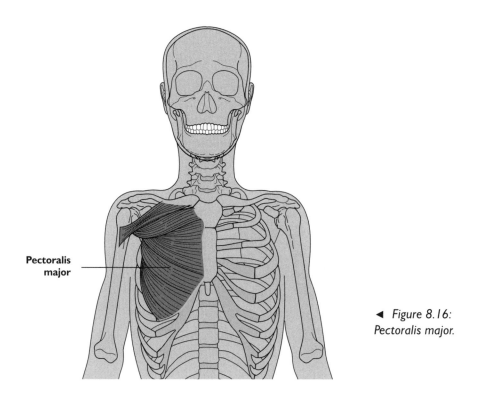

Pectoralis
major

◀ *Figure 8.16:*
Pectoralis major.

Pectoralis major (the 'big chest' muscle) comes from the underside of the clavicle and the edge of the sternum. The fibres gather together to form the front of the armpit as it crosses to a small area of attachment on the top of the humerus.

It draws the arm across the front of the body (adduction with flexion), so it is used much of the time in regular daily activities. It works with latissimus dorsi to medially rotate the arm and to lift the body towards the arm, e.g. when doing chin ups on a bar.

This muscle is, of course, present in both men and women, but you need to take special care when working with women. In women, the breast sits on the front of pectoralis major, so the muscle can only be massaged at the front of the armpit, just below the clavicle and along the edge of the sternum. This should be done carefully, with guidance from the recipient, as it may be sensitive at certain stages of the woman's menstrual cycle, particularly in the pre-menstrual and menstrual phases (or she may prefer no touch here at all).

Pectoralis major may also be sensitive in pregnancy, but, if not, massage of the upper pectorals can be appreciated because of the extra pull of the enlarging breasts. Note that when people speak in general terms of the pectoralis muscle, they are referring to pectoralis major (not minor).

Latissimus dorsi (the 'broadest of the back') covers most of the back below the scapula. It connects via a wide aponeurosis – the *thoracolumbar fascia* covering the lower erector spinae – to the iliac crest, the sacrum and the lumbar and lower thoracic vertebrae. The upper part is covered here by the lower fibres of trapezius. The fibres gather together towards the side of the midback to thicken as they form the back of the armpit. They twist around the medial edge of the humerus to attach to the front of it, just under the pectoral insertion.

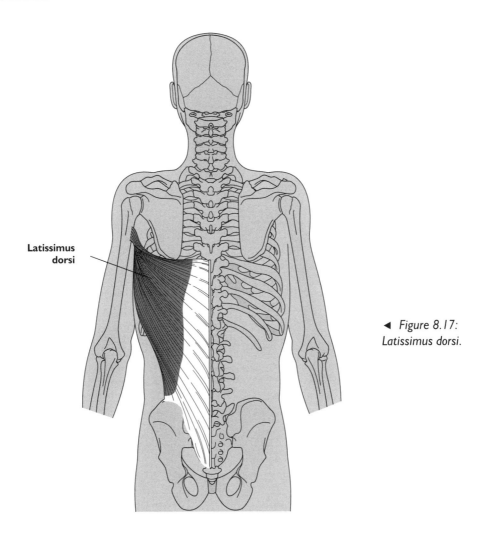

Latissimus
dorsi

◄ *Figure 8.17:*
Latissimus dorsi.

Its strongest actions are to pull the arm down across the front of the body, e.g. in over-arm swimming or chopping, or the complementary action – aided by pectoralis major – of lifting the body towards the arm, e.g. in climbing or swinging through the trees.

It can also sweep the arm back and behind the trunk or, with pectoralis, rotate the arm medially (turn the arm in), echoed and assisted in its actions by teres major (*see* page 136).

Deltoid is roughly triangular, like the delta of a river. Unlike the previous two muscles, it only moves the humerus in relation to the shoulder girdle. Although it doesn't have the length of pectoralis or latissimus, it is quite bulky and can therefore pull strongly through its smaller range, while simultaneously helping to stabilise the glenohumeral joint (the joint between the humerus and the scapula).

The upper end attaches to the undersides of the clavicle and the spine of the scapula, directly below the attachments of the trapezius. The fibres converge to insert into a small bulge just under halfway down the outside of the humerus. The deltoid covers and, by its bulkiness, protects the attachments of muscles that cross the shoulder joint, particularly the pectoralis, latissimus, the rotator cuff (*see* overleaf) and the tendons of biceps.

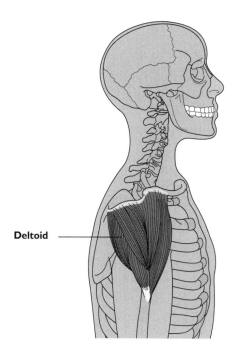

Deltoid

◄ *Figure 8.18:*
The deltoid.

Although the anterior section can be involved in flexion, and the posterior in extension, its main action is abduction, lifting the arm up to the side that is produced by the middle fibres. Like trapezius, it is well used in everyday life, as well as sport, DIY, etc., because most activities involve lifting the arm, or at least stabilising the upper arm for the activities of the hands.

When not moving the arm, the deltoid may still be working to support the rotator cuff in maintaining the stability of the shoulder joint, particularly when one is lifting an object. Even such activities as working at a computer or driving make significant use of it. It cries out for massage in anyone who uses their arms.

Rotator Cuff

There are four 'SITS' muscles that form the rotator cuff that crosses the shoulder joint; *supraspinatus, infraspinatus, teres minor* and *subscapularis*. The muscles arise from the scapula and their tendons form a flexible four-pronged 'clamp' around the head of the humerus, underneath the deltoid. Their main role is to keep the head of the humerus closely connected to the glenoid fossa (the socket) of the scapula, while allowing the arm to move through its multi-directional range of movements. They are also involved in lateral and medial rotation, and in taking the arm behind the body.

In order to allow this great mobility, the shoulder joint is only weakly held by ligaments. This is in contrast to the equivalent joint in the leg (the hip joint) which, because of its importance in weight bearing, fits into a much deeper socket, and has considerably thicker and stronger ligament wrappings for stability and thus a smaller range of movement. The integrity of the shoulder joint, combining movement and stability, is therefore dependent on these cuff muscles and the deltoid, aided by the other muscles whose tendons cross

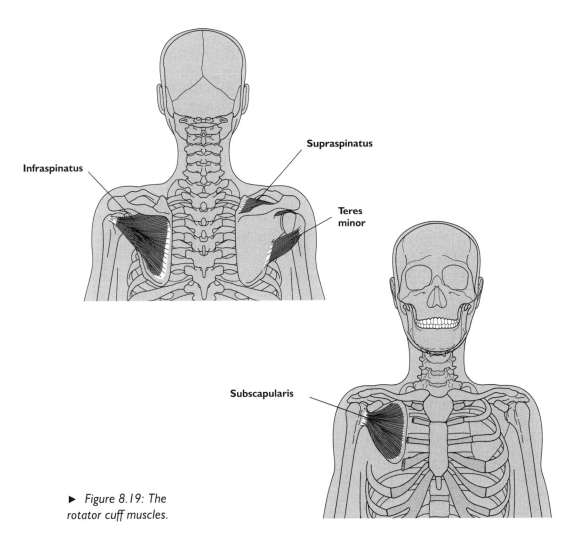

Infraspinatus

Supraspinatus

Teres minor

Subscapularis

► *Figure 8.19: The rotator cuff muscles.*

the joint (pectoralis major and latissimus dorsi, biceps and one head of triceps). Although subscapularis is hard to get at, the other three 'cuff' muscles deserve attention in massage treatments.

Supraspinatus ('above the spine' of the scapula) has a compact muscle belly sitting in the 'trough' formed between the scapular spine and the top part of the back of the scapula. Its tendon passes under the joint between the clavicle and the acromion of the scapula to fix onto the top of the humerus. It is a weak abductor, acting with the middle fibres of deltoid. It is the most commonly damaged of the cuff muscles, particularly through sports activities that involve throwing.

This muscle is worth seeking out in massage, palpating through the covering of the upper trapezius, as it can often be an area of tension, caused by consistently bracing the head of the humerus.

Infraspinatus ('below the spine' of the scapula) runs from the 'dish' of the back of the scapula, crossing the back of the armpit to attach to the top of the humerus a little below and behind supraspinatus. It is the major lateral rotator of the arm (turning the arm out), and also extends the arm (taking the arm back up behind the trunk), working with the posterior fibres of the deltoid.

Teres minor ('round, small') aids the actions of infraspinatus. It passes from the middle of the lateral edge of the scapula to attach just below it on the upper humerus. It's hard to distinguish between these two when massaging; they can be regarded as a unit as they do the same movements. They are hard working muscles, and can usually take firm sliding strokes that start at the back of the scapula and follow the muscle fibres across the back of the armpit.

Subscapularis ('under the scapula') acts at the front of the shoulder joint. It comes from the underside of the scapula, passing between the scapula and the serratus anterior, stretching to the front side of the top of the humerus. Only the lateral part can be directly palpated by carefully digging in through the deltoid at the front of the armpit. It works with pectoralis, latissimus dorsi and teres major muscles to medially rotate the humerus (turn the arm in).

Other Shoulder Joint Muscles

Teres major ('round, big') is another muscle that works across the shoulder joint. It originates lower down on the lateral edge of the scapula, twisting from the back of the armpit to attach to the front of the top of the humerus, just next to latissimus dorsi. It can in fact be regarded as a scapula equivalent to the latissimus, and is sometimes called the 'lats little helper' as its actions are the same and very different from teres minor. Massaging the back of the armpit, with kneading or sliding pressure strokes, works simultaneously on both teres major and the latissimus. Both tendons of biceps and one of triceps cross the joint, so they play a small role in stabilising it.

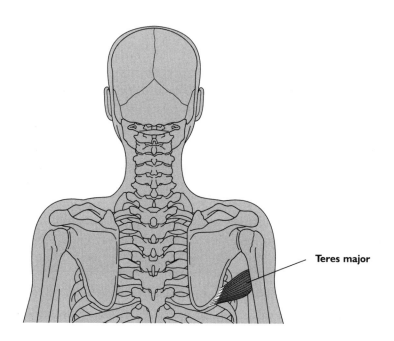

Teres major

◄ *Figure 8.20: Teres major.*

Review of the Muscles of the Scapula and Shoulder Joint

Scapula Movements

Elevation: upper trapezius, levator scapulae, rhomboids.

Depression: lower trapezius, serratus anterior.

Protraction: serratus anterior.

Retraction: rhomboids, trapezius (middle fibres).

Upward rotation (point of shoulder lifts towards neck): upper and lower trapezius, serratus anterior.

Downward rotation (point of shoulders lowers): rhomboids, levator scapulae.

Arm Movements

'Prime movers': pectoralis major, latissimus dorsi, deltoid.

Rotator cuff (SITS muscles): supraspinatus, infraspinatus, teres minor, subscapularis.

Flexion: anterior deltoid, pectoralis major, coracobrachialis.

Extension: posterior deltoid, latissimus dorsi, teres major.

Abduction: deltoid, supraspinatus.

Adduction: pectoralis major, latissimus dorsi, teres major.

Medial rotation: pectoralis major, anterior deltoid, latissimus dorsi, teres major, subscapularis.

Lateral rotation: infraspinatus, teres minor, posterior deltoid.

The Arm

The muscles of the arm are more numerous and larger on the front surface, more used, and thus more in need of massage. The muscles of the front of the upper arm that bend the elbow give strength and coordination to the important activity of bringing the hand to the front of the body, e.g. to bring food to the mouth.

To complement this in the forearm, the flexors of the wrists and fingers at the front are bigger than the extensors at the back. Bending the hand and fingers back is not as important as being able to grasp. The front surface of the hand contains the fleshy areas that provide the fine-tuning for gripping movements of the thumb and fingers; these are in the heel of the hand, the upper palm and the fingers.

Remember, to work 'towards the heart' when doing firm massage strokes on the arms, i.e. up the arm, to assist the venous return of blood to the heart and to avoid damaging the valves in the veins ad lymph vessels that are close to the surface.

The Upper Arm

There are three muscles at the front of the upper arm that are concerned with flexion at the shoulder and the elbow; *biceps, coracobrachialis,* and *brachialis,* and the one at the back, *triceps,* which is primarily an extensor of the elbow. They play a subsidiary role to the rotator cuff and deltoid in stabilising the shoulder joint and in arm movements, apart from brachialis that only works across the elbow.

Biceps brachii: Even young children have often heard of biceps, proudly bending up their forearm to show off the small bulge of the working muscle in the front of their upper arm. It is usually referred to as 'biceps', but its full anatomical name is biceps brachii – the 'two headed, of the upper arm'. This technical name is used to distinguish it from biceps femoris, one of the hamstring muscles in the leg.

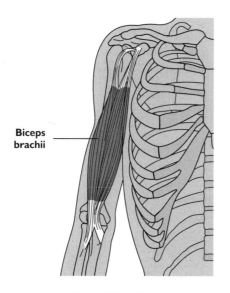

▲ *Figure 8.21: The biceps.*

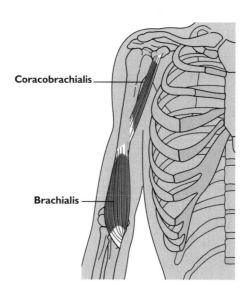

▲ *Figure 8.22: Coracobrachialis and brachialis.*

Although it crosses the shoulder joint, it acts primarily at the elbow. It is a sausage-shaped muscle, covering the two deeper, flatter muscles, coracobrachialis and brachialis, which only cross one joint each.

Both its heads arise from the scapula. The 'short' head passes from the coracoid process across the front of the shoulder joint. The 'long' head arises from the top of the shallow socket of the shoulder joint (glenoid fossa) and then travels down a groove (the bicipital groove) on the outer side of the head of the humerus. They join together about halfway down the front of the humerus and continue across the front of the elbow.

The principal attachment is to the front of the radius, a short distance below the elbow, so biceps mainly acts as an elbow flexor (bending the forearm), working with brachialis and brachioradialis. It also has a short lip that inserts into the fascia covering the muscles of the inner forearm, allowing it to work with *supinator* in supinating the forearm.

The tension and tone in this muscle vary widely from person to person, depending on how much they use their hands. Having the forearm bent will help relax biceps and brachialis, making them easier to massage. Sliding pressure works well on them, and so does kneading.

Coracobrachialis: The name of this muscle describes the two places where it attaches to bones – the coracoid process at one end and the upper arm at the other, close to halfway down the front of the humerus. It assists the anterior deltoid to flex the arm and plays a small role in adduction, which is primarily executed by latissimus dorsi, pectoralis major and teres major.

Brachialis ('of the arm') arises from a little further down the front of the humerus and inserts into the top of the front of the ulna. It works only across the elbow joint, acting with biceps in flexion of the forearm. Coracobrachialis and brachialis are wider and flatter than biceps, and are often harder and less pliable than it.

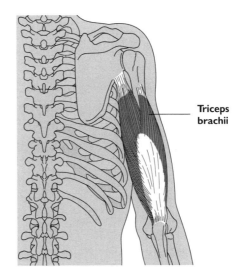

Triceps brachii

▶ *Figure 8.23: The triceps.*

Triceps brachii ('three headed') is commonly referred to as just 'triceps'. Like biceps, it crosses both the shoulder joint and the elbow.

Its long head, coming from the back of the scapula just below the socket, helps stabilise the shoulder joint. The other two sections come from the back of the humerus, converging to form the bulge of the muscle belly midway down the back of the humerus, which is where massage should therefore be concentrated.

The distal tendon inserts into the back of the point of the elbow, the olecranon of the ulna, where it acts as the major extensor of the elbow, working antagonistically to the biceps. Anconeus aids triceps in extension (*see* figure 8.28).

Although *brachioradialis* lies within the forearm, it is described here because its action is only on the elbow joint. Its name describes its attachments – the upper arm and the radius. It lies on the outer edge of the forearm on the thumb side, originating from the lower end of the humerus. The spindle-shaped muscle belly stretches from here to the mid-forearm, from where the tendon runs to insert into the lower (distal) end of the radius.

It works with biceps to flex the forearm, being most effective when the hand is turned so that the thumb is uppermost. It is used when one lifts food / drink to the mouth;

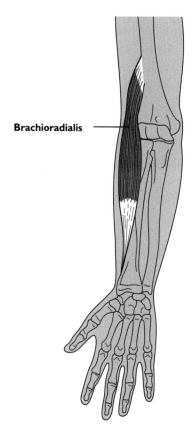

Brachioradialis

▲ *Figure 8.24: Brachioradialis.*

hence it is commonly referred to as the 'drinking muscle'. Massage it as you work on the flexors and extensors of the forearm.

Forearm and Hand

Apart from *brachioradialis* and the *pronators* and *supinator*, the muscles of the forearm are all concerned with movements of the wrist (*carpi muscles*), thumb (*pollicis muscles*) and fingers (*digitorum muscles*). They have long muscle bellies that are capable of producing a powerful pull on the wrist, fingers and thumb causing the hand to either close into a grip or open up. If these muscles were only in the hand itself they would not be nearly as strong, nor give such a long movement of the fingers; and the hand would also be too bulky to function very effectively. In fact most of the larger muscles that control wrist and finger movements also cross the elbow joint. This attachment to the humerus gives greater stability to hand and finger movements than would be the case if they only originated in the forearm.

The forearm muscles are well used in most activities in daily life. If a client wants a shoulder massage, pay attention also to the forearm and hands, as it is very likely that these areas are also quite tight. In fact, most people are surprised when they begin to discover through massage how much tension they hold here.

These muscles belong to three groups, the *flexors* at the front, the *extensors* at the back, and the muscles moving the thumb along the radial side (partly covered in the upper part of the forearm by the brachioradialis). The flexors and extensors each have two groups; muscles that move the wrist and, mostly below them, muscles that move the fingers.

The bellies of all of these muscles form the bulky mass of the forearm, with only the tendons crossing the wrist. Deep under them lie the two *pronator* muscles (at the front of the arm under the flexors), and the *supinator* (wrapping from the back of the humerus around the outside of the upper radius).

It is possible to identify the bellies of the outer layer of muscles when they are working, and to gain an impression of the deeper muscles when they are activated. At the wrist, because of the absence of muscle tissue, most of the tendons can be easily felt when the muscles are working.

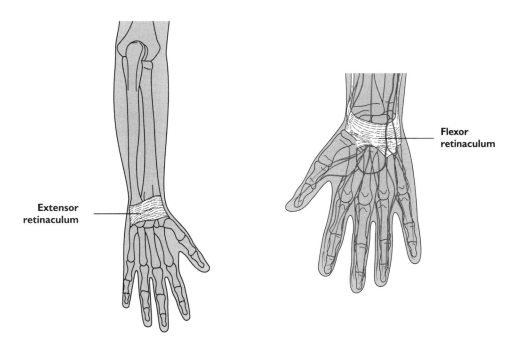

▲ *Figure 8.25: The retinacula of the wrist.*

These tendons are covered by thin layers of connective tissue; the *flexor retinaculum* at the front, and the *extensor retinaculum* at the back, which hold them down as they cross the wrist. Many of the tendons are also enclosed in protective synovial sheaths as they pass under the retinacula. The flexor retinaculum also protects all the nerves and blood vessels that feed the hand, which pass under it in the carpal tunnel, the space between it and the carpal bones.

If the forearm muscles are overused, particularly via repetitive activities, the tendons can become inflamed. This is more common in the flexor muscles because of their greater use. If the flexor tendons swell, they can put pressure on the nerves as they pass through the tunnel, particularly the median nerve that supplies much of the hand. This swelling and nerve compression can lead in turn to pain, tingling, numbness and/or dysfunction in the wrist and hand, known as *carpal tunnel syndrome*.

This is an important condition for massage practitioners to be aware of, for they can be vulnerable to it themselves, due to over-using strokes that are demanding on the flexor muscles. Excessive kneading, applying pressure through bent wrists, and working in ways that overuse the upper limb seem to be the predominant causes. This can be compounded by doing other activities that demand consistent hand use when not massaging, such as computing, playing musical instruments, or racquet or bat sports, or DIY.

If you begin to experience lingering pain, tingling, numbness or weakness in your wrists **AFTER** doing massages, especially if these symptoms begin to persist over time, **DO NOT IGNORE** the symptoms and **DO NOT** continue to work in the same way.

Change the way that you work, try to use less demanding techniques and perhaps reduce your workload for a while if that is feasible.

Front of the Forearm (flexors and pronators)

Apart from the pronators, most of the muscles of the front of the forearm are flexors of the hand (bending the wrist forward) or of the fingers (curling them up). They have long muscle bellies in the forearm, with tendons that start just above the wrist, cross the wrist joint, and extend to the base of the hand, the palm or the fingers.

Their importance in the gripping activities of the hand means that they are constantly used in everyday life, and used even more in most sports, crafts, building and factory work, DIY and computer work – in fact in most activities.

Although they are not often painful, they can sometimes be sore after unusual activity or over-activity. Keeping these muscles relaxed is important in preventing overuse strains in the wrist and hand. When these muscles are massaged, most people are surprised to realise how much tension they are holding there, and how good it feels to have them massaged. This can include massage practitioners!

The five *superficial flexors* all come from the medial epicondyle of the humerus, which is the bulge at the lower end of the humerus, on the side nearest the body.

This common origin can become inflamed in activities that involve gripping and twisting, especially when there is a forceful grip, such as when using a screwdriver, or in playing golf with a faulty grip. This problem is commonly called *golfer's elbow*.

Pronator teres is the shortest of the group, stretching diagonally across the front of the forearm to about halfway down the outside edge of the radius. It works with *pronator quadratus*, a small square muscle in the deeper layer that connects the lower ends of the radius and ulna. You can palpate the teres in action, but the quadratus is covered by the flexors. Together, they pronate the forearm, turning the palm down.

Two flexors attach to the base of the hand to flex the wrist, *flexor carpi radialis* on the thumb side and *flexor carpi ulnaris* on the little finger side. Flexor carpi ulnaris works with extensor carpi ulnaris to adduct the wrist, bending the hand to the little finger side; flexor carpi radialis works with the radial extensors to abduct the wrist.

Between the wrist flexors lies *palmaris longus* (although some people do not have one), which stretches to the palm where it helps to hold the skin of the palm in place and to flex the wrist.

The *flexor digitorum superficialis* ('superficial flexor of the fingers'), the largest superficial flexor, lies beneath the others. In addition to arising with them from the humerus, it attaches to the front of the radius and ulna. It divides into four long tendons which cross the palm to the middle phalanges of the four fingers, to curl the fingers.

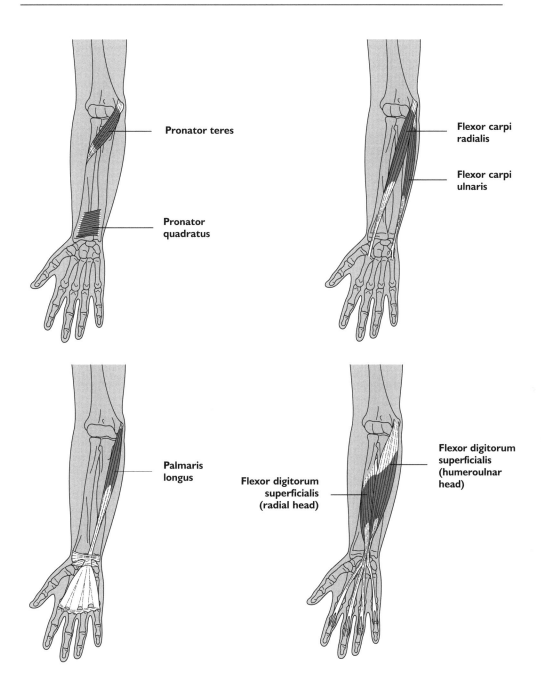

▲ *Figure 8.26: The superficial flexors and pronator quadratus (right lower arm, anterior view).*

Deep flexors arise from the front of the forearm bones. *Flexor digitorum profundus* comes from a large section of the front of the ulna, and has tendons running to the end of each of the four fingers, acting to curl them up.

Flexor pollicis longus ('pollux' is the thumb) stretches from the middle of the front of the radius to the end of the thumb to flex it.

Pronator quadratus, described above, runs between the ulna and radius near the wrist.

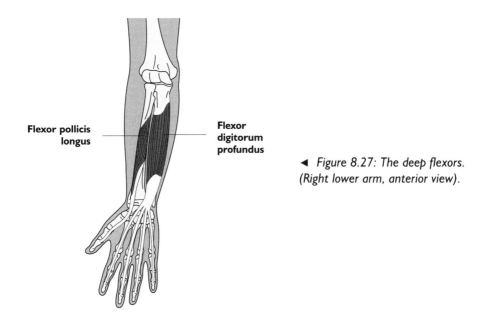

Flexor pollicis longus

Flexor digitorum profundus

◄ *Figure 8.27: The deep flexors. (Right lower arm, anterior view).*

Back of the Forearm (brachioradialis, supinators, extensors and thumb muscles)

The outer layer of muscles here bend back the wrist and fingers, while the deeper layer act primarily on the thumb and index finger. The muscle bellies in the forearm, which are smaller than the flexors, have long tendons crossing the back of the wrist. Many of these tendons are contained in protective synovial sheaths as they pass under the *extensor retinaculum*. When the muscles are working, the tendons acting on the fingers and thumb can be seen on the back of the hand or the outside edge of the base of the thumb.

This group of muscles can often become quite tight as they work to balance the pull of the flexors. They are quite compact, so massage on them generally needs to be firm to have much impact.

The *superficial extensors* all come from a tendon that attaches to the lateral epicondyle of the humerus, which is the bulge on the outer edge of its lower end. *Tennis elbow* is the name given to inflammation of this common tendon, which arises from overuse of the extensors in forceful racquet or bat sports and/or other activities, such as gardening. Tennis elbow is usually accompanied by pain and tenderness.

This group comprises of: *brachioradialis* (previously described with the upper arm muscles), three muscles that bend the wrist back (*extensor carpi radialis longus, extensor carpi radialis brevis* and *extensor carpi ulnaris*), two that bend the fingers back (*extensor digitorum* and *extensor digiti minimi*), and *anconeus*, a short muscle running to the upper ulna which assists triceps to extend the elbow. The radial extensors also work with flexor carpi radialis to abduct the wrist. Extensor carpi ulnaris works with flexor carpi ulnaris to adduct it.

Extensor digitorum bends back the fingers via attachments to each section of the fingers.

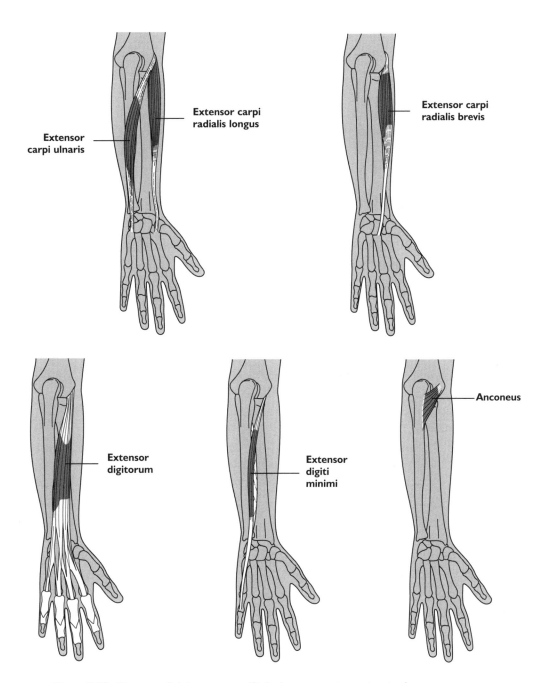

▲ *Figure 8.28: The superficial extensors. (Right lower arm, posterior view).*

Extensor digiti minimi (the 'tea drinker's muscle') lifts back the little finger.
The *deep extensors* are comprised of three muscles that act on the thumb, one that acts on the index finger and *supinator*. Even when the muscles are working, you will only be able to get a vague feeling of the muscle bellies by pressing through the superficial extensors. However, apart from supinator, the tendons are palpable in the wrist and hand, when the muscles are working.

Supinator is the only one of this group that arises with the superficial extensors from the lateral epicondyle of the humerus. It runs diagonally to the outer edge of the upper radius.

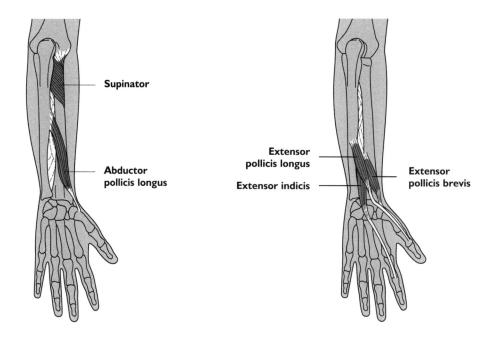

▲ *Figure 8.29: The deep extensors. (Right lower arm, posterior view).*

The rest come from the back of the radius and ulna. They are *abductor pollicis longus*, *extensor pollicis longus* and *extensor pollicis brevis* to the thumb, and *extensor indicis* to the index finger.

Hand

There are small intrinsic muscles in the hand. The heel of the hand is made up of a group of muscles that form the base of the thumb and a smaller group of muscles that make up the base of the little finger. These muscles move the thumb and little finger respectively, and can give a finely-tuned 'precision grip' to complement the strength of the forearm muscles whose tendons move the hand and fingers into a 'power grip'. There are also tiny muscles between the fingers. These are all hardworking areas that usually enjoy firm massage. The *thenar eminence*, the muscle bulge at the base of the thumb, is formed by intrinsic muscles that move the thumb. The 'webbing' between the thumb and the index finger is also formed by a thumb muscle called *opponens pollicis*. The *hypothenar eminence* is made up of muscles that act on the little finger.

Between the metacarpal bones, there are small palm muscles called *interossei* ('between the bones') that spread and bring together the fingers, called abduction and adduction respectively.

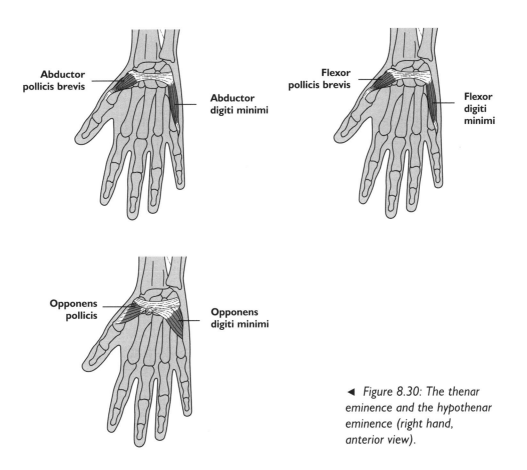

◀ *Figure 8.30: The thenar eminence and the hypothenar eminence (right hand, anterior view).*

Review of the Muscles Involved in Movements of the Forearm and Hand

Movements of the Forearm

Flexion: biceps (brachii), brachialis, brachioradialis.
Extension: triceps (brachii), anconeus.
Pronation: pronator teres, pronator quadratus.
Supination: biceps (brachii), supinator.

Movements of the Wrist

Flexion: flexor carpi radialis, palmaris longus, flexor carpi ulnaris.
Extension: extensor carpi radialis longus, extensor carpi radialis brevis, extensor carpi ulnaris.
Abduction (bending to thumb side): flexor carpi radialis, extensor carpi radialis longus, extensor carpi radialis brevis.
Adduction: flexor carpi ulnaris, extensor carpi ulnaris.

Movements of the Fingers and Thumb – Forearm Muscles

Flexion: flexor digitorum superficialis, flexor digitorum profundus, flexor pollicis longus.
Extension: extensor digitorum, extensor indicis, extensor digiti minimi, extensor pollicis longus, extensor pollicis brevis.
Abduction: abductor pollicis longus.

Movements of the Fingers and Thumb – Intrinsic Hand Muscles

Thumb – thenar eminence.
Little finger – hypothenar eminence.
Between the fingers: interossei of the palm.

Trunk

This section covers the postural muscles of the back, the muscles involved in breathing, the muscles of the abdomen, the muscles of the lower trunk that relate to the leg, and the pelvic floor muscles.

The muscles of the arm and shoulder girdle that cover the back, shoulders and chest are described in the earlier section on the arm. These are *trapezius, levator scapulae, rhomboids*, and *serratus anterior* in the upper back, *latissimus dorsi* in the mid and lower back, and *pectoralis major* and *pectoralis minor* at the front of the chest.

Postural Muscles of the Back (the Para-vertebrals)

There are two groups of postural muscles stretching from the sacrum up to the base of the skull; the *erector spinae* group which form the intermediate level and the deep network of small muscles. They are covered in the upper back and neck by the muscles involved in the movements of the shoulder girdle and arm. In the neck, these two groups have a third group covering them called *splenii* muscles that control the movements of the neck and head. In the lower back, the *quadratus lumborum* forms the back of the abdomen.

The *erector spinae / sacrospinalis* are the large postural muscle group arising from the sacrum and running up along each side of the spine, with attachments to each of the vertebrae and the back of each rib. They are commonly known either as the *erector spinae* group ('keeping the spine upright') or *sacrospinalis* ('from the sacrum, of the spine'). The largest part of the group (and the easiest to feel) is in the lower back, where the muscles do the most work in maintaining the uprightness of the spine and there is only a layer of fascia covering them.

This is a complex group of overlapping strands of muscle, which collectively extend the spine either straightening it from forward bending or hyperextending it (back bending). It is made up of three groups of muscles, each of which is further divided into three:

1. The *iliocostalis* is the most lateral group. Its lowest section runs from the lumbar fascia to the lower ribs, the middle section from the lower to upper ribs (with the upper

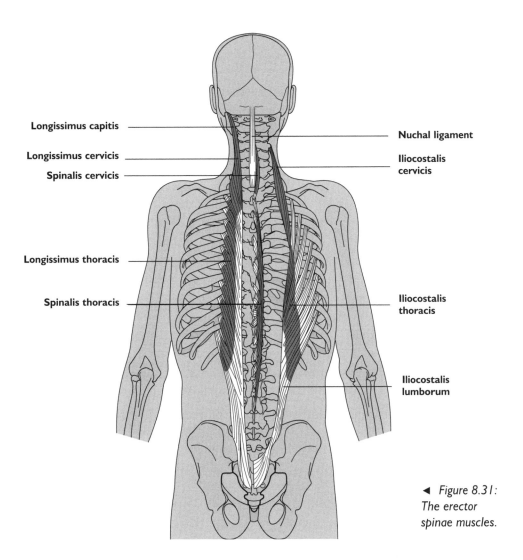

Longissimus capitis

Longissimus cervicis

Spinalis cervicis

Longissimus thoracis

Spinalis thoracis

Nuchal ligament

Iliocostalis
cervicis

Iliocostalis
thoracis

Iliocostalis
lumborum

◄ *Figure 8.31:*
The erector
spinae muscles.

part of this section often being covered by the scapula), and the upper section from the upper ribs to the lower cervical vertebrae. Because they are the furthest from the vertebral column, they can also act in lateral flexion of the spine, working with quadratus lumborum.

2. The *longissimus* group is the middle and largest part of the erectors. It originates from the lumbar vertebrae and the lowest section inserts into the thoracic vertebrae and lower ribs, the middle section runs from the upper thoracic vertebrae to C2–6, and the upper section from the upper thoracic and lower cervical vertebrae to the base of the skull.

3. The *spinalis* group is closest to the spine. The lowest section is from the upper lumbar and lower thoracic vertebrae to the upper thoracic, the middle section from the lower to the upper cervical, where it often blends into the longissimus, and the upper section from the upper thoracic and lower cervical to the occiput. This top section, *spinalis capitis*, is usually blended with the *semispinalis capitis*, the top section of one of the para-vertebral muscles (below).

Most people wanting a general massage want you to work on their shoulders and/or back, so this is an important group of muscles to know about, because of their role in balancing the posture of the whole back. They are easy to work on in the midback, where there is only a thin layer of covering muscle and in the lower back where there is none. In the shoulder and neck area, you need to work firstly on the superficial muscles and may not get this deep in a short massage session.

Although the whole muscle may be quite toned, there are usually some tighter sections, and it is often different on the left and right sides. When massaging near the spine, you will usually find lines of tension within some sections of the muscle group, running up and down alongside the spine in a superior-inferior direction. There may even be lines of tension in the upper back, which you will only feel by palpating through the superficial muscle layers, e.g. trapezius and rhomboids. For example, tension lines that you encounter running alongside the spine in the area between the shoulderblades are clear indicators that you are feeling tension in the erectors, as they are the only muscles with fibres running in this direction.

Tightness in the lower back can be chronic and fairly solidly 'locked in', often the result of a sedentary occupation. This is not usually sensitive and can be massaged using long sliding pressure strokes applied with a large contact area, such as your palm. More pressure can be applied, if appropriate, with your knuckles or forearm, *if you have been trained in using these*. You can also push or pull transversely across the muscles here, stretching them by moving them towards or away from the spine.

However, when this area has been strained or damaged by an injury, awkward lifting, sudden twists, or it hasn't settled back after childbirth, it can be quite painful and too sensitive for much pressure to be applied.

It can also be inflamed by extended activity in bending positions, such as gardening or a burst of DIY activity. Gentler sliding and kneading strokes would then be more appropriate, and perhaps stretches applied from above and below the painful area. In both cases, gentle side bending and twisting exercises, *performed within a carefully monitored comfortable range, with no sudden or forceful movements*, will help clients regain some flexibility.

Tension in the midback between the shoulder blades, is common in those whose job entails long periods of leaning over, because as the erectors are stretched, they also have to support the upper body. Most middle-aged office workers, for example, have chronic locked-in hardness in the midback, and the prevalence of computers is contributing to this happening in younger people.

Jobs that involve people repeatedly or constantly leaning over while using their hands can strain the lower back as well and also lead to pain in the upper back and shoulders as the muscles struggle to keep the head upright. This is a common problem for laboratory technicians, factory workers, sewing machinists, many musicians, and especially for dentists.

Mid back tension is not normally sensitive. You can generally apply more pressure than on the upper and lower back, and you can usually use the full range of common massage strokes. If you can ease some of the tension and help the client regain some flexibility here, it will take the strain off other parts of the back. Increased flexibility here and in the lower trunk also helps sustain flexibility in the shoulders.

The upper back and base of the neck can vary from being an area of 'rock hard' tension, to quite sensitive scattered knots of tension, or combinations of these, so you'll need to have a versatile approach to massaging here. Tension in this upper part of the erectors can be due to a number of factors. It is usually allied to tensions and stresses in the overlying muscles:

- In the other neck muscles due to stress, posture or adjustments to strain or problems lower in the back;
- In the shoulder muscles in response to stress;
- In response to considerable use of the arms and hands;
- Combinations of these factors.

Massage of this area should therefore be carefully applied, adapting to the client's responses, and concentrating first on the more superficial muscles.

The deepest muscles of the back (the 'gutter muscles') are a network of tiny muscles which fill the 'gutter' formed by the spinous and transverse processes of the vertebrae; they fine-tune the posture and the movements of the spine, particularly extension and rotation. The *intertransversarii* muscles run between transverse processes of adjacent vertebrae; the *interspinalis* connect adjacent spinous processes running on both sides of the interspinous ligament; and the *transversospinalis* group run up from transverse to spinous processes (the *semispinalis* often spanning five or six vertebrae, the deeper *multifidis* spanning two to four, and the deepest *rotatores* connecting adjacent vertebrae).

In contrast to the lines of tension in the erectors, tension in these muscles form small *knots* right up against the spinous processes. Many chiropractors and osteopaths use these knots as diagnostic indicators of a restriction between adjacent vertebrae. They can be points of great sensitivity, in which case it is best to work around the area. If they are less sensitive, they can be massaged, provided you monitor the client's responses.

If there is considerable sharp pain at the same level on both sides of the spine, this can often indicate a herniated disc. Do not work on this area, but refer the client to an osteopath, chiropractor or doctor for a clear diagnosis.

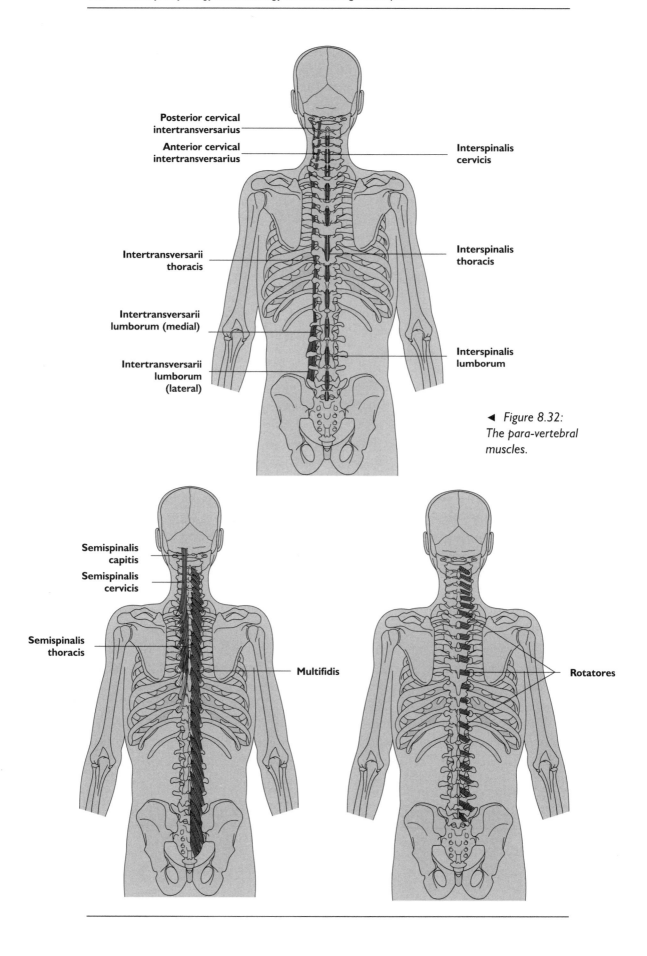

Posterior cervical intertransversarius

Anterior cervical intertransversarius

Interspinalis cervicis

Intertransversarii thoracis

Interspinalis thoracis

Intertransversarii lumborum (medial)

Intertransversarii lumborum (lateral)

Interspinalis lumborum

◄ *Figure 8.32:*
The para-vertebral
muscles.

Semispinalis capitis

Semispinalis cervicis

Semispinalis thoracis

Multifidis

Rotatores

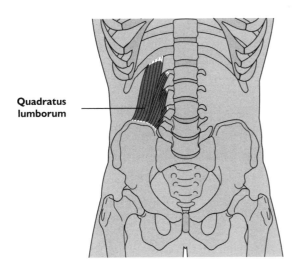

◀ *Figure 8.33:*
Quadratus lumborum.

Quadratus lumborum is a square sheet of muscle in the lower back, connected on three sides to bones; the lowest ribs, the lumbar vertebrae and the crest of the ilium. It is covered by the lumbar section of the erectors, except for its outer edge that stretches a little wider to link up with the fascia from the abdominals. It thus forms the back wall of the abdomen.

The quadratus muscles are part of the postural balance of the lower trunk, working reciprocally with the iliopsoas muscles. They also work with the abdominals in twisting, and with them and the erectors in side bending. Lower back problems in the erectors can also affect the quadratus, so gentle side bending and twisting exercises of the trunk will benefit both muscles. You can work on the outer part of quadratus when massaging in the lower back, by working in just under the outside edge of the erectors.

Breathing Muscles

The lungs are made of spongy, elastic material, which is stretched by the action of the muscles around it.

The main breathing muscles are the *diaphragm* which forms the base of the lungs and pulls directly down on the lung tissue, and the *intercostal muscles* between the ribs, which move the ribs to affect the lungs.

In everyday breathing, the diaphragm is the major muscle of inhalation, aided by the external intercostals. Breathing out is generally via relaxation of these muscles. The internal intercostals and abdominal wall muscles are called upon when one coughs or sneezes in an attempt to expel material from the lungs, and when we forcibly exhale.

Many of the neck and back muscles previously described can be called into play when one is very active or in breathing difficulties. This includes the *scalenes, sternocleidomastoid, quadratus lumborum, erector spinae,* and perhaps *pectoralis major* in forceful inhalation, and the *abdominal wall* muscles and *latissimus dorsi* in strong exhalation.

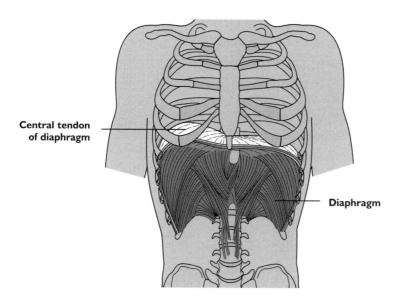

Central tendon of diaphragm

Diaphragm

◀ *Figure 8.34: The diaphragm. (Cross section through the lower ribs).*

Bear in mind that all of the main muscles of the trunk and shoulders can affect the breathing. If the muscles of the back and chest are tight, it is harder for the ribs to move. Therefore, even if you cannot apply much direct pressure on the diaphragm and intercostals (for reasons described below), encouraging these other muscles to relax will allow more freedom in the ribcage. Strong percussion, appropriately applied on the well-muscled areas of the midback, can penetrate to the lung tissue and stimulate it.

The *diaphragm* is a dome-shaped muscle, which forms the base of the lungs, separating the thoracic cavity from the abdominal cavity. It arises from the inside of the lower ribs and the front of the lumbar vertebrae, by tendinous 'straps' called crura, with fibres rising up towards its own central tendon.

When the fibres shorten, they lower the central part of the muscle, increasing the volume of the lung area, which pulls air into the chest. As the diaphragm relaxes, the central part rises, in part pushed up by a reflex action of the abdomen. This reduces the volume of the lungs and pushes air out.

This muscle can only be palpated just under the arch formed by the ribs at the top of the abdomen, and any massaging here should only be done by experienced practitioners.

The intercostals ('between the ribs') are two layers of short muscle sheets that run between consecutive ribs. In addition to their direct role in breathing, they maintain the integrity of the chest wall.

Each *external intercostal* runs obliquely forward to the rib below, and when active in inhalation, lifts the ribs to help expand the volume of the lungs. The *internal intercostals* run at right angles, obliquely backwards to the rib below, and can lower the ribs.

Many people respond well to long 'raking' slides with your fingers between the ribs at the side of the trunk to encourage softening, but some people may find this ticklish.

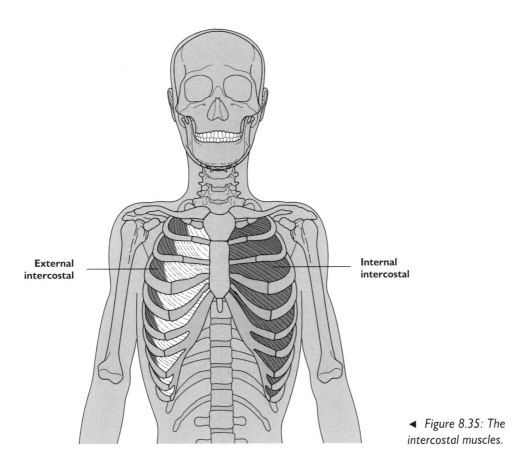

External
intercostal

Internal
intercostal

◀ *Figure 8.35: The intercostal muscles.*

Abdomen

This area is bounded by muscles – the muscles of the *abdominal wall* in front, the *quadratus lumborum* at the back, the *diaphragm* above which separates it from the thorax, and the *pelvic floor* below.

These muscles surround and contain the abdominal contents, the organs and digestive tract, and support the breathing. Those at the front and back of the abdomen play a role in the movements of the trunk and in posture.

The *iliopsoas* muscles, which are in the abdomen and are involved in posture, are described below in the section on trunk muscles that move the legs.

Abdominal Wall

The wall at the front of the abdomen is formed by four muscles, which stretch from the ribs to the hips and pubic bone, and at the side of the waist connect with the fascia of the lower back.

As previously mentioned, they are stretched when the diaphragm contracts on inhalation and pushes down on the abdomen. Their reflex contraction then helps push the diaphragm up as it relaxes on the exhalation.

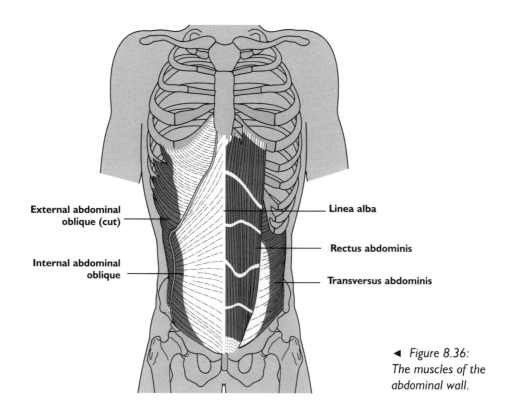

External abdominal
oblique (cut)

Internal abdominal
oblique

Linea alba

Rectus abdominis

Transversus abdominis

◀ Figure 8.36:
The muscles of the
abdominal wall.

Rectus abdominis is the central muscle, a long thick strap on either side of the *linea alba*, the 'white line' of connective tissue which forms the centreline of the front of the abdomen. The muscle is in short sections, with short strips of tendon, *'tendinous insertions'*, between them. This arrangement of alternating muscle and tendon gives rise to the characteristic belly ripples (the 'six-pack' effect) in body builders who have worked the abdominals ('abs').

It may be relaxed or toned when you are standing, but is most active when you lift your head or legs, or both, while lying on your back (supine). Doing sit-ups is the most common way of exercising it, and you'll often find tension here in those who do this exercise a lot, for example in sports warm-ups.

The other abdominals are in three thin layers to the side of the rectus, one on top of the other, with the fibres of each one running in different directions to give a plywood-like strength.

The outer abdominal, the *external oblique*, has its fibres running diagonally down towards the centre, the angle of putting your hands in your pockets. The next, the *internal oblique*, has fibres running diagonally upwards towards the centre. The deepest one, the *transversus abdominis*, sometimes called the 'corset muscle', has fibres running across the abdomen.

At the waist, the outer edges of their sheaths blend into the fascia of the lower back muscles, and at the centre the sheaths join the fascia around the rectus abdominis.

The abdominals support breathing and help push matter out of the body in such activities as coughing, defecating, or when giving birth. The three lateral abdominals work with the outer parts of the erectors and the quadratus lumborum of the lower back in twisting movements of the trunk and in side bending.

For the massage practitioner, the abdomen is the area where you can expect to work in a variety of ways and where you will find the most varied responses from recipients. Some people have well-toned abdominal muscles which relish firm kneading massage, as do the sides of the waist. When applying any significant pressure on the abdomen, strokes should be done in a clockwise movement to follow the direction of the large intestine.

If you are working firmly on or through these muscles, it can be helpful to have a pillow under the back of the client's knees, propping them up in order to relax the abdominal muscles.

In some situations, pressure that would affect the underlying organs is not appropriate. When a women is menstruating she may not want any touch here at all, although for some people the gentle 'laying on' of hands can be quite soothing. Gentle abdominal stroking is often appreciated in pregnancy. The practitioner should also be sensitive to the fact that this is an area of psychological vulnerability, which may affect people's willingness to be touched there.

Pelvic Floor Muscles

The main muscles here, the *levator ani* and the *coccygeus*, form a 'sling' that supports the abdominal contents, helped by the hip rotators. The tubes passing through them are controlled by the sphincter muscles. This area is not generally touched in professional massage.

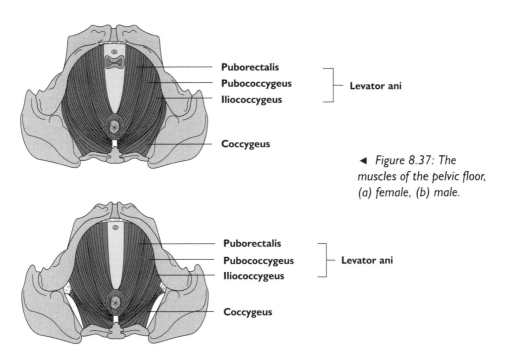

Puborectalis
Pubococcygeus
Iliococcygeus — Levator ani

Coccygeus

◄ *Figure 8.37: The muscles of the pelvic floor, (a) female, (b) male.*

Puborectalis
Pubococcygeus
Iliococcygeus — Levator ani

Coccygeus

Review of the Trunk Muscles

Movements of the Trunk

Flexion: rectus abdominis, external oblique, internal oblique.
Extension: erector spinae group, deep 'gutter' muscles, quadratus lumborum.
Lateral flexion: erector spinae group, quadratus lumborum, external oblique, internal oblique.
Rotation: external oblique, internal oblique, deep 'gutter' muscles.
Compress abdominal contents: external oblique, internal oblique, transversus abdominis.
Elevation of the hip: quadratus lumborum.

Respiration

Inhalation: diaphragm, external intercostals.
Exhalation: internal intercostals.

Accessory Muscles

Strong inhalation: scalenes, sternocleidomastoid, quadratus lumborum, erectors, pectoralis major.
Strong exhalation: abdominal wall muscles, latissimus dorsi.

Muscles of the Lower Trunk that Move the Leg

The *iliopsoas* can be viewed either as three separate muscles or as a three-part muscle. The two main components are the *iliacus* and the *psoas major*, which come from the lower trunk and join, via a common tendon, to the lesser trochanter of the femur, which is the bulge on the inside at the top of the shaft of the femur. The psoas comes from the lowest thoracic and all of the lumbar vertebrae, and the iliacus from the inside surface of the ilium.

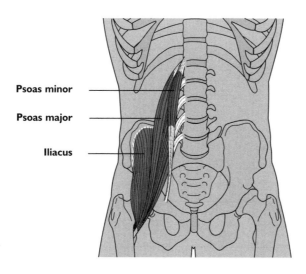

Psoas minor

Psoas major

Iliacus

◄ *Figure 8.38: The iliopsoas muscles.*

They move the legs and also maintain the postural relationship between the trunk and the legs. Psoas is the strongest flexor of the leg (lifting it forward); iliacus helps in lateral rotation of the leg; together they can bend the trunk forward on the legs.

Psoas plays a part in the postural balance of the trunk, via its attachments to the front of the lower spine and if it is contracted, it pulls the lumbar spine forward to give a 'sway back'.

Because of their origins deep in the abdomen, they are hard to palpate, except where they cross the pubic bone behind the inguinal ligament. This should only be done by a therapist with training and experience due to the potential risk to other structures in this area.

Leg Movements

The two hip joints are weight bearing joints and therefore need good stability, both from strong ligaments and from muscles that cross the joint. Although the movements of the leg at the hip joint are not as extensive as the actions of the shoulder girdle and arm, there is still quite a range of movement.

Therefore a large number of muscles cross the hip joint. They coordinate the two reciprocal functions of moving the leg in relation to the trunk, and of moving and stabilising the trunk on the legs. These two activities are always simultaneous when one is upright, e.g. walking involves lifting one leg while stabilising the other hip joint in order to maintain balance. Walking up stairs or climbing involves the stabilisation of the supporting leg and hip joint whilst also straightening the leg and perhaps moving the trunk as well.

Because the hip has this potential range of movement – abduction, adduction, flexion, extension, rotation and circumduction – it is important that the knee is very stable. The knee has a much more limited range of movement, primarily flexion and extension, and therefore less muscles crossing it, although they are all quite strong. The main ones are for flexion (quadriceps) and extension (the hamstrings). The side-to-side stability of the knee is balanced between gracilis on the medial side and the pull of the fascia lata (iliotibial tract) on the lateral side. Six muscles that cross the hip joint also work across the knee joint, helping to coordinate the relation between these two weight bearing joints.

Bear in mind the terminology for the actions of these joints. Lifting the leg forward is called flexion of the leg or flexion at the hip, while taking it backwards is extension. However bending the lower leg backwards is called flexion at the knee or flexion of the lower leg, while extension at this joint is straightening it.

Apart from the *iliopsoas* in the trunk, and the *tensor fasciae latae* and *sartorius* in the thigh, the muscles of the hip and thigh can be considered in five main groups. There are two

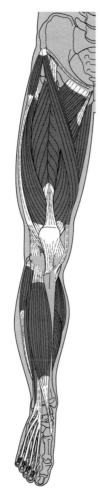
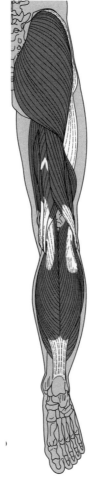

◄ *Figure 8.39:*
Main muscles of
the leg,
(a) anterior,
(b) posterior.

groups around the hips; the *gluteals* of the buttocks and the deep *lateral rotators* of the leg. There are three in the thigh; the *quadriceps* at the front which primarily straightens the knee, the *hamstrings* at the back which lift the leg back and bend back the knee, and the *adductors* on the inside of the thigh.

Buttocks and the Top of the Thigh

The small *tensor fasciae latae*, the three *gluteal muscles* of the buttocks and the *hip rotators* under the gluteus maximus can extend, abduct and rotate the leg, or act to move or stabilise the trunk or the thigh.

When giving a runner a leg massage, it is good to work on their buttocks if the situation allows, because of the significant role of these muscles in leg actions. You may need to get the client to lie on his side to work effectively on the *gluteus medius*, but try not to miss it out if possible.

Tensor fasciae latae (TFL – 'the tensor of the wide fascia') is a short strap of muscle from the top, front projection of the 'hip' bone called the *anterior superior iliac spine* ('ASIS'), running diagonally back to the *iliotibial tract*. This strong strap of connective tissue, also called the *fascia lata*, stretches from the top of the ilium down the outside of the thigh

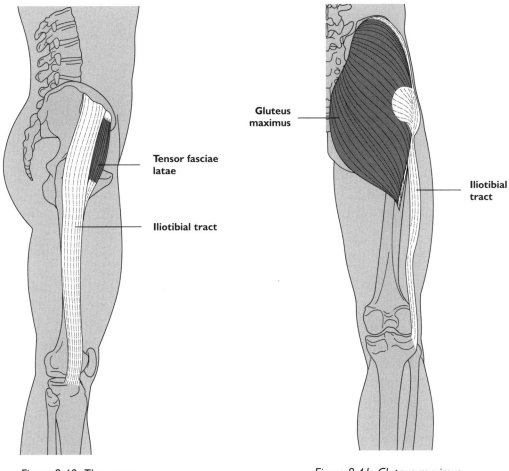

▲ *Figure 8.40: The tensor fasciae latae muscle.*

▲ *Figure 8.41: Gluteus maximus.*

to the top of the tibia, holding in place the outer muscles of the thigh and stabilising the outside of the knee joint. The TFL rotates the thigh medially, and assists *gluteus medius* in abducting the leg.

Gluteus maximus forms the mass of the buttocks. It is usually the bulkiest and strongest muscle in the body. Although it can extend the leg backwards, it's not usually active in easy walking. However, it is crucial for more forceful leg extensions (e.g. running and jumping) or in straightening the trunk (e.g. in climbing stairs, or standing from sitting). This is why we have large, well-muscled buttocks, unlike apes who cannot straighten their legs or lift them backwards because of the shape of their hip and knee joints. It also laterally rotates the leg to turn the foot out, working with the hip rotators that it covers.

From an origin on the outer edge of the sacrum and the back of the top edge of the hip bone (the crest of the ilium), it stretches to the greater trochanter of the femur, which is the 'bump' on the outside at the top of the shaft and also to the *iliotibial tract*.

If you are doing extensive massage on the gluteals, work with some pressure along the origin, which is the boomerang shape at the edge of the sacrum and just below the iliac crest, as there is often tension present. You can also usually apply pressure into the large

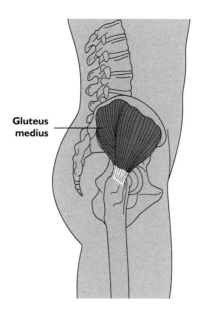
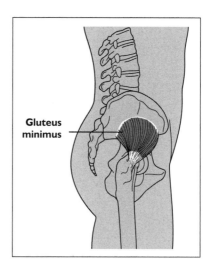

▲ *Figure 8.42: Gluteus medius and gluteus minimus.*

fleshy central mass of the muscle, taking care not to jab through into the sciatic nerve, which is at its largest, about the size of a finger, as it passes under the muscle. Towards the front of the muscle, you will also be working on the part of the gluteus medius that it covers, and also the deeper lateral rotators.

Gluteus medius is an equivalent at the hip of the deltoid in the shoulder. It originates from a wide area of the outer surface of the ilium, with its back third covered by the gluteus maximus. This thick mass of muscle converges onto the great trochanter of the femur. It can be quite tight in those with stiff hips.

Like the deltoid, it can be involved in a range of actions, depending on which part of the muscle is being activated, the position of the leg, and the actions of the other hip muscles. It can be involved, for example, in rotation of the leg in either direction, the front section helping to medially rotate it, and the posterior section involved in lateral rotation. Its main actions are side lifting of the leg (abduction) or, when we lift the other leg, stabilising the pelvis from tipping to the side.

Gluteus minimus is totally covered by the gluteus medius. It arises from below and slightly behind it on the ilium and inserts in front of it on the greater trochanter of the femur. Its actions are very similar. These two muscles are crucial for balance in walking; problems with them produce an awkward gait that cannot be compensated for by other hip muscles.

The lateral hip rotators lie under the gluteus maximus. These six small muscles come from the sacrum and the ischium to the great trochanter. The largest of them, the *piriformis*, which is the uppermost of these muscles, can be palpated by experienced practitioners. However, the unskilled practitioner should beware of pressing on the sciatic nerve, which is at its largest as it passes through this area.

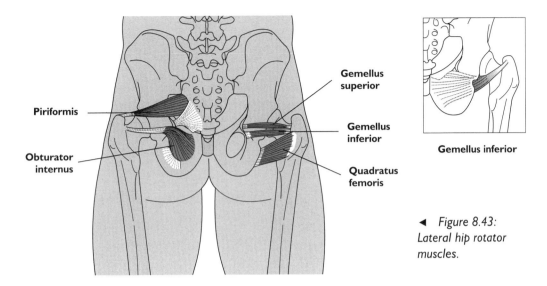

Piriformis

Gemellus superior

Obturator internus

Gemellus inferior

Quadratus femoris

Gemellus inferior

◄ *Figure 8.43: Lateral hip rotator muscles.*

Upper Leg

With the exception of *sartorius*, the muscles of the upper leg belong to three groups – the four parts of *quadriceps* at the front, the three *hamstrings* at the back, and the five *adductors* on the inside of the thigh.

As well as moving the leg, the quadriceps and hamstrings are postural muscles, maintaining a reciprocal balance between the body tilting backwards and forwards. They can usually take firm massage, especially in those with well-used legs. The adductors vary considerably in tone and sensitivity.

Quadriceps (femoris) is the large 'four-headed' muscle at the front of the thigh, sometimes described as four separate muscles. They all join to a common tendon housing the patella, which braces the tendon as it crosses the knee to insert into the front of the tibia. The primary collective action is to straighten the knee (extension) for example in kicking.

Rectus femoris ('straight, of the femur') is the only part of quadriceps that crosses the hip joint, coming from the front of the hipbone – the anterior *inferior* iliac spine (just below the ASIS) – and is therefore able to work with the iliopsoas in lifting the leg forward (hip flexion).

It covers the *vastus intermedius*, the central one of the other three, which arises from the front of the femoral shaft. On either side of the intermedius are the *vastus medialis* and *vastus lateralis*, coming respectively from the inside and outside edge of the front of the femur.

Because the quadriceps is such a large strong muscle group, there is a bursa just above and another just below the knee to stop the tendon rubbing on the bones. The tendon attaches to the large tuberosity at the front of the tibia.

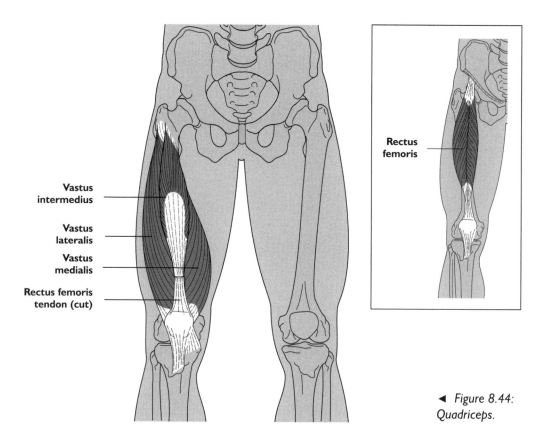

Vastus intermedius

Vastus lateralis

Vastus medialis

Rectus femoris tendon (cut)

Rectus femoris

◄ *Figure 8.44: Quadriceps.*

The patella helps hold the tendon from being pulled sideways out of place when either the medialis or lateralis is pulling without the other. The section of the quadriceps tendon below the patella is often called the patellar ligament because it runs between two bones, the patella and the tibia.

The large strong muscles of the quadriceps can take a lot of pressure, both sliding pressure along the muscles and kneading and wringing across them. The tightest area is usually the vastus lateralis and the fascia lata that lies over it and helps hold it in place. When you are massaging here, you will also be working on the sartorius that crosses it (*see* below). Remember to do heavy strokes on the leg 'towards the heart'.

Be careful about working on this area immediately after your client has been involved in contact sports, as it is the most common area of impact. If the client has been bumped here, and there is a reason to suspect bruising, i.e. internal bleeding, this needs to be referred to someone who is trained to deal with sports injuries.

Sartorius is the 'tailor's muscle' (dressed in 'sartorial splendour' means wearing well-tailored clothing). Sartorius draws the legs to a crossed-legged position, the sitting position used by tailors when sewing until recent centuries. It was, in fact, a common sitting position for many people in the past – the drawings of Leonardo da Vinci from five centuries ago show the sartorius larger than on present day charts of the body.

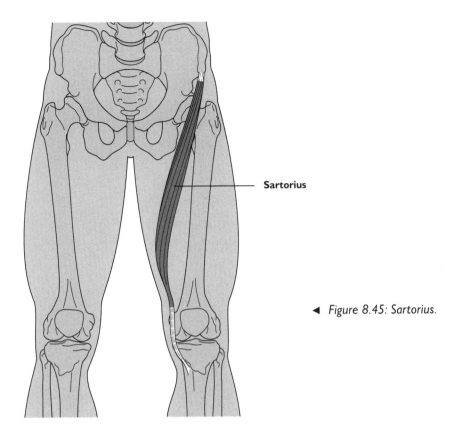

Sartorius

◀ *Figure 8.45: Sartorius.*

This strap muscle, which can be hard to distinguish on many people, is usually the longest in the body. It crosses the front of the quadriceps diagonally, extending from the front projection of the 'hip' bone (the ASIS) to the inside of the tibia just below the knee. Its action is technically described as flexing both the hip and the knee, while also abducting and laterally rotating the leg.

The *hamstrings* are three muscles at the back of the upper leg, which cross the back of both the hip and the knee joints. The 'hams' are the bellies of the muscles and the 'strings' are the tendons that frame the back of the knee.

Semitendinosus and *semimembranosus* both run from the ischial tuberosity, which is the prominent 'bump' of the sitting bone, to the medial side of the upper tibia. Semitendinosus, with a shorter muscle section and longer tendon, lies over the top of the other.

Biceps femoris ('two headed, of the femur') has one head also coming from the ischial tuberosity, and the other from the back of the femur. They merge into a tendon that attaches to the upper tibia and head of the fibula on the lateral side of the leg.

These muscles flex the knee and work with gluteus maximus to extend the hip. If the leg is held in place, they can help straighten the trunk from a bent forward position. They are constantly working like this in a small way to maintain an upright posture, and are

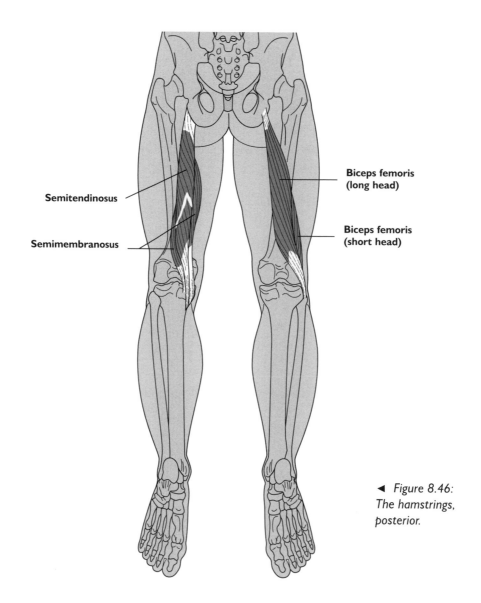

Semitendinosus

Semimembranosus

Biceps femoris
(long head)

Biceps femoris
(short head)

◄ *Figure 8.46:*
The hamstrings,
posterior.

thus often tight, particularly near the midpoint of the back of the thigh. They can also affect small rotations of the knee on their respective sides.

The muscles can usually take reasonable pressure in massage. Again, however, be cautious after sports events, as they are often strained or overstretched in the heat of the moment, or can be bruised in contact sports.

The *adductors* are often referred to as the 'horse-riding muscles'. They are five muscles on the inside of the thigh between the hamstrings and vastus medialis. They act primarily as adductors of the leg, but can also be involved in a small way in flexion if the leg is extended, or in extension if it is flexed.

They all arise from the pubic bone, and cross the hip joint. The longest, *gracilis*, is a thin strap reaching to the tibia just below the knee. It acts as a stabiliser for the medial side of the knee, to balance the fascia lata on the lateral side.

The others, *pectineus, adductor brevis, adductor magnus*, and *adductor longus*, go to the inside of the femur. Pectineus, the uppermost, is also the shortest. Adductor brevis, just below it, lies mostly between the adductor longus in front, and the larger adductor magnus behind.

Some people use the adductor muscles very little, and others use them a great deal. Therefore the tone and tension vary greatly from person to person, so your pressure needs to be adapted accordingly.

Review of the Muscles of the Hip and the Knee

Movements of the Leg at the Hip

Flexion: iliopsoas, rectus femoris, sartorius, anterior gluteus medius, gluteus minimus.
Extension: gluteus maximus, hamstrings, posterior gluteus medius, adductor magnus.
Abduction: gluteus medius, gluteus minimus, sartorius, tensor fasciae latae, gluteus maximus, hip rotators.

Adduction: adductors, iliopsoas, biceps femoris (long head), gluteus maximus.
Medial rotation: tensor fasciae latae, anterior gluteus medius, gluteus minimus.
Lateral rotation: gluteus maximus, hip rotators, posterior gluteus medius, sartorius.

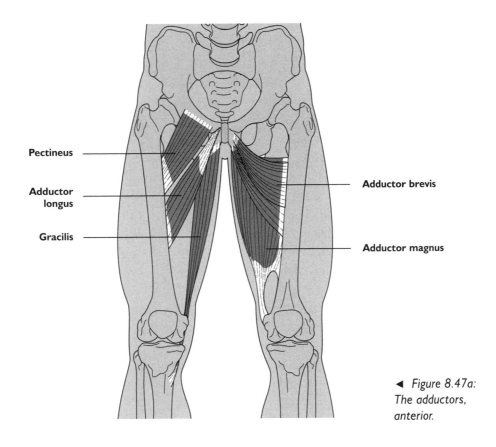

Pectineus

Adductor longus

Gracilis

Adductor brevis

Adductor magnus

◄ *Figure 8.47a: The adductors, anterior.*

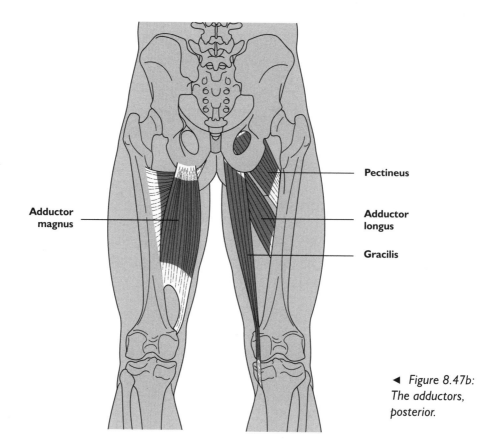

Pectineus

Adductor magnus

Adductor longus

Gracilis

◄ *Figure 8.47b: The adductors, posterior.*

Movements at the Knee

Flexion: hamstrings, gastrocnemius, sartorius, gracilis.
Extension: quadriceps.

The Lower Leg and Foot

In a similar way to the muscles of the forearm that act on the hand, the main muscles of the lower leg cross the ankle to control parts of the foot. The muscle bellies lie in the lower leg, with tendons crossing the ankle joint. The tendons at the front are held down by one retinaculum that forms a strip across the front of the ankle and, just below it, a group that forms a 'Y' shape that extends to the sides of the ankle.

These muscles belong to four groups; those on the outside of the shin, the calf muscles, the deep muscles of the back of the leg under the calf, and the intrinsic muscles of the foot.

Humans have the potential for considerably more 'dexterity' in the foot than most of us ever attempt to use. We mainly use the lower leg muscles to maintain upright posture and to balance in walking or running. While most walking surfaces in cities are flat, city dwellers will notice the unaccustomed work that is demanded of these muscles in order to adapt to uneven ground, e.g. hill walking.

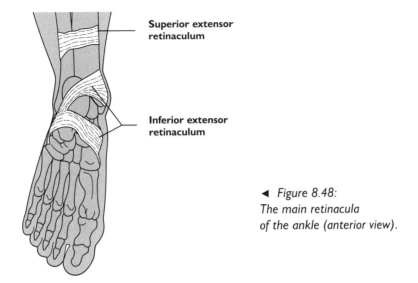

Superior extensor retinaculum

Inferior extensor retinaculum

◄ *Figure 8.48:*
The main retinacula
of the ankle (anterior view).

People who spend a reasonable part of their time in standing, walking or running usually respond well to massage on these muscles. However, in those with a mainly sedentary lifestyle, massage can also be beneficial, as the muscles can become quite hard through lack of movement. You will often notice more tension in the right lower leg, the accelerator leg, of someone who does considerable long-distance driving.

Even well-used calf muscles can be sensitive, so you need to be careful about the pressure you apply. However, the muscles on the outside of the shin usually need quite strong pressure to have any effect on them.

The Outside of the Shin

This area, on the front of the lower leg lateral to the tibia, contains a group of hard-working muscles, *tibialis anterior*, the *toe extensors* and the *peroneals*. They can be difficult to massage, as clients often like firm pressure in this compact, dense area of muscle.

Here is a little reminder about terminology. Bending up the foot is described as *dorsiflexion*, and the opposite action that points the toes down, is known as *plantar flexion*. The terms for toe actions are the same as for the fingers – curling the toes under is *flexion*, while *toe extension* is bending them up from the floor. *Inversion* is rolling onto the outside edge of the foot to turn the sole inwards, and *eversion* is rolling onto the inside edge of the foot to turn the soles outwards.

The belly of *tibialis anterior* attaches to the upper two thirds of the shin. Its tendon crosses to the inside of the ankle, attaching just under the foot at the centre of the arch.

It supports the arch and, if working harder, inverts and/or dorsiflexes the foot. In this latter role, it can become considerably tighter in the right leg than the left in those whose job involves regular long-distance driving.

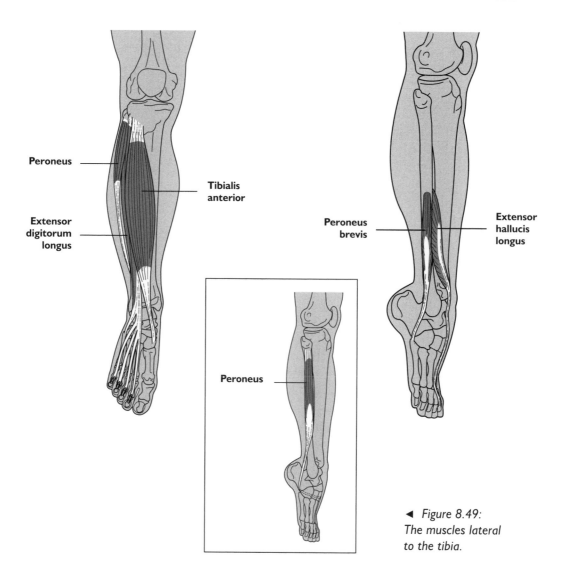

Peroneus

Tibialis anterior

Extensor digitorum longus

Peroneus brevis

Extensor hallucis longus

Peroneus

◄ *Figure 8.49: The muscles lateral to the tibia.*

The *toe extensors* lie next to tibialis anterior, attaching to the fibula as well as the tibia. *Extensor hallucis longus* has a tendon to the big toe, and *extensor digitorum longus* has tendons to the other four toes. The tendons can be seen in the top of the foot when the muscles are working. They bend the toes up from the floor and, with tibialis anterior, dorsiflex the foot.

There are two main *peroneals, peroneus longus* and *peroneus brevis*, which attach to the fibula on the outside edge of the lower leg, the longus on the upper half and the brevis on the lower. Their tendons pass behind the outside anklebone and under two retinacula. The tendon of peroneus brevis inserts onto the outside edge of the foot, while the tendon of the longus continues under the foot to attach almost next to the tibialis anterior. They therefore evert the foot, or aid the calf muscles in plantar flexion.

Peroneus longus forms a 'stirrup' under the foot with tibialis anterior; together they coordinate the side to side balance of the foot.

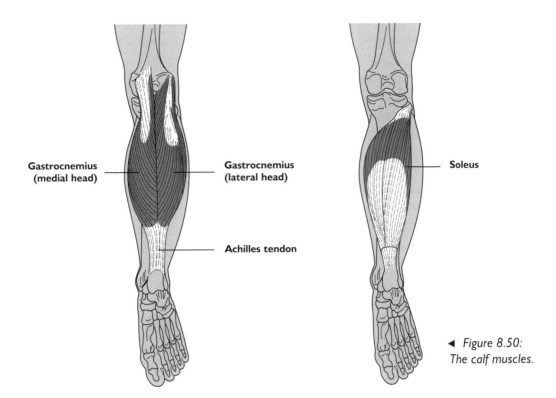

Gastrocnemius
(medial head)

Gastrocnemius
(lateral head)

Soleus

Achilles tendon

◄ *Figure 8.50:*
The calf muscles.

The Calf

Gastrocnemius ('belly-like') is the outermost part of the calf, forming the bulge from the midcalf upwards. The muscle arises here from the back of the Achilles tendon and then divides into two. A tendon goes round each side of the back of the knee joint to attach to the back of the lower end of the femur, just inside the hamstrings. This is the only lower leg muscle that also crosses the knee joint.

By crossing the back of both the ankle and knee, the gastrocnemius not only works with the soleus in plantar flexion, but also flexes the knee. In everyday life it therefore helps maintain the upright balance across the back of the knee. It works even harder in this way when a person is standing on tiptoe, which is why it can be so prominent in women who wear high heels. Gastrocnemius provides propulsion for walking, running and jumping.

The *soleus* is a wide, flat muscle just under the gastrocnemius, which comes from the front of the Achilles tendon to attach to the back of the upper tibia and fibula.

These two muscles both attach to the heel bone via the Achilles tendon. This is the largest tendon in the body because it needs to support the body's weight, via the action of these muscles, from falling forward. Together they are the strongest plantar flexors of the foot. They are used extensively in walking and running to push the body forward at each stride, or to lift it in jumping.

These muscles always cry out for massage in active people, especially those who do formal exercise or play sports. However, even when the calf muscles are tight, they can have quite sensitive spots. It is easiest to massage deeply into gastrocnemius and to affect soleus and the underlying muscles (described below) when the knee is bent and the muscle is therefore more relaxed, e.g. by propping up the leg when the client is lying face up.

Muscles Under the Calf and in the Foot

Under the calf muscles lie some deep muscles which are much harder to palpate, and therefore hard to massage directly. Even when they are working, one only gains an impression of them by pressing through the calf. Their tendons all pass behind the inside ankle bone (medial malleolus) to the underside of the foot.

Tibialis posterior runs from the back of the upper tibia and fibula to the underside of the midfoot. It plantar flexes and inverts the foot.

The *toe flexors* flex the toes and help in plantar flexion. *Flexor hallucis longus* and *flexor digitorum longus* run from the back of the lower tibia and fibula to the big toe and other four toes respectively.

The main intrinsic muscles of the *foot* are in layers on the sole. The superficial layer consists of muscles that run from the back to the front of the foot. The middle layers incorporate the tendons of the lower leg muscles, and two *interossei* muscles make up the deepest layers.

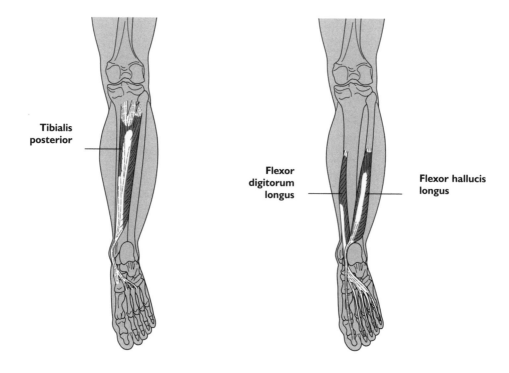

▲ *Figure 8.51: Muscles under the calf.*

These layers maintain the springiness of the foot. They are most important in propelling the body forward at each step when walking or running by flexing the toes; they also absorb the impact of each step forward by giving a little as the foot lands.

Some people have quite soft soles, and some may be ticklish. Both of these need the application of static pressure, ideally with the palm of the practitioner's hand. However, if clients have tough, well-used soles, they usually relish deeper pressure with the fist or even the knuckles. Extensive massage here is easiest to perform when the client is face down.

Summary of the Muscles of the Lower Leg and Foot

Movements at the Ankle

Dorsiflexion: tibialis anterior, extensor hallucis longus, extensor digitorum longus.
Plantar flexion: gastrocnemius, soleus, peroneus longus, peroneus brevis, tibialis posterior, toe flexors.

Movements of the Foot and Toes – the Extrinsic and Intrinsic Foot Muscles

Inversion: tibialis anterior, tibialis posterior, the toe flexors.
Eversion: peroneus longus, peroneus brevis.
Flexion of toes, extension of toes and abduction of toes (away from centreline of foot): flexor digitorum longus, flexor hallucis longus, extensor digitorum longus, extensor hallucis longus and intrinsic foot muscles.

Review of Muscle Actions

Muscles are usually described as doing one or a few limited actions. This is a useful simplification, but it's important to bear in mind a number of variables, all of which are the result of coordinated control in the central nervous system.

Muscles never act alone. Even when a muscle is the main activator of a movement, it is always aided by other muscles. For the muscle to act, antagonistic muscles must allow it to do so, with fine-tuning help from synergists and with the associated fixators stabilising other parts of the body. Biceps is aided in flexing the forearm by brachialis. Triceps relaxes to allow biceps to act, and shoulder muscles stabilise the forearm while this is happening.

Other muscles may be essential co-prime movers in an action. Flexor carpi radialis works with flexor carpi ulnaris to *flex* the wrist, but works with the radial extensors to *abduct* the wrist.

The action can be reshaped by other muscles working. Whether biceps acts merely to flex the forearm, to supinate the forearm, and/or in shoulder flexion, will depend on the relative actions of other muscles around the elbow joint, and around the shoulder joint. Muscle actions can change in different positions. The adductors of the inner thigh can act as flexors when the leg is extended backwards, and extensors when it is flexed.

Muscles do specific actions best in particular positions. Because of their geometry, they get the best leverage for their actions only in certain positionings of the body parts, so that the muscle pull (mediated, of course, by the associated muscles) is the most direct and least dissipated. Biceps, for example, is most effective in flexing the forearm when that is supinated.

Muscle actions can change in different positions. The adductors of the inner thigh can act as flexors when the leg is extended backwards, and extensors when it is flexed.

Gravity helps. If gravity can be used to do an action due to the body's position, this will be employed in preference to muscle work. Bending the trunk slowly forward from the standing position does not involve the abdominals.

Muscles can work while being stretched. In fact, in bending forward from standing, it will be the erector spinae muscles of the back that control the rate and extent of the forward bend, like playing out a rope over a pulley to lower an object to the ground. This means that the muscles are doing the opposite action to that normally ascribed to them.

The trunk can be moved rather than the limbs. Normally muscle actions are described as taking the extremities towards the centre of the body. However, in some actions, the trunk is moved in relation to the limbs, e.g. walking up stairs, climbing or swinging through the trees.

Muscles adapt to needs. We are all born with genetic pre-dispositions, which can encompass the relative size and strength of muscles, and also may mean the absence of muscles. The palmaris longus muscle, for example, is often absent from one or both forearms. And muscles, or their activating nerves, can be injured, requiring other muscles to do their job. These factors, as well as how we've developed specific muscles through activity and exercise, will all influence the way muscles work – in addition, of course, to the body's position and the other factors described above.

Many muscles are primarily active in posture maintenance. In the lower limbs, the trunk and the neck, the muscles on the front and back surfaces are constantly involved in a balancing act to maintain upright posture. They are aided by muscles on the lateral surface of the lower leg, the medial and lateral surfaces of the thigh and the iliopsoas muscles of the lower trunk.

The body's weight would cause it to slump forward if there was no muscular support so, in standing or in sitting still, the muscles of the back surface of the body, the extensors, are more active. When we are moving this becomes a much more complex interplay of muscular coordination, particularly in the legs which are simultaneously supporting us and moving us around.

Review of the Individual Muscles

Muscle	Origin	Insertion	Action

Muscles of the Head

Scalp

Muscle	Origin	Insertion	Action
Occipito-frontalis	skin of eyebrow	occiput	tenses scalp, raises eyebrows

Facial Expression

Muscle	Origin	Insertion	Action
Corrugator supercilii	mid eyebrow arch	skin at top of bridge of nose	frowning, squinting
Procerus	bridge of nose	skin of forehead	frowning, squinting
Orbicularis oculi	medial edge of eye socket	skin around eyelid	closes eye
Nasalis	maxilla (upper jaw) and nasal cartilage	bridge and corners of nose	widens nostrils
Orbicularis oris	maxilla and mandible	buccinator and other muscles around mouth	closes lips
Levators of lips	maxilla, cheek bones	orbicularis oris	lift corners of mouth
Depressors of of mouth	mandible	orbicularis oris	lower corners of lips

Chewing

Muscle	Origin	Insertion	Action
Masseter	cheek bone	corner of mandible	chewing
Temporalis	temporal bone	top of mandible	chewing
Buccinator	maxilla and mandible	orbicularis oris	compresses cheeks

Muscles of the Neck

Front of the Neck and Lower Jaw

Platysma	upper chest	mandible and skin of cheek	wrinkles skin of neck, depresses mandible
Suprahyoids	mostly edge of mandible	hyoid bone	lift hyoid bone
Infrahyoids	mostly sternum and first rib	hyoid bone	lower hyoid bone
Sternocleido-mastoid	sternum and clavicle	mastoid process of occiput	flexes and rotates neck

Side of the Neck

Scalenes	C2–C6 vertebrae	top of ribs 1 and 2	laterally flexes and rotates neck

Back of the Neck

Trapezius	occiput, C1–T12 vertebrae	clavicle, spine of scapula	raises shoulders, draws head back, rotates neck (upper part of trapezius)
Levator scapulae	C1–C4 vertebrae	scapula (superior angle)	raises scapula
Splenii (splenius capitis splenius cervicis)	C7–T6 vertebrae	occiput, C1–C2	extend, tilt and rotate neck
Erector spinae – spinalis, iliocostalis, longissimus (upper part)	lower cervical, upper thoracic vertebrae and upper ribs	upper cervical vertebrae and occiput	extends and rotates neck

| Para-vertebrals – multifidis, rotatores, interspinalis, intertransversarii (upper part) | lower cervical, upper thoracic vertebrae and upper ribs | upper cervical vertebrae and occiput | extend and rotate neck |
| Sub-occipitals | axis (C2) and atlas (C1) | atlas (C1) and occiput | rock, tilt and rotate head |

Scapula and Shoulder Joint

Scapula Movements

Trapezius	occiput, C1–T12	outer third of clavicle spine of scapula	*upper*: adducts, rotates and lifts scapula, rotates and laterally flexes neck *middle*: adducts scapula *lower*: depresses and rotates scapula
Levator scapulae	C1–C4	medial border of upper scapula	elevates and adducts scapula, laterally flexes and rotates neck
Rhomboids	C6–T4	medial border of scapula	adducts and elevates scapula
Serratus anterior	lateral surface ribs 1–8/9	underside medial edge of scapula	draws scapula forward and rotates it
Pectoralis minor	front of ribs 3–5	coracoid process (scapula)	tilts front of scapula down, lifts ribs

Prime Movers of the Arm

Pectoralis major	clavicle, sternum ribs 1/2–6/7	upper humerus, outer side	draws arm across chest, medially rotates arm
Latissimus dorsi	T7–12, iliac crest and sacrum	front top of humerus	adducts, extends, medially rotates arm
Deltoid	clavicle, spine of scapula	outside edge of mid humerus	abducts arm, *anterior:* flexes, medially rotates *posterior:* extends, laterally rotates
Teres major	lower lateral edge of scapula	front top of humerus	adducts and medially rotates arm

Rotator Cuff – the 'SITS' Muscles

Supraspinatus	top back of scapula	top of humerus	abducts arm
Infraspinatus	lower back of scapula	top of humerus	lateral rotation of arm
Teres minor	lateral edge of scapula	top of humerus	lateral rotation of arm
Subscapularis	underside of scapula	top of humerus	medial rotation of arm

Muscles of the Arm and Hand

Upper Arm

Biceps (brachii)	top of shoulder joint, coracoid process (scapula)	front of radius	flexion and supination of forearm
Coracobrachialis	coracoid process (scapula)	front of mid humerus	flexion of shoulder
Brachialis	front of mid humerus	front of ulna	flexion of forearm
Triceps (brachii)	edge of scapula (below shoulder joint) and back of humerus	point of elbow (back of ulna)	extension of forearm

Muscles of the Forearm – Anterior

Flexors – superficial	medial epicondyle of humerus	wrist, palm and fingers	flex wrist and fingers
Flexors – deep	front of upper and mid radius and ulna	fingers and thumb	flex fingers and thumb
Pronators	ulna	radius	pronate forearm

Muscles of the Forearm – Posterior

Extensors – superficial	lateral epicondyle of humerus	wrist and fingers	extend wrist and fingers
Extensors – deep	back of radius and ulna	thumb and index finger	extend and abduct thumb, extend index
Supinator	distal humerus	radius	supinates forearm

Muscles of the Forearm – Radial Edge

| Brachioradialis | distal humerus | distal radius | flexes forearm |

Intrinsic Hand Muscles

Thenar eminence	metacarpals 1–3	thumb	movements of thumb – flex, extend, abduct and across palm
Hypothenar eminence	metacarpals 4–5	little finger	movements of little finger – flex, abduct and across palm
Interossei	metacarpals 1–5	mid phalanges fingers 2–5	abduct, adduct fingers 2–5

Muscles of the Trunk

Postural Muscles of the Back

| Quadratus lumborum | iliac crest | twelfth rib lumbar vertebrae | tilts pelvis, lumbar hyperextension, lumbar side bending |
| Para-vertebrals | sacrum and ilium | upper cervical vertebrae | extend and rotate spine and neck |

Erector Spinae / Sacrospinalis Group

Iliocostalis	lumbar fascia	lower cervical vertebrae	extend and laterally flex spine
Longissimus	lumbar vertebrae	occiput	extend, laterally flex and rotate spine and neck
Spinalis	lumbar vertebrae	occiput	extend and rotate of spine and neck

Breathing

Diaphragm	lower sternum and ribs, upper lumbar vertebrae	central tendon	draws down base of lungs
External intercostals	each rib (except lowest)	next rib down	lift ribs
Internal intercostals	each rib (except lowest)	next rib up	lower ribs

Abdominal Muscles

Rectus abdominis	top of pubis	bottom end of sternum, front of ribs 5–7	flexes trunk
External oblique	lower 8 ribs	linea alba, iliac crest	flexes and twists trunk
Internal oblique	iliac crest, lumbar fascia	lowest ribs, linea alba	flexes and twists trunk
Transversus abdominis	lumbar fascia, iliac crest, cartilage of ribs 7–12	linea alba, pubis, iliac crest	compresses abdomen

Hip Muscles

Muscles Around the Hips

Iliacus	lateral surface of ilium	lesser trochanter of femur	flexes and rotates thigh
Psoas major	T12–L5	lesser trochanter	flexes thigh or lumbar spine
Tensor fasciae latae	iliac crest and iliac spine	iliotibial band	flexion, abduction, medial rotation of thigh

The Buttocks

Gluteus maximus	iliac crest, sacrum	upper femur, iliotibial tract	extends and laterally rotates thigh
Gluteus medius	outer surface of ilium	greater trochanter of femur	abducts and rotates thigh
Gluteus minimus	outer surface of ilium	greater trochanter	abducts and extends thigh
Lateral hip rotators	ischium and sacrum	greater trochanter	laterally rotate thigh

Thigh Muscles

Quadriceps

Rectus femoris	anterior inferior iliac spine	tibial tuberosity	flexes hip, extends knee
Vastus intermedius	anterior shaft of femur	tibial tuberosity	extends knee
Vastus lateralis	lateral shaft of femur	tibial tuberosity	extends knee
Vastus medialis	medial shaft of femur	tibial tuberosity	extends knee
Sartorius	anterior superior iliac spine	medial upper shaft of tibia	laterally rotates flexes and abducts hip, flexes knee

Hamstrings

Biceps femoris	ischium and lower lateral femur	top of fibula and lateral tibia	extends hip and flexes knee
Semimembranosus	ischium	top of medial tibia	extends hip and flexes knee
Semitendinosus	ischium	top of medial tibia	extends hip and flexes knee

Adductors

Pectineus	pubis	femur, just below lesser trochanter	flexes, adducts thigh
Adductor brevis	pubis	posterior shaft of femur just below pectineus	flexes, adducts thigh
Adductor longus	pubis	mid shaft of posterior femur	flexes, adducts and medially rotates thigh
Adductor magnus	pubis	whole length of shaft, posterior femur	extends, adducts and medially rotates thigh
Gracilis	pubis and ischium	medial tibia, at top	adducts hip and stabilises knee

Muscles of the Lower Leg and Foot

Front and Lateral Side of the Lower Leg

Tibialis anterior	top lateral shaft of tibia	first metatarsal	inverts and dorsiflexes foot
Extensor digitorum longus	upper fibula (antero-lateral)	top of ends of toes 2–5	extends toes, dorsiflexes foot
Extensor hallucis longus	middle fibula (antero-lateral)	top of end of big toe	extends big toe, dorsiflexes foot
Peroneus longus	upper lateral fibula	1st metatarsal	everts and plantar flexes foot
Peroneus brevis	lower lateral fibula	5th metatarsal	everts and plantar flexes foot

Back of the Lower Leg

Gastrocnemius	lower end of femur	calcaneus (heel bone)	Flexes knee and plantar flexes foot
Soleus	back of upper tibia and fibula	calcaneus	plantar flexes foot
Tibialis posterior	back of upper tibia and fibula	underside of tarsals and metatarsals	inverts and plantar flexes foot
Flexor digitorum longus	back of mid tibia	underside of ends of toes 2–5	flexes toes 2–5
Flexor hallucis longus	back of mid fibula	underside of end of big toe	flexes big toe

Section 3
The Communication Systems

Every moment of our life, even in deep sleep, even in coma, our body is alive with activity – the activity of communication. Every moment, every cell and tissue, every vessel and cavity and organ in our body, is sending out information. Every moment, our body receives input from the external environment, through specialised sense organs, our eyes, ears, nose and skin. Every moment, our brain is teeming with activity as information is received, relayed from one part to another, and processed. And every moment, responses to this incoming information are being relayed to our muscles and glands.

What enables this communication process to take place? How is this information carried round the body? There are three systems involved in information sending, receiving and processing in the body. The two well-known communication systems are the nervous system and the endocrine system. Information travels rapidly in the nervous system, up and down the spinal cord between the brain and the nerves that extend out to all tissues and organs in the body, carried by a combination of electrical impulses and chemical transmitters, called neurotransmitters. Unlike the nervous system, which structurally is one connected mass of identical specialised tissue, the glands that make up the endocrine system are found at separate locations around the body. But all glands have an identical function, namely the secretion of hormones. Hormones are information carrying chemicals, released from the glands into the blood supply where they travel to target organs. For example, one of the many hormones released by the pituitary gland, which is located in the brain, sends information to the kidneys, to retain or release water. The rate of communication in the endocrine system is much slower than in the nervous system.

The third communication system involves the aspect of our internal communication network that signals the presence of damage to tissues, or the presence of foreign organisms or chemicals in the body. The immune system, like the nervous and endocrine systems, also produces many kinds of information carrying chemicals, which facilitate or inhibit the action of white blood cells, and alerts the whole body to respond to potential disease. These three kinds of 'messenger molecules', neurotransmitters, hormones and immune system chemicals are now known to be able to communicate with cells in any of the three systems. A hormone can connect with a neuron, or a neurotransmitter with an immune system white blood cell. Not only can information be transmitted between these three systems, but cells in all three are capable of synthesising neurotransmitters and immune system chemicals.

So our internal environment is awash with information carrying chemicals and buzzing with continuous electrical activity. This information is processed by the brain. Some of this processing is conscious, that is, we are aware that it is happening. As you read these words, you are conscious that your eyes are seeing symbols on the page and that your brain is (hopefully) making sense of them. However, you are not aware of the various neural routes in your brain involved in processing this visual information, neither are you aware of the chemicals pouring into your duodenum to digest your breakfast, or the circulation of blood through your left foot. But as you read, parts of your brain are monitoring all of these and many more activities.

Most of this unconscious communication activity is designed to keep our body in a state of balance. Normal healthy functioning of each individual cell as well as the whole body requires that the internal environment of our body remains within certain parameters. This includes temperature, the rate at which the heartbeats and body fluids circulate, and the concentration of the hundreds of different chemicals needed for or produced as a result of basic life activities. Normal body temperature, for example, is half a degree either side of 98.5°F (37°C). When it rises, due to exercise, or on a very hot day, certain processes happen automatically to cool us down. These include sweating and dilation of blood vessels close to the surface. If these regulatory activities fail, and body temperature goes above 104°F (40°C), death can occur.

This process of maintaining inner equilibrium is called **homeostasis**. An important aspect of homeostatic mechanisms is the negative feedback loop. In the example above, a combination of neural impulses and messenger molecules alerts the brain to the rise in internal temperature and the brain alerts a different combination of neural impulses and messenger molecules to activate the 'cool down' mechanisms. As soon as body temperature returns to normal, this information is communicated to the brain, that switches off the 'cool down' messages. The body has thousands of these homeostatic processes, which are constantly assessing, monitoring and adjusting the state of our internal environment, through the complex interactions of the three communication systems; the nervous, endocrine and immune systems.

Each of these systems is considered in turn in this section; the structure and function of the component parts, and the most common disorders, and considerations for massage. In addition, phenomena that are of particular relevance to the massage therapist are covered in more detail; these include the physiology of stress, pain, and emotions.

Chapter 9 The Nervous System

Key Words

Structure and Function

Central nervous system (CNS)
Peripheral nervous system
Somatic / voluntary nervous system
Autonomic nervous system (ANS): sympathetic nervous system (SNS) /
parasympathetic nervous system (PNS)
Neuron
Glial cell
Dendrite
Axon
Myelin sheath
Synapse / synaptic end bulb / synaptic vesicle
Neurotransmitter
Motor / efferent neuron
Interneuron / association neuron
Sensory neuron: mechanoreceptor / thermoreceptor / chemoreceptor / nociceptor /
photoreceptor
Brain
Meninges
Spinal cord
Brainstem: medulla oblongata / pons / midbrain
Diencephalon: thalamus / hypothalamus
Cerebrum
Pineal gland
Pituitary gland
Cerebellum
Corpus callosum
Ventricles
Cerebrospinal fluid
Peripheral nerves / cranial nerves / spinal nerves
Nerve plexus
Dermatome
Reflex arc

Structure of the Nervous System

The nervous system can be divided into the following parts:

1. The **central nervous system** comprises the brain inside the cranium and the spinal
   cord inside the length of the vertebrae. This part processes information from the
   special senses, from skin and muscles, regulates the internal organs, and is the site of

memory, thought and feeling. The central nervous system initiates responses to incoming information; messages are relayed from the brain and spinal cord to the body.

2. The **peripheral nervous system** consists of all the nerves arising from the brain, called the cranial nerves, and those that arise from the spinal cord, called the spinal nerves, which branch throughout the body to all the muscles, bones and organs.

Nervous System Tissue

This tissue contains highly specialised nerve cells, called **neurons**. Within the central nervous system there are also supporting cells, called **glial cells**. We are born with our full complement of 10–12 billion neurons; neurons are not capable of regeneration when they die. There are between 10 and 50 times more glial cells than neurons, which can and do multiply throughout life. Glial cells are not nerve cells, and have various functions, including manufacturing the myelin sheath, protection of neurons from foreign particles, and regulating the contents of the intercellular fluid in the nervous system.

Neurons look and function differently from cells found in the other types of body tissues. A neuron has a cell body, which can be round, oval or spindle-shaped, with a nucleus and other organelles, but what distinguishes it from other cells is the number of extensions arising from the cell surface. Most of these extensions are short and stubby and branch out like the twigs on a tree. These extensions are called **dendrites** and their function is to carry information to the cell body. Most neurons also have one extension from the cell body that is long and thin, also ending in twig-like fibres. This single long extension carries information away from the cell body, and is called the **axon**. Some axons are coated in an insulating fatty substance called the **myelin sheath**, which facilitates rapid transmission of information.

The gap between two dendrites, or an axon and dendrite is called a **synapse**. Axons and dendrites end in small knobs called **synaptic end bulbs**, which contain many sacs called **synaptic vesicles**, full of **neurotransmitters**. Neurons can be classified according to their structure or function.

Structural Classification

Unipolar neurons, usually sensory receptors, have one extension that forms an axon and a dendrite. Bipolar neurons are found in the eyes, ears and olfactory bulb of the nose, and as the name implies, have two extensions. The majority of neurons are multipolar, that is they have multiple dendrite connections.

Functional Classification

Motor (or **efferent**) **neurons** transmit information from the brain to muscles and glands. The message to a muscle fibre to contract comes via a motor neuron. The synaptic junction between a motor neuron and the muscle fibres that it activates is called the motor unit (*see* Chapter 7).

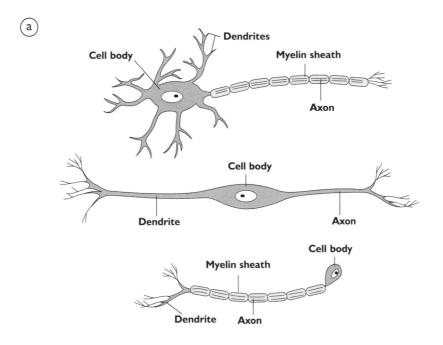

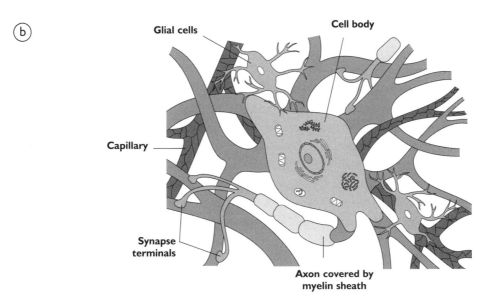

▲ *Figure 9.1: (a) Different kinds of neurons, (b) nervous tissue.*

Interneurons (or **association**) **neurons**, which, as their name suggests, connect one neuron with another, make up over 75% of neurons and are found mainly in the central nervous system.

Sensory neurons receive input through specialised receptors and transmit this to the brain. Exteroreceptors receive input from outside the body, and interoreceptors receive input from inside the body. There are five classes of sensory receptors, each reacting to different types of stimuli:

1. **Mechanoreceptors** are sensitive to mechanical stimuli including touch, pressure, vibration, stretch and proprioception. Mechanoreceptors in the skin include Paccini's corpuscles and Merkel's discs (*see* Chapter 12). Proprioceptive mechanoreceptors

include muscle spindles and Golgi tendon organs (*see* Chapter 7).
2. **Thermoreceptors** are sensitive to temperature changes.
3. **Chemoreceptors** include the receptors for smell and taste, and also those for changes in the chemical make-up of the blood.
4. **Nociceptors** are sensitive to pain, which is a signal that tissue is being damaged.
5. **Photoreceptors** in the retina of the eyes are sensitive to light.

The function of a neuron is to transmit information. This occurs through a combination of electrical and chemical impulses. A neuron must respond to a stimulus before it can 'fire' – the ability to respond is called its excitability. A neuron can be fired by a stimulus (heat, pressure, light etc.), by a neurotransmitter or by a hormone. Once fired, an electrical impulse travels the length of the axon from the cell body to the synapse. In the little synaptic knobs, the electrical impulse triggers release of chemical neurotransmitters from the vesicles (sacs) where they are stored, into the synapse. Some neurotransmitters make it to the other side, to the target site, but many are lost. If the target is another neuron, the neurotransmitters stimulate an electrical impulse and the neuron fires, and the message continues on its path. If the target is a muscle fibre, the neurotransmitters stimulate contraction. Examples of neurotransmitters are: acetylcholine (important for muscle contraction), dopamine, seratonin, adrenaline and noradrenaline (in America, adrenaline and noradrenaline are called epiniphrene and norepiniphrene).

Organisation of Nervous Tissue

Brain tissue consists of millions of interconnected neurons, and a plentiful blood supply. The brain requires more oxygen than any other organ in the body. In the brain, cell bodies are arranged in overlapping sheets. The parts of the brain known as grey matter consist of cell bodies, and the white matter of axons.

Nerves

Nerves are bundles of axons. Nerve cell bodies are located in the central nervous system, in the spinal cord or brain, or in specialised clusters outside the spinal cord called ganglia. All spinal nerves are a combination of motor and sensory nerves. Some cranial nerves contain only sensory fibres, such as the optic nerve from the eye. Some cranial nerves contain only motor fibres, such as those that innervate the muscles of the eyeball.

The Brain

If you imagine the top of the cranium removed to expose the brain, you would see first glistening whitish tissue with blood vessels over the surface. This is a layer of the **meninges**, the protective connective tissue covering for the brain and the spinal cord (meningitis is inflammation of the meninges). Remove the meninges, and you see a pink / grey / cream coloured, walnut-like structure, with two clear halves. These are the two hemispheres of the cerebrum. Remove the brain from the cranium – it weighs just over

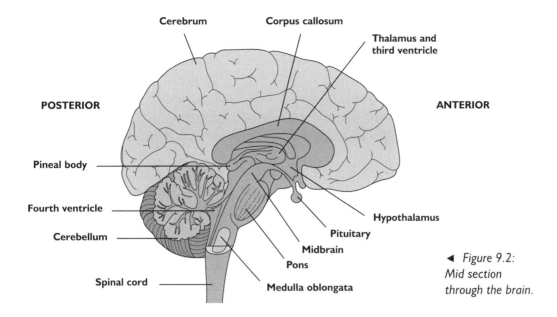

◄ *Figure 9.2:*
Mid section
through the brain.

a kilogram and feels like custard – and turn it over. At the back of the brain is a cauliflower shaped appendage called the **cerebellum**, or little brain. The whole brain sits on a stalk, the **brainstem**, which connects the brain to the **spinal cord**.

Function of the Different Parts

The brainstem has three distinct parts; nearest to the spinal cord, at the point where it enters the cranium, is the **medulla oblongata**. This widens out to become the **pons** (bridge), and then the **midbrain**. The majority of the cranial nerves connect to the brain at the brainstem level. One of the functions of the brainstem is to act as a relay station between the spinal cord and brain, and the cranial nerves and brain.

Enclosed within the brainstem is a network of cells called the reticular formation, which play a crucial role. Functions of the reticular formation include monitoring sleeping / waking patterns, maintenance of consciousness (damage here can cause coma), maintenance of normal heartbeat and breathing, regulation of autonomic functions and control of reflexes like sneezing and vomiting.

The **diencephalon** is located between the brainstem below and the **cerebrum** above. It is not a clearly observable structure like the cerebellum or brainstem, but more a dense network of nerve cell bodies, observable under a microscope. The two endocrine glands in the brain are both attached to the diencephalon by little stalks (infundibula). The **pineal gland** which secretes melatonin, and is associated with sleep / waking rhythms, is attached posteriorly, and the **pituitary**, or 'master' **gland** because of the role it plays in activating so many of the other endocrine glands, hangs inferiorly.

The largest part of the diencephalon is the **thalamus**, which relays sensory information to the cerebral cortex and also plays a part in influencing emotions. Underneath this is the **hypothalamus** that is the main control centre for the autonomic nervous system.

The **cerebellum** lies below and to the rear of the cerebrum. It is responsible for motor coordination and balance, and particularly automatic learned sequences. The ability to walk upstairs, swim, or lift a cup to your mouth, depends on cerebellum functioning.

The largest part of the brain is the **cerebrum**, with a convoluted surface that increases the total area. This part of the brain is much larger comparatively in humans than in animals, and is also the site of those activities we think of as exclusively human; reasoning and language.

The left and right hemispheres, which are joined by a band called the **corpus callosum**, are not exactly identical in structure or function. The left hemisphere processes information sequentially and is more involved with language and calculation tasks. The right hemisphere processes 'the whole picture', and is more involved with spatial awareness. This is where the 'grey matter' and 'white matter' of the brain is found; the outer layer of the cerebrum, the cerebral cortex, consists of cell bodies and has a greyish appearance, and the inner layers, the white matter are tracks connecting the cortex to the rest of the brain.

Observations of people with damage to specific areas of the cerebral cortex have made it clear that processing information is not straightforward but involves a number of areas and pathways between them. In order to recognise the object in front of you as a book, your brain is processing visual information about colour, size, shape, position in space, and relating this to stored memory; each bit of information going to a different part of the cerebral cortex. However, lobes within the cerebral cortex do have particular functions; there are areas which process sensory input, others which process motor input and others, the association areas, which receive and process information from many modalities.

The lobes are named according to the cranial bone they lie beneath. The frontal lobe is mainly concerned with cognition, motor output and speech. The temporal lobes on either side are concerned with understanding language (left hemisphere only), hearing and smell. The occipital lobe at the back processes visual input and the parietal lobes process somatosensory input, mainly from skin and muscles. The somatosensory area of the brain is interesting because, instead of being a one to one map of the parts of the body, the areas representing the lips, mouth and genitals are much larger and those to do with the back and abdomen much smaller than would be expected. This is due to the fact that some body parts, like the fingers and lips, have a much greater supply of sensory receptors than others.

The face and hands and, to a lesser extent, the feet are therefore the most sensitive and responsive areas of the body that are available for professional touch. Massage practitioners know how relaxing to the whole person a good head massage can be. A massage that combines nurturing with specific tension release will therefore include significant attention to these highly innervated areas.

There are four chambers in the brain called the **ventricles**. The walls of the ventricles

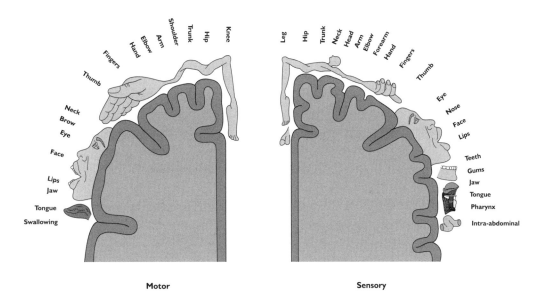

▲ *Figure 9.3: A map of the somatosensory areas corresponding
to the different parts of the body.*

produce **cerebrospinal fluid** that circulates around the inside and outside of the brain
and spinal cord. It bathes the whole central nervous system, and has nutrient as well as
protective functions. In the cranium it acts as a shock absorber, preventing damage to
soft brain tissue.

The **spinal cord** is about 40–45cms long, extending from the cranium to the lumbar
vertebrae, where it becomes a fine filament before fanning out into strands like a horse's
tail as it leaves the sacrum. It has a central core of grey matter, composed of cell bodies
and glial cells, like the writing in a stick of rock, surrounded by white matter, composed
of axons. The cord is wrapped in the meninges, cushioned by cerebrospinal fluid and
housed in the bony cases of the vertebrae. At the junction between each pair of
vertebrae, four nerve roots leave the spinal cord, two on each side. The anterior (ventral)
roots are motor nerves, taking messages to the muscles; the two posterior (dorsal) roots
are sensory nerves, bringing messages in from the body. Each pair converges shortly after
leaving the cord to become a single nerve.

There are 12 pairs of **cranial nerves** and include those in the head involved in the special senses of sight, hearing, smell and taste and the motor nerves that innervate the muscles and glands of the head, face and neck. The vagus nerve (vagus means wanderer) is
the only one that extends into the trunk, where it is involved in many of the autonomic
functions, including heartbeat.

There are 31 pairs of **spinal nerves**, each dividing and subdividing, sending branches
throughout the whole body. Each pair is named according to the place where they exit the
spinal column; for example, C1 refers to the first cervical pair, and S5 to the last sacral pair.

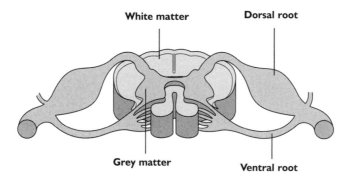

▲ *Figure 9.4: Transverse section of the spinal cord.*

Cervical nerves innervate the neck, shoulders, arms and diaphragm, thoracic nerves the back and abdomen, lumbar nerves the lower back, thighs and legs and sacral nerves the buttocks, pelvis and thighs.

At certain points, the peripheral nerves to particular body areas join up in a **nerve plexus** (which means braid). Nerves may join up in a plexus, then separate, then rejoin again. Nerves in the arm, for example, contain a mixture of spinal nerves; injury to one spinal nerve serving the arm is not incapacitating, because another one can take over the function.

The brachial plexus of nerves C5 to C8 and T1, innervates the neck, shoulder, arm and diaphragm. There is also a lumbar plexus, which gives rise to most of the nerves of the buttocks and thigh, and a sacral plexus, that gives rise to the sciatic nerve which innervates the back of the thigh and most of the lower leg and foot.

The skin of the body supplied by the peripheral sensory nerves can

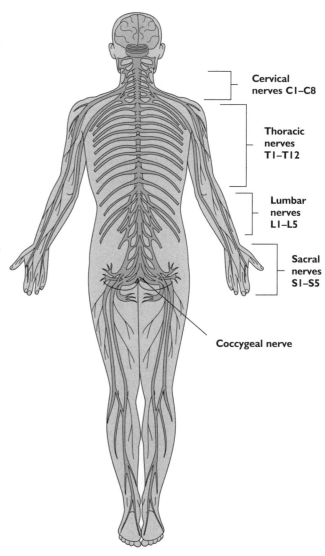

▲ *Figure 9.5: The peripheral spinal nerves.*

be divided into regions called **dermatomes**. Each dermatome is the area of skin supplied by nerves from a single spinal root. The map created by these dermatomes is useful for identifying problems in spinal nerve transmission.

A **reflex** is an involuntary response to a stimulus. The time taken for a sensory input to travel to the brain, and for the brain to initiate a motor response out to the body is bypassed by a reflex. Often only three neurons are involved; sensory input to the spinal cord, where an association neuron connects directly to a motor neuron for the output response. The most common sort is flexor withdrawal reflexes that involve a body part moving away from pain. We pull our foot out of the bath when the water is too hot, or drop a burning match when the flame reaches our fingers. The knee jerk reflex that occurs when the knee is tapped just below the patella is a reflex; this is done to test the condition of that part of the spine. Visceral reflexes include shivering in the cold, coughing, sneezing or blinking. Many reflexes can be overridden by conscious awareness; if the very hot object we have picked up is also a priceless dish, we might risk burnt fingers rather than drop it.

Functions of the Nervous System

The nervous system, as we have seen, consists of the brain, spinal cord and peripheral nerves; the specialised sensory receptors; and the chemicals of the nervous system, the neurotransmitters.

The central and peripheral nervous systems can be subdivided into two other systems:
The **somatic** (or voluntary) **nervous system** that sends messages to the skeletal muscles and glands.
The **autonomic nervous system** that sends messages to the internal body organs.

The **somatic nervous system** transmits information from the central nervous system to the skeletal muscles and the glands through the motor, or efferent, nerves. The areas of the brain particularly concerned with motor activity are the motor cortex in the cerebrum, and the cerebellum. This branch is also known as the voluntary nervous system because many of its activities are under our conscious control. We can chose to move our limbs, to tighten our postural muscles or to smile; we cannot chose to contract our arteries, or control peristalsis in the digestive tract.

Feedback from the proprioceptors, our eyes and, to a small extent, our skin, enables us to monitor and thus control and coordinate our activities. Learning new tasks or refining acquired skills is a process of forging new connections in the cerebral cortex; once a task is learned, it is controlled primarily through the cerebellum.

We feel the effects of massage on muscular tension via the proprioceptors. It is through the sensory nerves in the muscles, tendons and ligaments that massage helps us to notice specific areas of tightness in our muscles. Then we can monitor how our muscles soften, as we are encouraged to relax and reduce the unconscious motor messages to the muscles. All relaxation training uses this proprioceptive awareness to distinguish between the feelings of tension and relaxation in muscles, in order to learn how to initiate relaxation.

Relationships of different parts of the nervous systems

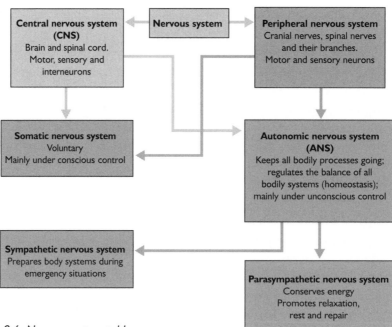

▲ *Figure 9.6: Nervous system table.*

The **autonomic nervous system** (**ANS**) controls the body's automatic functions of breathing, circulation, digestion, and the automatic accommodations of the eyes to light. These are all slow, involuntary processes, ones that happen automatically without our conscious awareness. There are specific autonomic centres in the brain and spinal cord, including the hypothalamus and reticular formation, that monitor and regulate these processes and transmit information to the smooth muscles, the glands and the cardiac muscle.

The autonomic nervous system has two branches, the sympathetic and the parasympathetic branch. The former is sometimes called the thoraco-lumbar branch, because the nerves involved arise from the mid-section of the spine. The parasympathetic is also called the cranio-sacral branch, because the nerves involved arise from the brain (particularly the vagus nerve) and the sacrum. Nerves from both branches go to the same organs, with a few exceptions, and they work in a complementary way, switching between branches all the time. This balance is controlled by the hypothalamus in the brain.

The Sympathetic Nervous System (SNS)

This is often called the 'fight or flight' branch. When we are excited, startled, or challenged, a cascade of reactions is initiated in the body that mobilises energy in the muscles in readiness for action. Processes that are involved with energy production, like respiration, metabolic rate and release of stored foods, are enhanced, while those that are unhelpful in an emergency, like digestion of food or sexual arousal, are suppressed. Emotions associated with sympathetic arousal are joy, anger and fear.

The structure of the sympathetic branch involves neurons in the central nervous system which exit the spinal cord and connect with a chain of ganglia (cell bodies of neurons) on either side between the thoracic and lumbar vertebrae. Axons from the neurons in the ganglia then spread out through the body to the eyes, heart and lungs, salivary glands, liver and intestines, kidneys and bladder, the adrenal glands, the muscles and the skin (fig. 9.7)

Physiological Changes in the Body When the SNS is Activated

1. Heart rate and blood pressure increase, to pump blood faster to the skeletal muscles.
2. Breathing rate increases, and bronchial tubes dilate, to supply more oxygen to the blood.
3. Blood vessels of skeletal muscles dilate, to increase blood supply, while peripheral vessels to the skin constrict, diverting blood to where it is needed. This reduces potential blood loss from superficial injuries, and explains why people often seem to go pale in stressful situations.
4. Glucose is released from the liver into the blood to supply more food for muscle contraction.
5. Pupils in the eyes dilate to let in more light and increase the field of vision, so that the situation can be monitored.
6. Erector pili muscles in the skin contract, causing hairs to stand on end. This has no useful function in humans, but in mammals, gives the appearance of looking bigger and more frightening.
7. Digestive functions slow down, because they are not immediately useful in a life-threatening situation.
8. Urinary functions decrease for the same reason, although part of the initial response may be to evacuate the contents of the bladder and rectum.
9. The medulla of the adrenal glands is stimulated to produce adrenaline and noradrenaline that pour into the bloodstream and reinforce and maintain the action of sympathetic nerves. Because they are circulating outside the nervous system, this also stimulates metabolic activity in all tissues in the body, and has a more long lasting effect.

The Parasympathetic Nervous System (PNS)

This is the part of the autonomic nervous system directed towards normal, relaxed functioning of the body processes. When this branch is active, heartbeat and breathing are slowed down, and digestion is promoted. Processes concerned with maintenance and repair of body tissues occur. Emotions associated with parasympathetic arousal are shame, disgust and sadness, peace, calmness and contentment.

The PNS has fibres in four cranial nerves, and three sacral nerves. One cranial nerve in particular contains many parasympathetic fibres; the vagus nerve, with branches to the oesophagus, heart, lungs and intestines. The parasympathetic nervous system sends nerve fibres to nearly all of the same areas as the sympathetic, with the exception of the skeletal muscles, the adrenals glands, the blood vessels of the skin and skeletal muscles,

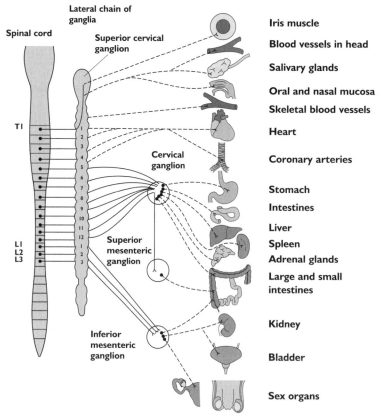

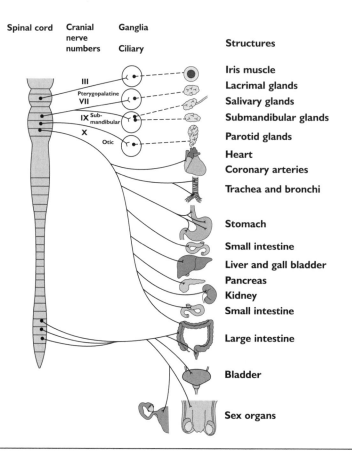

◄ *Figure 9.7: The structure of the, (a) sympathetic nervous system and; (b) parasympathetic nervous system.*

and the sweat glands. The actions of this branch are more localised, and less coordinated than sympathetic activity.

Physiological Changes in the Body When the PNS is Activated

1. Heartbeat slows, and blood pressure is reduced.
2. Breathing rate slows and may become deeper.
3. Blood vessels to skeletal muscles return to normal, while those to the skin, digestive, urinary and reproductive systems dilate.
4. The pupils of the eyes constrict.
5. Peristalsis and secretion of digestive juices in the intestines increase.

Relevance to the Massage Therapist

The ability to recognise signs of SNS or PNS activation is a useful way of determining changes in levels of arousal or relaxation in a client. If the intention of the massage is to relax the client, then breathing rate slowing down, or sounds of peristalsis, or skin becoming warmer and more flushed, (in a white skinned person the skin would appear redder, and in a dark skinned person darker) are all good signs. If someone's breathing suddenly quickens, muscle tension increases and skin becomes paler, then SNS arousal has occurred, which could be a reaction to pain, or to an emotional response. Touch experienced as invasive for example, would elicit SNS arousal. It may be helpful to ask the client what they are feeling if they are showing signs of SNS activation.

Physiology of Stress

Stress is a term that has become part of our everyday vocabulary, used to describe a wide range of reactions to all sorts of events. We are familiar with the idea of counselling for post-traumatic stress, or with exam stress, or the stress of trying to meet a deadline at work. We have our own individual experiences of what it feels like to be 'stressed'.

Key Words

Stressor
Fight or flight response
HPA axis: hypothalamus / pituitary / adrenal
Adrenocorticotrophic hormone (ACTH)
Corticosteroids / cortisol
The general adaptation syndrome (GAS)
Because there are so many different events, situations or stimuli that could be classed as stressful, a useful definition of stress is the physiological or psychological change in a person's internal state resulting from a **stressor**. Consider the following stressors:

- Caring for a relative with dementia.
- Moving house.
- Taking exams.
- Witnessing a road accident.

- Falling in love.
- Falling over a kerb.
- Being stuck in a traffic jam.
- Persistent negative thoughts.
- Constant back pain.

As you can see, a stressor can be external to the body, something that impinges from the environment, or internal, like our own thought processes. Stressors can be acute, causing effects that are short lived and reversible or chronic, causing long-term changes to the body.

Individual Differences

People differ in their responses to stressors. The constant phone ringing that makes Jane feel like exploding has no affect at all on John. Some stressors do affect all people. Anyone living in a war zone, or forced to become a refugee, or caring for a relative with dementia, experiences stress. The common life events of moving house, changing jobs, or losing a loved one through death or a relationship break-up are also stressful, but to varying degrees in different people, partly depending on other external factors and partly on psychological characteristics. 'Hardy characters' are those with a strong sense of control, commitment and flexibility who enjoy stressful situations, seeing them as a challenge. At the other end of the scale, research suggests that people who are psychologically vulnerable are more likely to experience illness resulting from stress.

Fight or Flight Response

Although the event that stresses one person may have no affect on another, the physiological response in the body to stress is always the same, and starts when the brain registers a stressor. If the stressors are the person's own thoughts (I'm useless, I'll never learn all this stuff) the message arises within the brain. But if the stressors are physical stimuli from inside the body (stomach ache, or a pulled muscle) or outside (a fire alarm), the infomation reaches the brain from the spinal cord or cranial nerves.

Behavioural and Emotional Responses

In the brain, certain neural pathways are activated which are concerned with arousal, alertness and vigilance, and with aggressive behaviours. The systems that are concerned with feeding or sexual behaviours are suppressed, since these are not useful in what may be a potentially life-threatening situation.

Interestingly, the emotions that accompany the 'fight or flight' response vary according to the person and the context. If experienced while waiting to meet a close friend off a plane, they may be felt as excitement, but the same sensations in the dentist's waiting room are more likely to be felt as anxiety or terror. The part of our brain that makes connections between what's happening now, our stored memories of past similar events, and what we know about this sort of situation, also provides input which determines our overall response.

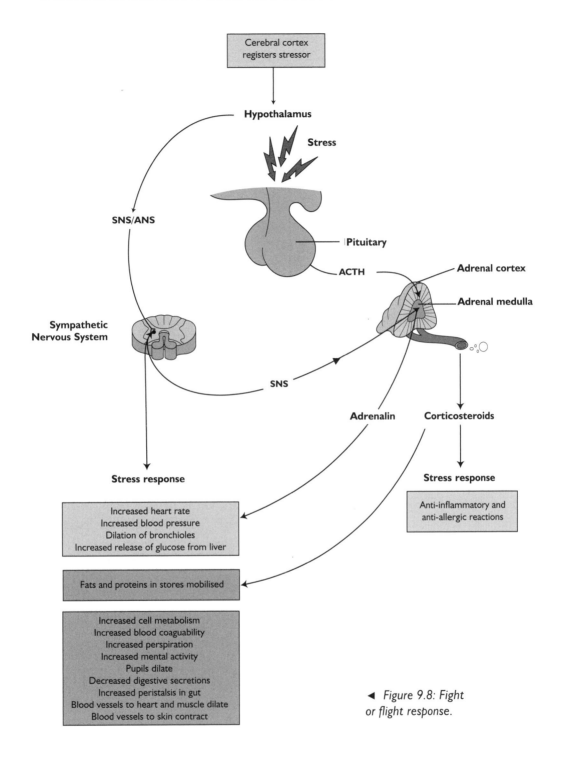

◄ *Figure 9.8: Fight or flight response.*

Physiological Responses

At the same time, the hypothalamus initiates a cascade of chemical responses, which involve the nervous, endocrine and immune systems.

The **hypothalamus – pituitary – adrenal (HPA axis)** part of the stress response begins with the release of a hormone called **ACTH (adrenocorticotrophic hormone)** from the pituitary to the adrenal cortex, which in turn produces hormones called **corticosteroids**, the main one being **cortisol**. The corticosteroids enable more energy to be released into the body for the fight or flight response, by facilitating the conversion of protein and fat stores into glucose. When released into the blood in large quantities, as in the initial stage of the stress response, they also inhibit the normal inflammatory response of the tissues to damage, and the body's allergic response. This suppression is helpful in the short-term. For example, to experience no pain or swelling from a sprained ankle until after one has run away from a dangerous situation is life-saving.

Another way that the body has to deal with severe acute stress, the kind of situation where the options of fight or flight are just not feasible, is to freeze. When attacked by a tiger, a deer will appear to go dead, and fall to the ground unconscious. This is a good survival mechanism, since in this state, the pain of injury is felt less; also, tigers are not so interested in dead meat. In physiological terms, what happens in the body is very different from the fight or flight reaction; both the SNS and the PNS are switched on together and muscles lock into immobility. Anyone who has experienced being paralysed by fear knows what this feels like.

Resolution of the Stress Response

If the stressor is removed, the physiological activity in the body gradually returns to normal. The adrenal glands stop pumping out hormones, sympathetic nervous system activity decreases, parasympathetic activity resumes and homeostasis is attained. However, these physiological mechanisms were designed to facilitate a physical response to an external event, such as running away from a fire, or fighting with an attacker, and such responses are inappropriate in many of the situations that we find ourselves in day to day. Many stressors are psychological in origin; people suffering from Post-traumatic Stress Disorder are unable to process and resolve the affects of their trauma and live with continuous heightened SNS arousal. The body resources that are mobilised by the stress response have no outlet.

Chronic Stress and the General Adaptation Syndrome

If the stressor is ongoing, then the possibility of the body returning to parasympathetic nervous system activity, of shifting from fight or flight to a state of rest and repair, is excluded. The balance of many body processes is upset, and disease may result. This is called the **General Adaptation Syndrome** (**GAS**) and was first described by Hans Selye. There are three overlapping stages:

1. Alarm stage (fight or flight). The changes described above are easily reversible.
2. Resistance stage. In the resistance stage, cortisol output from the adrenal glands into the blood continues to suppress certain aspects of immune system functioning. Sympathetic nervous system activity maintains an increased heart rate and high blood pressure. Skeletal muscles, contracted and ready for action, become tense and sore. Digestion remains suppressed.
3. Exhaustion stage. The immune system eventually loses its ability to fight infection,

repair damaged tissues or destroy cancer cells. The adrenal glands enlarge, and lose their stores of hormones. Continued stress on the cardiovascular system may contribute to stress-related disorders such as angina and heart attack. The tissues, which are in a constant state of stimulation, particularly the muscles and endocrine glands, become fatigued. Stress-related muscular tension occurs in muscles that have forgotten how to relax. Continued suppression of digestive function may lead to ulcers or Irritable Bowel Syndrome (IBS).

Stress-related Disease

Research has demonstrated the following connections: Chronic Fatigue Syndrome and severe depression are linked to malfunctioning of the HPA axis. Psychological stress connected with major life events increases susceptibility to respiratory infection, bacterial infections, herpes reoccurrence, TB, Epstein–Barr virus. Stress may contribute to progression of disease from infection with HIV to AIDS, and may be an aggravating factor in asthma, and IBS. Stress increases time taken for a wound to heal by up to 40%.

There is no convincing evidence of a relationship between stress and cancer, partly because there is such a long time lag between onset of cancer and appearance of symptoms. But women with advanced breast cancer have shorter life expectancy if leading a stressful life compared with women leading less stressful lives (Evans, P., et al., 2000).

Massage and Stress

The autonomic nervous system can be stimulated or soothed by massage, depending on the techniques used. Percussion or deep tissue strokes will tend to stimulate the SNS, whereas slow effleurage or holding techniques will have a sedative effect. Relaxing massage stimulates parasympathetic activity. Regular treatment may facilitate an improvement in the balance of autonomic nervous system (ANS) functioning in someone with a tendency towards high stress levels. Massage can also relieve chronic tension patterns in the muscles resulting from elevated SNS activity.

Brain and Emotions

How do we feel certain emotions? Are mind and brain made of the same stuff or of completely different material? How do we know that we are conscious beings? Questions like these have been discussed by philosophers for centuries, and it is only recently that clear links are being made between mind, feelings, memory and the neural structure and chemistry of the brain.* A few of the current ideas, those that might be helpful for a massage therapist to think about, are summarised here, in particular those that throw some light on the well-known phenomena that massage elicits feelings of wellbeing. How might this happen?

Antonio Damasio (2000) describes consciousness as the interface between our perception of the outside world as it is at this moment and our perception of our internal world as it is at this moment. That is, the point where all that I know of my environment meets all that I know of my body state. As I type, I am aware of the feel of the keyboard and mouse, the hum of the computer and the text on the screen. I am also aware, when I pay attention, that my mouth is dry, my fingers stiff, my shoulders tense, and my bladder full. I also have a background sensation that I can only describe as a mixture of frustration and focusing hard. Our brain surfaces are flooded constantly with messages from both sources, and are reacting to this information; messages are sent to the body to act on the outside world (to speak or to move) and to the internal world (to adjust its rhythms or chemical balance). As human beings, our history of learned experience plays a part in this process as well; memory alters our consciousness of the lived in moment. It is four o'clock; I often have a cup of tea around this time and this habitual behaviour is also part of my consciousness of my self right now.

The neuroscientists distinguish between emotions, feelings, and consciousness of feelings. The process of knowing what we feel involves a chain of three processes:

1. A stimulus (such as watching a horror movie, or winning the lottery) activates cell nuclei in certain clearly defined areas in the brainstem. These release neurotransmitters that flood the brain, producing an emotional state.
2. This emotional state produces changes in the body; there are alterations in the overall chemical balance, the state of the viscera and the degree of contraction in the skeletal muscles, especially those of the face and throat. (The main emotions have easily recognisable facial expressions).
3. Finally, information about the changes in the body is transmitted back to the brain and the bodily sensations are registered in consciousness as feelings. The function of knowing what we feel may be mainly evaluative; Is this (what I am experiencing at this particular moment) good for me or not good for me? Do I want more of it or to stop it?

Not only do stimuli activate emotional states in the brain, but different kinds of stimuli activate specific neural pathways in the brain and patterns of neurochemical release, which are associated with clear physiological changes in the body, behavioural patterns and emotional states.

Imagine that you are sleeping alone in a strange house that has a reputation for being haunted, and are woken suddenly by a loud noise. Neural pathways and chemicals in your brain are activated, your heart pounds, your muscles contract and freeze while your mind races trying to locate and understand the source of the noise. The emotion you're feeling is fear, or terror. But in another scenario, imagine yourself as a small child suddenly alone in a crowded shopping centre. A different set of neural pathways and chemicals are activated, and your heart pounds, your muscles tense ready to search, your eyes scan the horizon, and you experience panic, or separation distress.

*   *The ideas presented here are very new and represent the state of understanding at this moment. As understanding of pathways and chemistry of the brain improves, understanding of mind, emotions and feelings will alter correspondingly.*

Circuits have been identified for arousal / seeking / alertness, for anger and rage, for separation distress, for fear and anxiety, and for sexual / intimacy behaviours and emotions. In animals, these patterns are known as instincts. In humans, they are often less easy to observe because of our ability to use our higher cognitive skills to modify or suppress instinctual behaviours and emotions. Fights resulting from road rage are a direct behavioural expression of the anger circuit; swearing under your breath at the driver who overtakes you dangerously is a modified behavioural response with identical physiological and emotional stimuli.

Massage and Emotional Mood

We experience low intensity feelings all the time from our bodies, as well as the clearly defined feelings described above. This background of feeling depends on the state of contraction in both smooth and cardiac muscle, the chemical profile of the internal environment and the presence or absence of threats to homeostasis or tissue damage. The kinds of words we use to describe these feelings if our internal world is out of balance are 'out of sorts, tense, fatigued, or low in energy'. If we feel good in our skins, we might say that we feel comfortable, balanced, in harmony or relaxed. These are also the sort of words often used to describe how a person feels after a massage. Massage clearly effects the state of the skeletal muscles. But it also seems possible that massage can affect our whole 'internal milieu', and therefore our awareness of how we feel in our bodies. Facial massage, by directly altering the degree of tension in facial muscles, alters the direct facial representation of emotion. Massage can interrupt SNS and HPA activity, and activate the PNS. These ideas are discussed in more detail on page 199.

Pain

Nociception is the response of the nervous system to real or potential damage to the tissues. Nociceptive receptors respond to extreme temperatures, pressures, light and sound, and to irritants released from damaged cells, and transmit this information to the spinal cord and then to the brain.

Pain is the subjective experience of tingling, burning, stabbing, aching or painful sensation. Pain and nociception are not identical phenomena; the feeling of pain can come and go even when the nociceptive receptors responsible are firing continuously in response to tissue damage. Sometimes pain is felt when there is no nociceptive activity.

Pain has an important protective function since it alerts the person feeling it to the fact that something is amiss and needs to be done. A hand that comes into contact with a flame is instantly withdrawn; muscles that are stiff and sore indicate a build up of lactic acid, and the need for stretching, a hot bath or massage.

Referred Pain

Superficial nociceptive nerve fibres and those from the interior of the body converge in the same spinal column pathway to the brain, which results in the CNS perceiving pain as originating near the surface of the body. A good example of this is the pain from a heart attack, which is not experienced in the heart but behind the sternum, down the left arm and left side of the neck. The area to which pain is referred is called a dermatome, and the pain is experienced as general, with no clear boundaries, and usually clearly on one side of the body.

Chronic Pain

Pain is diagnosed as chronic when it persists past the time normally expected for healing to take place; sensory pathways continue to fire even after the initial stimuli are no longer present.

Massage and Pain

Within the spinal cord, there are two pathways for sensory information to ascend to the brain. One transmits information rapidly, and the other more slowly. The fast pathway transmits information from the mechanoreceptors sensitive to light pressure, vibration and touch and the slow pathway transmits information about pain, temperature, and pressure. When the former pathway is activated, the pain pathway is inhibited. Sensations arising from touch to the skin, or from non-painful manipulation of soft tissue, arrive at the brain before pain sensations and can help to displace the awareness of pain.

Disorders of the Nervous System and Considerations for Massage

Key Words

Meningitis   Headaches
Brain haemorrhage   Epilepsy
Brain tumour   Parkinson's disease
Stroke   Myalgic encephalitis (ME)
Transient ischaemic attack (TIA)   Multiple sclerosis (MS)
Cerebral palsy   Herniated or 'slipped' disc
Muscular dystrophy   Trigeminal neuralgia
Neuralgia   Lumbago
Shingles   Sciatica
Carpal Tunnel Syndrome   Migraine

Total Contra-indications

Some disorders, including those that involve the blood supply to the brain, are potentially life-threatening, and, although most forms of massage are very unlikely to precipitate a fatality, these disorders are total contra-indications in order to protect the practitioner. **Meningitis**, **brain haemorrhage** and **brain tumours** are all serious conditions requiring hospitalisation not massage.

A **stroke** occurs when the blood supply to the brain tissue is affected, either by a clot (thrombosis) or by a blood vessel bursting. Some of the brain tissue may be damaged, which may result in loss of speech, movement, thinking ability, and sphincter control. Strokes are fairly common in the elderly, and can be fatal. There is a very high risk of a second stroke occurring within one month of the first; do not massage someone at all during this period, for your own protection. There is a lower risk of a stroke occurring up to six months after the first; during this period, it is probably sensible to ask for a doctor's letter regarding advisability of massage.

Transient Ischaemic Attack (**TIA**) is a mini-stroke from which the person recovers with no or little damage. TIA's are more often caused by clots in the vessels in the neck than clots in the head. Since there is a high risk of further TIA's, medical advice should be sought before massage is given.

Headaches affect everyone at some time or another. If someone has a severe headache that came on suddenly, with no previous history of similar headaches, and dizziness or numbness or sleepiness, refer them for medical attention. Sudden onset headache is one of the initial symptoms of meningitis.

Local Contra-indications

About 3% of all people will have an **epileptic fit** at some time in their lives. There are different forms of epilepsy, caused by abnormal electrical activity in the brain, and ranging from momentary lapses in attention, to the 'grand mal', or major fits. Epileptics often have warning signs of an impending fit. Except in severe cases, fitting is usually controlled by medication. Some practitioners who work with energy have reported that working with energy around the head area has brought on epileptic fits. Massage is probably safe, but it may be advisable for those who intentionally work with energy during massage to avoid input to the head area, and to work with grounding energy instead.

Other Neurological Disorders

For people with disorders that affect motor nerve supply and result in muscle tremors or weakness, massage may be beneficial as a means of stimulating circulation bringing nutrients to the muscles and removing wastes. Take care with pressure and joint movements since there may also be sensory loss and the client may not be able to give good feedback. People who are non-ambulant can develop thin skin on the soles of the feet and may be at risk of developing pressure sores. Take care when assisting the person into position for treatment if he suffers poor muscle control or tremors.

Negotiation with the client is always important, since symptoms vary from person to person, and may vary for the same individual over time. If in doubt, ask the client to get medical clearance from his doctor.

Parkinson's disease is a progressive disease, caused by degenerative abnormalities in the brain and characterised by a tremor, or shaking in the hands and limbs, and by a stiffness in movements.

Myalgic encephalitis (**ME**) is a chronic fatigue syndrome and is possibly caused by a virus. It results in extreme fatigue that is worse after exercise, and general aches and pains in the muscles. There is some evidence that muscle physiology may be affected. It is important to negotiate the pressure and quality of touch with the client because the pain may be severe at times.

Multiple sclerosis (**MS**) is caused by degeneration of the myelin sheath around the axons in the CNS. The symptoms include loss of vision, weakness and numbness in the legs, but the severity of the symptoms can vary considerably.

Cerebral palsy refers to various conditions that result from damage to the brain during or soon after birth. There is always some lack of muscle control, and, sometimes, learning difficulties.

Muscular dystrophy is a rare, incurable inherited disease causing weakness and degeneration of skeletal muscle.

Neuralgia, also called neuropathy, refers to any condition affecting the peripheral nerves. Inflammation of a nerve is neuritis. Nerve entrapment occurs when a nerve presses against surrounding soft tissue, and nerve impingement when it is trapped against hard tissue like bone or cartilage. The symptoms range from the familiar pins and needles, and tingling, to pain, numbness and loss of muscular function.

Muscles contract protectively around pain, so massage to relieve muscle tension is beneficial, but deep massage on the site is contra-indicated, and on areas of inflammation. Osteopathy may be more beneficial to alleviate some problems.

Shingles, is inflammation of the sensory nerves in the intercostal area causing a blistery rash, and is caused by toxins released from the herpes zoster virus after an attack of chicken pox. This condition is a local contra-indication to massage.

Carpal Tunnel Syndrome is a repetitive strain injury, where the tendon sheath to the wrist and finger muscles becomes inflamed, causing compression of the median nerve. Osteopathy can be helpful.

A **herniated** or '**slipped**' **disc** is compression of a nerve root arising when a vertebral disc ruptures and part of the contents is displaced onto the nerve.

Trigeminal neuralgia is a disorder of one of the facial nerves, causing acute pain.

Lumbago is a general term for lower back pain.

Sciatica is a condition that refers to pain along the sciatic nerve. It is most often felt in the buttocks and thighs, and is commonly caused by entrapment of the long sciatic nerve as it exits from the spine.

Migraines are a particular form of headache and affect about 10% of people. Constriction of the blood vessels around the temples may contribute to the cause, and so may stress. Daily massage of the temporalis and masseter muscles can play an important part in a treatment programme. Regular massage can help reduce stress levels. Massage during a migraine is not advisable and probably unwanted.

Conditions That Affect Awareness of Reality

Some neurological disorders affect a person's sense of reality, or the ability to comprehend or communicate about what is happening. When treating people with severe learning difficulties, or autism or dementia, it is important to ensure as much as possible that the treatment and procedure is fully understood, and to be sensitive to nonverbal cues from the client.

Alcohol, recreational and some prescription drugs have an affect on the nervous system, and can distort perception of sensory input. It is advisable to avoid massaging a person whose perception is seriously distorted.

Chapter 10 The Endocrine System

Structure of Endocrine Tissue

Endocrine tissue consists of areas of cells specialised to produce and secrete the chemical messengers called **hormones**. In some parts of the body, endocrine tissue occurs as patches of tissue within other organs; for example, the hypothalamus in the brain contains endocrine tissue, and there are patches in the intestines. The main, large areas of endocrine tissue are called **glands**. Endocrine cells secrete their products directly into the copious blood supply of the surrounding tissue. This distinguishes them from exocrine glands, such as the salivary glands, which secrete their products through a tube or duct. (*Endo-* and *exo-* as prefixes mean inside and outside respectively).

Key Words

Structure and Function

Endocrine gland
Hormone
Glands
Neuropeptide
Receptor site
Pituitary gland
Pineal gland: seratonin / melatonin
Thyroid gland: thyroxin
Parathyroid glands
Thymus gland
Pancreas gland: insulin / glucagon
Andrenal glands: adrenaline / noradrenaline / cortisol / cortisone
Testes: testosterone
Ovaries: oestrogen / progesterone

Disorders

Myxoedema   Cushing's disease
Goitre   Diabetes
Addison's disease

Hormones and Neuropeptides

Many of the hormones of the body, including ACTH (adrenocorticotrophic hormone), prolactin and insulin, are now known to exist in the brain, where they play an important role in brain processes, including those that determine emotional states. The hormones of the brain are called **neuropeptides**. When CRF (corticotrophin releasing factor), the neuropeptide that stimulates the hypothalamus to release ACTH, is released in the brain, the corresponding emotional state is stress, anxiety or panic.

Functions of the Endocrine System

Like the nervous system, the endocrine system is designed to transmit messages around the body. Nerves carry information immediately, and to specific sites. If you want to lick your lips, only the nerves affecting your tongue, certain facial muscles and the joint at the mandible are activated, not the nerves to the rest of your musculoskeletal system.

Hormones, on the other hand, when released into the bloodstream and transported around the body, are available to cells in any tissues. But not all cells will react to the information carried by the hormones, only those with **receptor sites** onto which the hormones can attach. The bulk of these for any one hormone will be in the target tissue. For example, prolactin is a hormone secreted by the **pituitary gland** after childbirth, which acts on the mammary glands to start and maintain milk production. Prolactin will circulate throughout the body once released, but since the receptor sites for prolactin are located mainly within the mammary glands, this is the target tissue that will respond to this hormone.

Like the autonomic nervous system, the endocrine system is controlled by the hypothalamus, and plays an important role in homeostasis. Hormones are involved in regulation of blood sugar, of calcium, sodium and water levels in the body, of metabolic rate and in the arousal response. This system is also responsible for the growth and maturation of the body. Hormones influence growth during childhood and the massive changes in the body at puberty, pregnancy, and menopause.

Endocrine Glands

The **pituitary gland** is located in the brain, and attached under the hypothalamus by a little stalk. The pituitary gland is tiny, about the size of a pea and is divided into two lobes. The anterior lobe produces hormones which stimulate the thyroid, adrenal and reproductive glands. The posterior lobe produces a hormone that regulates water levels (anti-diuretic hormone) and prolactin, mentioned previously. Because of its role in activating other endocrine glands, the pituitary is sometimes called 'the master gland'.

The **pineal gland** is also located in the brain, and works in conjunction with the pituitary. It produces two hormones; **seratonin**, an important neurotransmitter which affects mood, and **melatonin**, which is concerned with the body's biological clock, and the way that our systems fluctuate according to circadian – twenty-four hourly – and seasonal rhythms. The monthly menstrual cycle of women is regulated by the pineal. Melatonin is made at night, and is linked with sleep. If the pituitary can be thought of as the gland that switches on many of the body's activities, then the pineal can be considered the 'off' switch.

The **thyroid gland** is a butterfly-shaped gland, which wraps round the trachea just below the larynx, with four tiny parathyroid glands embedded in the back part. The hormone it produces is called **thyroxin**, which is produced continuously and acts on most cells in the body, causing them to speed up their activity. Thyroxin regulates the body's

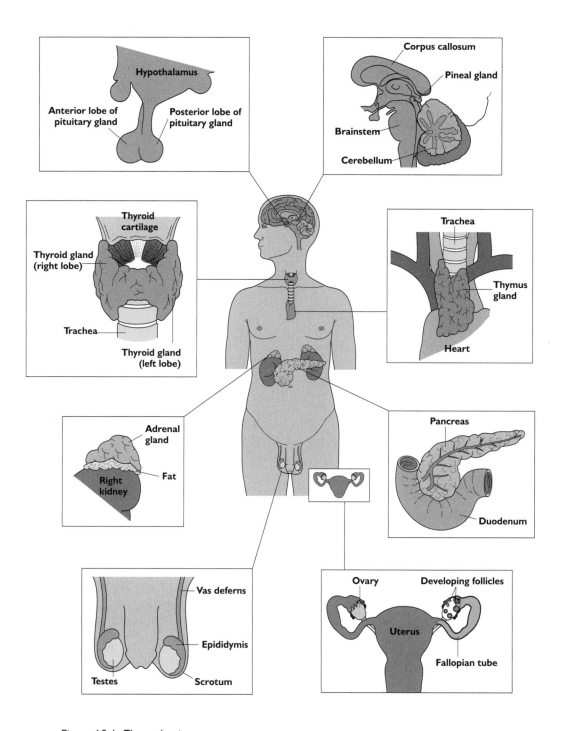

▲ *Figure 10.1: The endocrine system.*

metabolic rate. The **parathyroid glands** are concerned with controlling calcium levels in the blood. Calcium is vital to bones, teeth, muscles, the lining of nerve cells, and blood coagulation.

The **thymus gland** is located inferior to the thyroid, at the front of the body, just posterior to the top of the sternum. This gland is very large in newborn babies, covering much of the space in the thorax between the heart and lungs, but atrophies after puberty, when it ceases to be so active. The function of the thymus is to programme certain white blood cells, the T cells, to recognise and defend the body against foreign invaders.

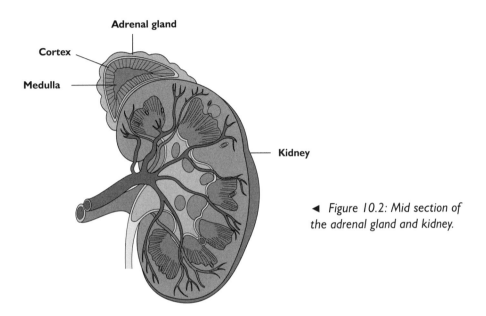

◄ *Figure 10.2: Mid section of the adrenal gland and kidney.*

The **pancreas** lies below the stomach in the loop of the duodenum, and is shaped like a long thin leaf. It functions both as an endocrine gland, secreting **insulin** and **glucagon**, the hormones which regulate blood sugar level, and as an exocrine gland, secreting digestive juices into the duodenum.

Each kidney has an **adrenal gland** perched on top of it, like a little cap (renal is the original word for kidney). Like the pituitary, the adrenal glands have two distinct parts, producing different sets of hormones. The hormones **adrenaline** and **noradrenaline** are made in the central adrenal medulla. Release of these into the bloodstream stimulates the heartbeat, production of glucose from the liver, causes dilation of skeletal arteries and the windpipe, and diminishes digestion, all of which are part of the 'fight or flight' response.

Surrounding the adrenal medulla is the adrenal cortex, which produces three groups of hormones. The hormones **cortisol** and **cortisone** have a part in regulating blood sugar, and also have an anti-inflammatory effect. Injections of cortisol are sometimes used to reduce symptoms of inflammation in soft tissue. Another group of hormones secreted by the adrenal cortex regulate the body's sodium and potassium balance. A small amount of the sex hormones are also produced by the adrenal medulla.

The sex glands have the dual function of producing the basic cells of reproduction, and the sex hormones. In men, the **testes** produce sperm, and the male sex hormone, **testosterone**. In women, the **ovaries** produce the ova, and the female sex hormones, **oestrogen** and **progesterone**. These hormones are responsible for the development of secondary sexual characteristics at puberty, and for the menstrual cycle in women.

Disorders of the Endocrine System and Considerations for Massage

Pituitary / Pineal Glands

Imbalance of pineal / pituitary functioning underlies conditions like Seasonal Affective Disorder (SAD). Relaxing massage may be helpful to relieve depression and tiredness.

Thyroid Glands

Insufficient production of thyroxin in adults results in a condition called **myxoedema**. The person suffering from this condition experiences weight gain and fatigue. Overproduction of thyroxin causes hyperactivity and weight loss. Both can be treated with drugs, or in the case of overactivity, surgical removal of part of the gland. **Goitre** refers to an enlarged thyroid gland, resulting from too much or too little thyroxin, infection or inflammation. Massage is not contra-indicated, except to avoid the neck area in a person with goitre.

Adrenal Glands

Addison's disease and **Cushing's disease** are both malfunctions of the adrenal glands. Overproduction of one of the adrenal hormones causes Cushing's disease with symptoms of obesity, body hair, and high blood pressure. Underproduction causes Addison's disease, with the reverse symptoms. Massage is not contra-indicated.

Pancreas

Diabetes is a disorder of the pancreas. When the gland fails to produce enough insulin, blood sugar levels in the blood and urine rise. Symptoms include frequent urination, thirst, and tiredness. There are two kinds; a sort which develops in people under twenty (Type 1), which although fairly rare, carries the risks of long-term damage to the eyes and circulation, and another much more common type that develops after the age of forty (Type 2). Mild diabetes is controlled by medication, but more severe forms require regular injections of insulin. Avoid massage of the injected muscle for an hour or so to avoid altering the rate of absorption of the drug.

Complications that the massage therapist should be aware of include the possibility of thin skin in the peripheral areas of the body due to circulatory problems, and the risk for the long-term diabetic of developing gangrene in the feet or lower legs, for the same reasons. Massage feet and ankles gently, and take particular care over hygiene. Diabetics may experience other skin conditions, including itchy skin, spots or boils.

Chapter 11 The Immune System

Key Words

Structure and Function

Bacteria

Virus

Fungus (**pl.** fungi)

Worms

Protozoa

Innate immunity

Adaptive immunity

Acute inflammatory response

Fibrinogen

Leucocytes

Phagocytosis

Lymphatic system

B cells / T cells

Spleen

Tonsils

Specific immune response

Antigens

Humoral immunity

Cell mediated immunity

Immunisation

Disorders

Allergy

Anaphylactic shock

Auto-immune disease

Acquired Immuno-deficiency Syndrome (AIDS)

Human Immuno-deficiency Virus (HIV)

Tumours

The immune system provides the body with surveillance and defence mechanisms against attack and potential disease. Threats to our physical wellbeing can come from outside the body, or within. The immune system is part of the whole communication network in the body, and like the nervous and endocrine systems, also produces many kinds of information carrying chemicals, which both play important roles in the defence strategies but also communicate with cells in any of the other two systems. The nervous, endocrine and immune systems keep 'up-to-date' with each other.

This section covers ideas of health and disease, our natural defences against disease, the immune system and acquired immunity, and disorders of the immune system and considerations for the massage practitioner.

Health and Disease

Health and disease are very difficult to define. We say we are well when we're not suffering from anything, but this might not mean we are in optimum health. Western medicine tends to define disease as starting at the point when symptoms show themselves. For example, when a person visits the doctor complaining of a skin rash, the doctor may diagnose dermatitis and prescribe steroid cream. The problem may have been building up for some time, before the symptoms began to manifest. Another way of looking at health and disease is to understand the symptoms as a manifestation of an underlying imbalance somewhere in the body. A practitioner of traditional Chinese medicine would treat the same patient by looking for imbalances in the person's energetic system. Some approaches treat the symptoms of disease, while others treat the underlying imbalance. Many practitioners, medical and complementary, are adopting a more holistic approach to disease, believing that a person's mental and emotional state, and lifestyle, all have a part to play in the disease process.

Some Factors That Cause Disease

1. Our hair, skin and eye colour are inherited from our parents, and determined by the genetic make-up in our cells. Certain disorders are also **genetically determined**; these include haemophilia, cystic fibrosis and sickle cell anaemia. Tendencies to develop other conditions, including some allergies and cancers, can also be inherited.

2. **Trauma** includes any mechanical or chemical injury to the body. A fractured radius after a fall, whiplash injury from a car crash or repetitive strain injury from occupational use are all examples of mechanical trauma. Exposure to chemicals, pollution and poisons, on the skin or taken internally are examples of chemical trauma. Prolonged or severe emotional disturbance may also have a traumatic effect on body tissues.

3. **Iatrogenic** applies to a condition that occurs as a result of medical treatment, surgery or medication. Prolonged use of steroid cream, for example, causes thin skin. Medication may have side-effects. Surgery can result in adhesions in the fascia, which may affect the ability of tissues and organs to move smoothly in relation to each other within the body cavities.

4. **Degeneration** of all the body tissues gradually begins as we age. Skin looses its suppleness, fascia tends to stiffen, and the rate of nerve transmission slows down. We are more prone to arthritic joints, and loss of sight and hearing. These are not disorders but part of the normal process of ageing.

5. **Tumours** occur when cells begin to grow and divide much too rapidly, for no apparent reason, and the immune system fails to recognise and deal with this irregular cell or tissue growth. Tumours can be benign, and not life-threatening, such as fibroids, or they can be malignant, such as breast, lung or skin cancers.

6. There is increasing evidence linking **stress** (prolonged activation of the HPA axis and sympathetic nervous system) to certain disorders (*see* pp. 203–206).

7. **Infection** occurs when the body is attacked by another living organism. The usual routes of entry to the body are through cuts in the skin, through the respiratory tract inhaled as droplets in the air, or in food or drink absorbed through the digestive tract.

Causes of Infection

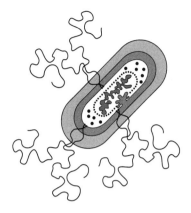

◀ *Figure 11.1: Bacterial cell.*

Bacteria are minute organisms, of varying shapes and sizes, with some of the characteristics of a cell. They are found everywhere; in the air, soil, water and on living creatures. Most bacteria are beneficial. The skin and the mucous membranes of the body are home to millions of bacteria that destroy harmful organisms, and help the digestive process. Bacteria can multiply very fast in the right conditions but are destroyed by heat (boiling milk prevents it from turning sour) and inactivated by freezing.

Very few types of bacteria cause disease. If one of these enters the body, then illness is caused by the toxins which are released by the bacteria that effect the tissues. Diseases caused by bacteria include diphtheria, tetanus, pneumonia, tuberculosis, tonsillitis, and food poisoning.

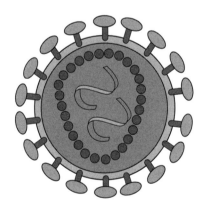

◀ *Figure 11.2: HIV virus.*

Viruses are micro-organisms that cannot exist independently but need to find their way into the live cells of another organism where they use the food and energy resources of the cells, multiply and invade neighbouring cells. Unlike bacteria, they are resistant to antibiotics. All living organisms can be infected by viruses. Human viral diseases include the common cold, flu, measles, mumps, chicken pox, polio, herpes and HIV infection.

Fungi are a simple form of plant, a group which includes mushrooms, toadstools and the mould that grows on unprotected food. Fungal infections occur on the skin, for example, Athlete's foot and ringworm, or on the mucous membranes of the mouth and genitals, for example, thrush.

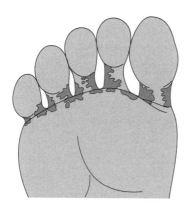

◄ *Figure 11.3: Fungal infection – athlete's foot.*

Infection by **worms** is less common than by bacteria, virus or fungi. There are a variety of worms that can enter the digestive tract, usually in food, and live and multiply there. The most common variety is the threadworm that affects children.

Dysentery, malaria, and giardia are examples of diseases caused by **protozoa**, a class of very simple organisms. For example, dysentery is caused by an amoeba.

◄ *Figure 11.4: Tapeworm.*

The body has two lines of defence against invasion by potentially disease-causing organisms. **Innate** (from birth) **immunity** is the routine protection provided all the time, against all invaders. It is activated immediately and by anything – it doesn't discriminate. The immune system provides **adaptive immunity**, which is highly specific, by 'remembering' infectious agents that it has met previously, and mounting an attack to destroy them.

Innate Immunity

Physical barriers such as the skin are natural barriers against invaders. The linings of the nasal passages, mouth and throat secrete mucus, which traps dust, chemicals and microbes. Little hairs in the lining help propel the mucus out of the body.

Chemical barriers such as sweat and tears contain anti-bacterial enzymes that destroy some bacteria on the skin. The gastric juices in the stomach contain a high level of hydrochloric acid that kills many of the bacteria or viruses taken in with food and drink. Unwanted substances that have survived the physical and chemical barriers may be ejected from the body more forcibly by various reflex actions such as sneezing, coughing or vomiting.

The **acute inflammatory response**, another of the body's innate defence mechanisms, is a non-specific response to tissue injury, which aims to remove disease-causing organisms, remove dead tissue and replace it with new tissue or scar formation. It lasts from a few hours to a few days. The symptoms are redness, swelling, heat, pain and loss of function. Inflammation is always a local contra-indication to massage. The sequence of events in the inflammatory response is as follows:

1. Damage to tissues (mechanical, chemical or infection) occurs.
2. Damaged cells release chemicals including histamines, which cause local vasodilation i.e. expansion of the capillaries. The increased local blood flow causes redness and heat. Capillaries become more permeable, fluid leaks into the tissues, causing swelling, and pressure on nerve endings which causes pain.
3. **Fibrinogen** (a blood protein) clots tissue fluid, preventing further flow, and platelets clot bleeding from damaged capillaries. The affected area becomes 'walled off' and the spread of infection is halted.
4. At the same time, white blood cells (**leucocytes**) are called to the area and begin to ingest damaged tissue, foreign matter and bacteria. They do this by extending portions of the cell around the object until it is completely engulfed. This is called **phagocytosis**.

Resolution of Inflammation and Tissue Healing

Healing of acute inflammation occurs in a number of different ways:

1. Abscess formation. Pus, which is a mixture of dead tissue, dead white blood cells and foreign matter, accumulates at the site of inflammation before being emptied into the body cavity or onto the surface of the skin.
2. Regeneration. Some tissues, like epithelium, have the ability to regenerate themselves. If the damage is not very extensive, or the edges of the wound close enough, new tissue grows to make good the damage.
3. Fibrosis (scarring). If the damage is extensive, or the tissue has little ability to regenerate, the repair is made by collagen fibres, which are secreted into the area in a haphazard way to form a patch of scar tissue. Because this is different from the original tissue, it cannot perform the same functions. Fibrosis in skeletal muscle, for example, can result in impaired mobility. Remedial massage of strains once the inflammatory stage is over and while collagen formation is occurring can help the new fibres to align with the muscle fibres and limit the degree of impairment.

The Immune System and Adaptive Immunity

The organs and tissues of the immune system, which provides specific immune responses, are the red bone marrow, the thymus gland, the spleen and the **lymphatic system**.

Red bone marrow is the site of manufacture of all blood cells. In the infant, red marrow is found in all bones and in the adult, mainly in the ribs, sternum, vertebrae and pelvis.

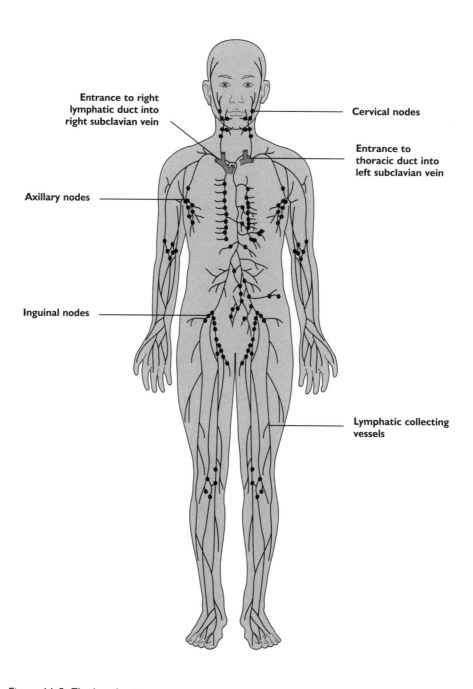

▲ *Figure 11.5: The lymphatic system.*

As well as erythrocytes (red cells) and platelets, there are six different kinds of white blood cells. Those involved in acquired immunity are called lymphocytes. Some remain in the bone marrow to mature (**B cells**) while others travel to the thymus gland for programming (**T cells**). Most of this activity occurs during infancy, when the thymus is proportionally very large; after puberty it stops growing although it still produces T cells.

As part of the circulatory system, the lymphatic ducts of the lymphatic system filter intercellular fluid back to the heart from the tissues through the lymphatic ducts. On route, the lymph passes through several lymph nodes. The ducts begin as tiny, open-ended tubes, picking up fluid and wastes that haven't returned to the capillaries from the tissue spaces. Flow of lymph, like venous blood, depends on suction and muscle pumping.

The capillaries join into lymph vessels, which then feed into the main lymph trunks that lead towards the heart. Lymph in three trunks from the right arm and right side of the head and chest drains into the right lymphatic duct. Four lymph trunks from the rest of the body feed into the large throacic duct. The lymph fluid from these two ducts drains into the two subclavian veins, just below the clavicles, to rejoin the main circulation.

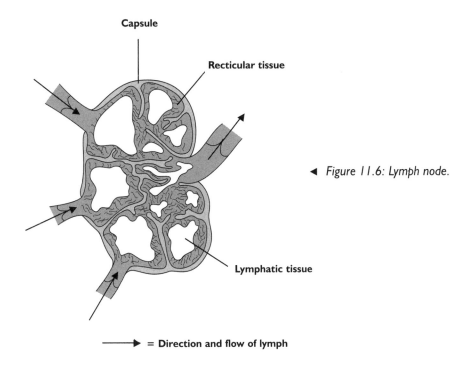

Capsule

Recticular tissue

◀ *Figure 11.6: Lymph node.*

Lymphatic tissue

= **Direction and flow of lymph**

The lymph nodes are masses of lymphatic tissue inside a fibrous capsule. The spaces between the tissue are full of white blood cells that ingest waste, bacteria and foreign material. When there is an infection to deal with, white blood cell activity increases, the nodes swell up and may feel sore. When this happens, we complain of 'swollen glands'. (From a structural point of view the nodes are not glands at all, since they don't produce hormones, sweat, sebum or saliva but act as filtering stations). The nodes mostly occur in clusters in the neck, armpit and groin, and deep in the abdomen.

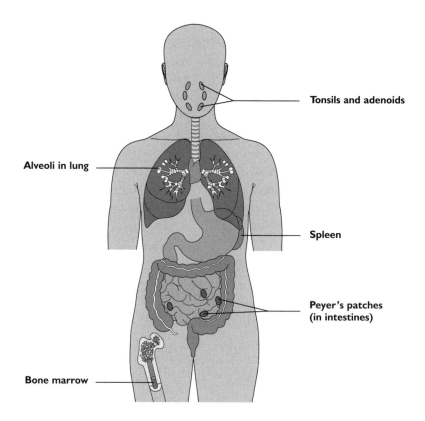

▲ *Figure 11.7: Lymphoid tissue.*

The **spleen** consists of masses of lymphatic tissue, but unlike the lymph nodes that filter lymph, the spleen filters venous blood. The white blood cells in the spleen ingest not only waste, bacteria and foreign matter but also damaged or old red cells and platelets.

Nearly all organs and tissues (the central nervous system, bone marrow and cartilage are exceptions) contain lymphatic tissue. The sites of entry into the body are guarded by lymphatic patches of tissue. The **tonsils** at the back of the throat and the **adenoids** under the tongue are made of lymphatic tissue that protects the upper respiratory tract. In the intestines, sites of lymphatic tissue are called Peyer's patches.

The **specific immune response**, involving the cells and tissues of the immune system, is activated when the inflammatory response fails to contain infection, or a disease-producing substance gets past other innate defences, and enters the circulation or lymphatic tissue.

All foreign matter, bacteria, viruses, toxins, and pollutants have molecules called **antigens** attached on the outside of the cell membrane. If the body has encountered a particular antigen previously, a memory of that antigen is activated in the lymphocytes and an attack mounted following one of these two routes:

1. **Humoral immunity** is where B cell lymphocytes produce antibodies, which are chemicals that circulate in the blood, recognise antigens and trigger a variety of

destructive responses. This includes clumping of cells to hinder movement within the body, or direct invasion and cell death.

2. **Cell mediated immunity** is where T cell lymphocytes summon other white cells to infected areas and the antigens are destroyed by phagocytosis.

Immunisation is a way of creating artificial memory in the immune system. There are two kinds; in active immunisation, a very small harmless amount of an organism is injected into the body, and the immune system develops antibodies to it. When the organism is encountered again, these antibodies recognise it and attack. In passive immunisation, blood from a person or animal who has recently had the disease is treated so that the antibodies are separated out, and these are then injected into the body. Passive immunisation is used when someone has risked exposure to infections such as tetanus or rabies.

Disorders of the Immune System

When the immune system over-reacts to harmless antigens and treats them as dangerous invaders, **allergic** symptoms are produced. Common allergies are hay fever, allergic asthma and skin rashes, including eczema. Some people have allergic reactions to foods, such as shellfish, eggs, milk, and strawberries. A severe allergic response can cause a sudden drop in blood pressure, breathing difficulties and even death. This is called **anaphylactic shock**.

Recommendations for Massage – Respect a person's allergies by avoiding use of essential oils in massage oil or aromatherapy burners; by using vegetable rather than nut-based carrier oils; and by not using perfumed soaps, deodorants or body lotions yourself.

Auto-immune disease is the term for overreaction of the immune system, but whereas an allergic response is to a substance foreign to the body, in auto-immune disease the body is reacting to its own tissues. These diseases are poorly understood. They include Addison's disease (affecting the adrenal glands), vitiligo (the skin), multiple sclerosis, myasthenia gravis (the muscles) and rheumatoid arthritis.

Acquired Immuno-deficiency Syndrome (**AIDS**) is caused by the **Human Immuno-deficiency Virus** (**HIV**). The virus is transmitted in infected body fluids. Blood, semen and vaginal fluid contain high concentrations and for infection to occur the virus must enter the bloodstream directly. Symptoms of HIV infection include insomnia, night sweats, weight loss, diarrhoea, and skin disorders. A person is diagnosed with AIDS when he has a T cell count below 200 (normal is 1200) or has three opportunistic infections such as pneumonia.

Recommendations for Massage – The benefits include relief from aches and pain, reduction in the emotional stress of living with the condition, possible improvements in breathing, sleep patterns, and digestion, and possible improvements in the functioning of the immune system. The virus cannot be transmitted through massage if the normal rules of hygiene and avoiding open or weeping skin are observed. If the person is fatigued, weak or unwell, use gentle massage. If medication is being injected, don't massage the site of an injection for an hour or so after injection. If someone has one of the opportunistic diseases they may well be in hospital, and a doctor's advice should be sought.

No-one really understands the process that causes some cells to proliferate too rapidly, or to develop abnormal forms. The immune system deals with these cells by destroying them, but sometimes this process fails and the cells grow out of control and large masses of abnormal tissue develop. These are called **tumours**, and there are two kinds. Benign tumours are not harmful, unless they are exerting pressure on other internal organs. Malignant tumours are the ones commonly called cancers, and can spread rapidly, invading other types of tissues. The most common cancers in men are of the lung, colon, prostate and pancreas: in women, of the lung, colon, uterus and breast.

Recommendations for Massage – Massage is generally beneficial for people with cancer. Although it is true that some cancers are spread through the lymphatic system, and that massage may affect the flow of lymph, there is no evidence that massage can spread cancer cells. Massage can provide a valuable source of comfort and relief from emotional stress. It may help to relieve pain on a temporary basis, and it may help with sleeping difficulties, minor digestive problems, and muscular stiffness.

Never massage directly over any tumour or site of cancer, or areas currently receiving radiotherapy. Depending on the vitality of the person, use gentle massage. Observe the usual contra-indications about broken skin, infections, recent scar tissue, and cardiovascular complications. Be aware that chemotherapy and radiotherapy can cause thin skin.

Lymphoedema is a painful oedema resulting from damage to the lymphatic system. Massage is part of the treatment programme, but this is a specialised technique called manual lymphatic drainage. Do not attempt to do this unless you are trained to do so.

Chapter 12 Skin, Touch and Massage

Our skin is the boundary between what is inside us, our blood and guts, and what is outside. We become very aware of this fact when the boundary is breached, and a bit of inside spills over into outside. Skin is also a psychic boundary, the point where all that I think of as 'me' stops and all that I think of as 'not me' begins. Once upon a time as very small babies, none of us were aware of that separation; we all had to learn it gradually.

Skin, together with eyes, ears, nose and tongue, provides us with information about the outside world. With over half a million sensory nerve receptors embedded in its surface, skin is our largest sense organ, weighing approximately 3kg and covering an area of 2m². As part of the nervous system, the skin is constantly sending information to the brain. Right now, your brain is registering the contact of clothes on different parts of your body, the pressure on the skin of your legs and buttocks (if you are reading this sitting down) and the temperature of the air around you. This information is filtered through your memory; your perception of all this might be different from another persons'. There is evidence that early experiences of touch determine how we understand touch when we grow up. There are implications here for the massage therapist. And, since it is the surface that we contact first, before muscle, fascia or bone, a knowledge of the structure, function and conditions that affect the skin is essential to the massage practitioner.

The skin consists of three layers of tissue, within which are found nerves, capillaries, hairs and exocrine glands. The whole organ, skin and appendages, is known as the **integumentary system**.

Key Words

Structure and Function

Integumentary system
Collagen and elastin
Epidermis: germinative / granular / clear / cornified layers
Papillae
Melanin
Keratin
Dermis
Hair follicle
Erector pili muscle
Sebaceous gland
Sweat gland
Sensory receptors: mechanoreceptors, thermoreceptors, nociceptors
Free nerve endings / Meissner's corpuscles / Merkel's discs / Ruffini's corpuscles / Paccini's corpuscles
Hair end organs / root hair plexus
Adipose layer

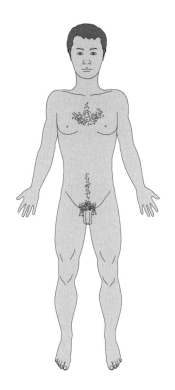

Integumentary system

Disorders

Dermatology	Acne vulgaris
Thin skin	Impetigo
Bruise	Boils / carbuncles
Blister	Herpes
Bedsore	Warts
Vitiligo	Verrucas
Liver / age spots	Ringworm
Skin tags	Athlete's foot
Eczema	Scabies
Contact dermatitis	Head lice
Psoriasis	Skin cancer
Stretch marks	

Structure of the Skin

The skin consists of three layers of tissue; the most superficial is epithelial tissue, and underlying that are two layers of connective tissue. The epithelial layer is called the epidermis, which consists of sheets of epithelial cells, plentifully nourished by blood and

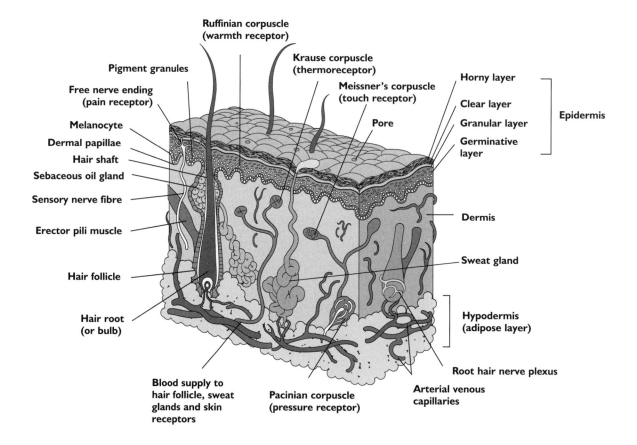

▲ *Figure 12.1: Skin.*

continuously replacing themselves. The next layer is the dermis, connective tissue with loosely arranged strands of **collagen** and **elastin** fibres, which give the skin its elasticity and mobility. The last layer connecting skin to fascia is the hypodermis, also called the subcutaneous layer or adipose layer, which is connective tissue with fat stores.

The Epidermis

When looked at under a microscope, it is easy to identify two aspects of the **epidermis**. One is that it is composed of sheets of cells, one on top of the other, and that the structure of the cells alter as they get further away from the dermis. The other is that the base layer of the epidermis is not flat, but has a corrugated appearance, with lots of bumps protruding into the dermis. These bumps are called **papillae**, and their function is to increase the surface area of the deepest layer, called the **germinative layer**. This is where new epithelial cells are constantly being formed by division of existing cells. The capillaries in the skin only reach to the germinative layer, so the nutrients required for cell function are no longer available as the cells divide and get pushed towards the surface. The pigment **melanin**, which gives the skin its colour and protection from the ultraviolet rays of the sun, is produced here. Exposure to the sun increases both the amount and the colour of melanin.

In the next identifiable layer, the **granular layer**, the cells are beginning to flatten, and deposits of a chemical called **keratin**, which is waterproof, are being formed. By the time the cells have passed through the **clear layer**, and then the outer horny or **cornified layer**, they are quite dead, flat and full of keratin. These outermost cells are constantly being rubbed away; we replace the whole of our outer epidermis every four weeks.

The cornified layer has important protective functions; the dead cells form an impenetrable barrier to bacteria and viruses, unless cut. This is one of the body's routine defence mechanisms against disease. Areas of the body that are exposed to continuous friction are protected from damage through the development of a thicker cornified layer in the epidermis. The soles of the feet are the obvious example; callouses on the hands of workers using certain tools are another. The ends of our fingers and toes are protected by nails, which are horny plates of cornified epithelium growing out of the epidermis.

The Dermis

Interspersed in the ground substance of the **dermis** are the organs and tissues that impart to the skin its multifunctional aspect; the blood vessels and lymphatic ducts, the nerves, the hairs, and two sorts of exocrine glands. The blood vessels consist of networks of fine capillaries, which fill each papillae, bringing blood to the surface of the skin, and to the germinative layer of the epithelium. Each hair follicle and gland also has its own capillary network. These capillaries are connected to arterioles and venules deeper in the tissues of the body.

Hair grows most plentifully where it is needed to trap sweat or protect the skin; on the head, eyebrows, armpit and groin. Each hair grows in its own sheath, or **follicle**, attached to which is a tiny muscle, the **erector pili muscle**. These are involuntary muscles, which contract in cold temperatures, causing the hairs to stand up away from the surface of the skin. This traps a layer of air, which has an insulating effect. These muscles also contract as part of the fight or flight response; in mammals, fur standing on end gives them a larger and more threatening appearance.

Sebaceous glands, a type of exocrine gland, secrete an oil called sebum, that keeps the hair and skin moist and pliable. Sebaceous glands mainly open into the hair follicles. Overproduction of sebum at puberty is one of the causes of blackheads and acne.

The other kinds of exocrine glands in the dermis and adipose layer are the **sweat glands**. These are found all over the body except in the lips and nails, but are larger and more numerous in the palms, soles, forehead, groin and armpit. They are coiled glands with a duct passing up to open on the surface of the epidermis. They secrete sweat, which is a combination of water, salt and traces of other wastes, to cool the body by evaporation.

Sensory Receptors in the Skin

It is the sensory nerve endings, spread throughout the dermis, which give the skin its function as the largest sense organ in the body. There are a number of different kinds of nerves, registering between them touch, pressure, vibration (the **mechanoreceptors**), heat and cold (the **thermoreceptors**) and damage to the tissues (the **nociceptors**). Information from these nerve endings is relayed via the spinal cord to areas in the cortex of the brain.

Free nerve endings are found everywhere in the skin and connective tissue, and register pain and temperature, but some also respond to pressure as well. They are considered to be the main pain receptors. **Meissner's corpuscles** are encapsulated nerve receptors found in great quantities in hairless skin areas of high sensitivity like the lips, palms, eyelids, genitals and nipples. They respond to light moving touch, and vibration. They help locate the source of sensation on the body, and possibly the texture of the touching object.

Merkel's discs, so called because of the shape of the receptor, are found in the epidermis, particularly non-hairy areas, and, unlike Meissner's corpuscles that respond to fleeting touch, these receptors respond to continuous light touch and pressure.

Ruffini's corpuscles register continuous deep pressure, and are found in the joint capsules and deep in the body as well as in the dermis of the skin. **Pacini's corpuscles** are found in the dermis, where they register rapid continuous movement, or vibration, and fleeting pressure. They are also found in the walls of blood vessels and in joint capsules.

Each hair has a sensory receptor wrapped round the follicle, called a **hair end organ** or **root hair plexus**, that registers movement of the hair, whether to light touch, or change of position on contraction of the erector pili muscle.

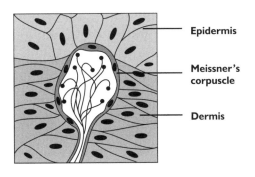

▲ Figure 12.2: Meissner's corpuscle.

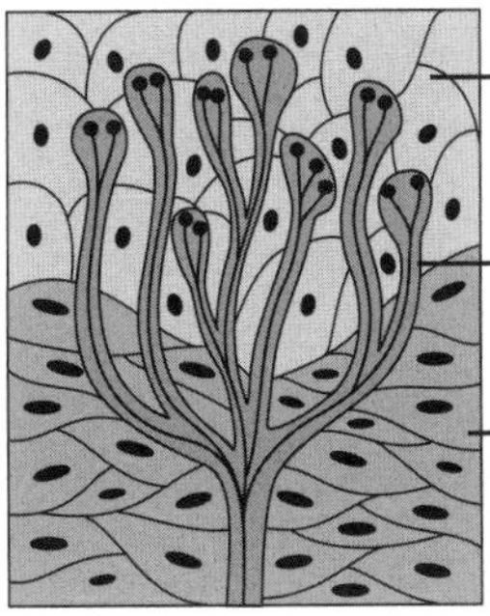

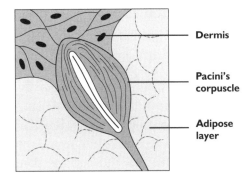

▲ Figure 12.3: Merkel's disc.

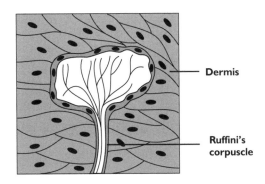

▲ Figure 12.4: Ruffini's corpuscle.

▲ Figure 12.5: Pacini's corpuscle.

The Hypodermis

The **hypodermis** or **adipose layer** is a layer of connective tissue containing stores of fat which varies in thickness over the body. In some areas of the skin it is connected directly to the periosteum of underlying bones or the fascia of muscles. There are sex differences, with women tending to accumulate adipose tissue on the abdomen, hips and thighs, and men on the abdomen. Race, age, lifestyle and climate also determine thickness and distribution of adipose tissue.

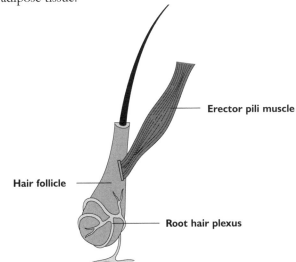

◀ Figure 12.6:
Root hair plexus.

Functions of the Skin

- Protection. The dead cells of the cornified layer act as a barrier to microorganisms, protect the underlying tissues from friction, and the keratin content prevents excessive entry of water. Melanin protects against ultraviolet rays in sunshine. Sebum kills many bacteria on the skin, and phagocytic cells act as a defence against bacteria and viruses in the dermis. The fat stores in adipose tissue may insulate the body against heat loss.
- Self-maintenance. Epithelial cells are constantly renewed and replaced, and kept supple by sebum from the sebaceous glands.
- Sensitivity. The skin is a major sense organ, registering light and firm touch, pressure, pain and temperature, thus providing us with information about our environment.
- Manufacture of vitamin D. In the presence of sunlight, certain cells in the skin are able to manufacture vitamin D, which is important for bone health.
- Temperature regulation. The skin plays a major homeostatic role in maintaining the internal temperature of the body at the optimum level. If this temperature rises, due to illness, or on a very hot day, two things happen. One is that the capillaries near the surface of the skin dilate, bringing blood-carrying heat from the inner parts of the body to the skin where it can be cooled. In white skinned people, the skin is seen to become redder. At the same time, the sweat glands are activated, releasing sweat onto the surface of the skin, where it evaporates and cools the skin. When the internal temperature is back to normal, sweating stops, and the superficial capillaries constrict again. If the internal temperature drops, the superficial capillaries constrict thereby reducing the flow of blood at the surface of the body, and the erector pili muscles contract, causing hair to stand on end and trap a layer of insulating air next to the body. All of these homeostatic activities of the skin are controlled by the hypothalamus in the brain.
- Elimination. The skin has a small excretory effect when we sweat; it excretes water, salts and urea.
- Absorption. It also has limited absorption abilities. This can be useful for introducing fat-soluble substances through the skin, such as oxygen, carbon dioxide, some vitamins and essential oils, and for the slow release of medication from skin patches. Unfortunately, it can also be the point of entry of heavy metals and toxic chemicals.

Touch and Early Development in Infancy

Skin and nerves are closely linked; in the embryo, the cells that eventually become our skin derive from the same tissue as the brain and spinal cord. Touch is the first sense we develop in the womb. Floating in amniotic fluid, foetuses have been observed to move when parts of their bodies are touched. The vaginal birth process is an experience of intense touch, over a long period of time, as the baby moves out of the uterus and down the birth canal, aided by the muscular contractions from the mother's body. This could be thought of as the first massage, although the degree of arousal and anxiety experienced by many babies during the birth process indicate that it may not be an entirely pleasurable affair. Touch is the newborn baby's medium of communication. Far more than through sight or hearing, this is how the baby learns about the environment, and the way in which she is handled by her caregivers informs her whether the world is a cold, unfriendly or rejecting place, or whether it is warm, welcoming and caring. Early touch experiences may lay down a 'template' through which all later interpersonal communication is filtered.

There are now many, many studies that demonstrate the importance of touch in early childhood. A structured regime of child care, which ruled out cuddling, petting or handling except for procedures like feeding or bathing, was common in care institutions in America during the first decades of the twentieth century and there was an exceptionally high infant mortality rate from 'wasting disease'. Contemporary research has demonstrated that premature babies who receive massage develop faster than those who receive standard care. The sort of physical contact a child has with her primary caregiver determines her pattern of attachment to that person, and her ability to form close connections in subsequent adult relationships. Children who are sexually or physically abused experience too much touch, or inappropriate touch, which can lead to distortions in touch perception. An absence of touch can also have serious consequences for later development.

Touch and Memory

When the skin is touched, a flood of physiological reactions occur in the body, most of which are unconscious. Not only do the skin receptors relay information to the cerebral cortex (the parietal lobes, to be precise) about what is happening in the here and now, but this information is also relayed to the association cortex to be compared with memory of similar events. Messages from both centres are sent to the hypothalamus, which downloads messages into the body, activating physiological and emotional responses. A medium pressure, static touch on the shoulder may be interpreted as calming by someone with a personal history of nurturing touch, but an extremely disturbing one by someone with a history of abuse, particularly if that sort of touch was a signal for the abuse to begin. In a person with such a body memory, the physiological response to touch in the 'here and now' will be activation of the sympathetic nervous system. If the touch evokes conscious memory, the person may be able to connect distress to past event.

So, although the physiology of touch can be understood in terms of different combinations of sense receptors in the skin firing when different kinds of touch are experienced which activates a physiological response in the body, it also has to be remembered that touch experiences are subjective, and the meaning of touch depends on the individual's personal history and stored body memories. Massage therapists, and clients, need to remember that our assumptions that massage is an enjoyable and pleasurable experience is not always true. Emotions associated with touch include anxiety, fear, shame, longing, joy, and sexual arousal, and even the more pleasurable ones may be suppressed, or experienced as shameful during a massage treatment. Many of us are touch starved, and feel ashamed of our hunger for physical contact. Some people cut off from their feelings associated with touch by living in their heads, others by leaving their bodies altogether.

In fact, there is a suggestion that unfamiliar touch is always arousing rather than relaxing, so a first experience of massage is likely to induce alertness in the receiver, a sense of, 'What's going on here? What is this person doing to me? Do I like this sensation or not?' The trust that develops during subsequent massages experiences derives from the sense of familiarity.

Skin Disorders and Massage

Dermatology is the study, diagnosis and treatment of skin disorders, some of which, like eczema, are very common and some very rare. Since many rashes, spots, lesions or sores can be quite hard for a doctor to diagnose, it is certainly not part of a massage therapist's job to identify clients' skin disorders. However, it is important to know the names of the common disorders and whether or not a condition is infectious. People with chronic skin conditions know whether they have psoriasis or eczema, for example, and will be able to give you that information. Undiagnosed conditions require that you follow commonsense guidelines for massage, and maybe refer your client to a doctor.

General Guidelines

- A contagious disorder is an infection that is transmitted through direct contact. Infectious skin conditions are always local contra-indications to massage.
- Never massage areas of skin that are bleeding, broken or weeping fluid. Body fluids (blood, lymph, pus) may contain infectious agents, which could be transmitted to the therapist or other parts of the client's body.
- Always clean towels and couch surfaces afterwards.
- Negotiation is important with a person who has a non-infectious skin condition. Someone with a skin condition, particularly a severe or chronic one, may feel very sensitive or embarrassed about their appearance, and may be concerned that you might not want to touch it.

Thin skin is common in very elderly people. If the blood supply to the skin becomes restricted, nourishment fails to reach epidermal cells and new growth slows. The skin becomes thin and papery, less elastic and liable to tear easily. Massage over areas of thin skin should be gentle (*see* Chapter 13), with no stretching or friction that could cause tearing.

Thin skin may also be found:

1. Over varicose veins.
2. Over areas of chronic oedema.
3. Where there has been prolonged use of steroid creams.
4. On extensive healed scar tissue from burns, injury or medical treatment.

Non-infectious Conditions

Bruising is discolouration and pain caused by internal, superficial bleeding. A local contra-indication, but massage of surrounding areas may help healing by bringing nutrients to and removing wastes from the area.

Blisters are caused by an accumulation of lymph below the surface of the skin in response to friction or pressure. This is a local contra-indication.

Bedsores / pressure sores occur when an area of skin is subjected to continuous pressure, the blood supply to the area is cut off and cells begin to die. This can happen to people who are bedridden, or who wear casts or braces. A local contra-indication, but gentle massage of surrounding areas may help improve circulation flow.

Vitiligo is a disorder of the melanin pigment in the skin, which may be an auto-immune problem. Patches of skin lose their colour, and their protection against the sun's rays. This is not a contra-indication.

Liver or **age spots** are brown spots found on the skin of older people. This is not a contra-indication.

Skin tags are little growths attached to the skin by a tiny stalk, or peduncle, and are common in older people. This is not a contra-indication, but avoid vigorous massage or friction that could break the stalks and cause bleeding.

Eczema is a group of diseases, also called dermatitis, characterised by inflammation of the skin with redness, itching or burning, and at times, weeping or blistering or formation of scales. Not a contra-indication unless the skin is weeping.

Contact dermatitis is skin inflammation caused by contact with a chemical such as washing powder, perfume, or fabric dye. Not a contra-indication unless the skin is weeping.

Psoriasis is a chronic condition where the epidermal cells grow too fast, and reach the surface of the skin without being properly keratinised. The cells clump together to form thick red scaly plaques. It affects most commonly the elbows, knees, scalp and back. Not a contra-indication unless the skin is broken.

Stretch marks are white lines caused by sudden stretching of the skin as a result of pregnancy, weight gain, or body building. Deep massage or friction is contra-indicated (*see* 'thin skin').

Infectious Conditions

1. Bacterial infections

Acne vulgaris is commonly found in teenagers when hormonal changes increase sebaceous gland activity, and sebum builds up in the pores. Bacterial infection then causes whiteheads, accumulations of sebum, pus and dead cells, and inflammation.

Severe acne can leave scarring. A local contra-indication depending on the severity and degree of inflammation.

Impetigo is typified by raised fluid filled sores and crusts on the face, particularly round the mouth and nose, most commonly found in children. Highly contagious, so definitely a local contra-indication, and take particular care with hygiene precautions.

Boils and **carbuncles** are caused by infection round a hair root or sweat gland, with pain, swelling and formation of pus. A carbuncle is a collection of boils. These are local contra-indications although massage of surrounding areas may help healing by improving circulation flow.

2. Viral infections

Herpes is an infection causing clusters of sore blisters. Once present in the body the herpes virus cannot be removed; it may lie dormant, but erupt in times of stress. There are two kinds; the common cold sores found round the mouth, and genital herpes that are transmitted sexually. Cold sores are a local contra-indication. The virus can survive outside the body for a few hours, so extra care is needed with hygiene.

Warts are small, rough, non-malignant tumours caused by viruses, which can disappear spontaneously. There are local contra-indications with this condition.

Verrucas are warts on the soles of the feet. Again, there are local contra-indications.

3. Fungal infections

Ringworm is not as the name implies, caused by a worm, although it looks as if a little worm has burrowed a red itchy shiny circle under the skin. If large areas of the body are affected, this is a total contra-indication because the condition is contagious. If only a small area is affected and can be covered, it is a local contra-indication. Take particular care with hygiene precautions.

Athlete's foot is an itchy infection between the toes, causing mushy skin. This is a local contra-indication.

Scabies is caused by a tiny parasite that crawls under the skin and lays its eggs and is commonly found on the wrists, between the fingers or on the genitals. Since it is so extremely itchy it is unlikely a scabies sufferer could lie still enough for a massage. A total contra-indication until cleared up, to protect the practitioner.

Head lice are blood sucking lice, with a preference for the head (other varieties prefer the pubic area). The white eggs are called 'nits'. A total contra-indication until cleared up, to protect the practitioner.

Skin cancer is the most common form of cancer, and the quickest to diagnose, since it is visible on the surface of the body. There are three main kinds; basal cell carcinoma (rodent ulcer), squamous cell carcinoma and malignant melanoma. Kaposi's sarcoma is a rare form of skin cancer found in people with AIDS. All skin cancers are local contra-indications (*see* page 224). The massage therapist is in a good position to notice moles, lumps or patches of skin which darken in colour, grow rapidly, bleed or ulcerate and bring these to the attention of the client. While there are many harmless reasons for changes in lumps on the skin, there is always a small possibility that a growth may be cancerous, particularly in a person with a history of overexposure to the sun.

Chapter 13 Physiology of Massage

Many claims are made regarding the benefits of massage, and the positive effects that it can have on the body, mind and emotions. How accurate or well-founded are these claims? There are two aspects that need consideration. One is that we need to be specific about what we mean by 'massage'. Sports massage, 'holistic' massage, Swedish massage, lymphatic drainage and myofascial release all involve manual manipulation of the soft tissues, but use different techniques, with varying degrees of pressure, to achieve different results. Even a stroke with a generally accepted meaning such as effleurage can be performed in diverse ways; consider effleuraging a back very quickly, with minimal pressure, and then imagine doing the same stroke using your full body weight, slowly. Even though your hands are moving identically both times, the affect on the underlying tissues, and the feel of the strokes to the receiver, are very different.

Also, to what extent can claims about the effect of massage be backed up by research findings? When we notice the skin on someone's shoulder reddening during massage, we assume that this is due to localised vasodilation, bringing more blood to the surface of the skin as capillaries dilate. However, it would be inaccurate to claim from this observation that this proves that massage improves circulation. All we can say is that, for that person, on that day, the techniques we were using caused vasodilation in the skin on the shoulders. Generalised statements like 'massage improves circulation' are meaningless until we have evidence-based research. This might include flow in arteries or veins or capillaries that are observed consistently when measured before and after a massage – stipulating duration, type and amount of pressure. And then we might want to know how long the change in circulation lasts and whether it is temporary or permanent.

This section attempts to address these problems by categorising massage strokes in order to provide a framework to relate these to the possible effects of each category of stroke on the physiology of the body. It then looks at the possible effect of massage on the different systems of the body. The categories are not definitive and other practitioners of massage might use the terminology differently.

There is a growing body of research that does validate some of the claims that have been made concerning the affects of massage. All massage therapists know that people sometimes fall asleep during a treatment, and assume therefore that massage has a relaxing effect. From this we could also assume that massage stimulates the parasympathetic nervous system. We could even try to work out the likely pathways between touch and the relaxation response. Now, with evidence that massage reduces levels of noradrenalin and cortisol, two hormones associated with stress, there is some scientific back up for the claim (Field, et al., 1999).

Some of the claims made in this section have scientific validation and some are theoretical; given our knowledge of the body as it is at the moment, this is what may be happening.

Key Words

Holds
Stroking / feathering
Effleurage
Vibration
Petrissage / kneading
Compression
Trigger points
Skin rolling
Connective tissue massage
Friction
Percussion: hacking / cupping / tapping / pummelling
Passive stretches
Shaking
Rocking
Joint mobilisation
Gentle massage

Physiology of Massage

Although at this time we cannot say for certain how a particular touch effects the body in terms of the exact input / response pathways, we can speculate. The effects of massage are mediated via the communication systems. Put very simply, when the therapist touches the receiver's body, the touch is registered by sensory receptors in the skin, joints or muscles and messages are relayed to the spinal cord and up to the brain where they are processed. As a result, messages flow down the spinal cord and via motor nerves to the skeletal muscles. At the same time, neurotransmitters are released at the synapses, the neurochemical balance in the brain also responds to the incoming information, and the homeostatic balance of the body is subtly altered. Memories of previous experiences of touch are stimulated in the cortex of the brain and this information added to the neurochemical response. The balance of the autonomic nervous system is affected.

Some of these input-response routes have been carefully mapped. We understand how a reflex arc works, for example the path taken when the patellar tendon is tapped. There are hypothesis regarding other effects of touch, for example the 'pain gate theory'. Other effects, particularly those involving the messenger molecules in the body, we can only guess at this stage.

Categories of Massage Strokes

Classical Swedish massage defines five types of stroke: effleurage, petrissage, friction, vibration and tapotement (percussion). Additional techniques now widely in use are holding, feathering, compression, trigger points and passive movements. Strokes are classified here according to the level of tissue activated as well as the broad technique involved.

238 Anatomy, Physiology and Pathology for the Massage Therapist

1. **Holds** – One or both hands in contact with the body, no or minimal movement, and minimal pressure.
2. **Stroking, feathering, light effleurage, light vibration** – Strokes that engage the skin and subcutaneous tissue (superficial fascia, capillaries and lymphatic vessels).
3. **Deep effleurage, petrissage, kneading, compression (palming), trigger points** – Strokes that engage the muscles, using a rhythmical compression and release of the tissues.
4. **Skin rolling, connective tissue massage, friction** – Techniques that address the connective tissues.
5. **Percussion: hacking, cupping, tapping, pummelling** – Techniques that use repeated rhythmical light striking, and affect the skin, connective tissue and muscles.
6. **Passive movements: stretches, shaking, rocking, joint mobilisation** – Techniques that involve movement of muscles in relation to bones or joints, or joints in relation to the torso. The structures engaged are the muscles and joints.

Massage strokes and sensory receptors affected:

1. **Holds** – Hair end organs in skin on limbs, free nerve endings and Merkel's discs to light touch. Thermoreceptors to heat.
2. **Stroking, light effleurage, feathering, light vibration** – Hair end organs in skin on limbs, Meissner's corpuscles in non-hairy skin and free nerve endings.
3. **Petrissage, kneading, deep effleurage** – Stretch receptors in muscles, Golgi tendon organs in tendons. Ruffini's endings to deep pressure.
4. **Skin rolling, connective tissue massage, friction.**
5. **Percussion: hacking, cupping, tapping, pummelling** – Paccini's corpuscles, and Meissner's corpuscles to light percussion.
6. **Passive movements: stretches, shaking, rocking, joint mobilisation** – Ruffini's endings and Paccini's corpuscles in joint capsules, Golgi tendon organs in tendons, stretch receptors in muscles.

Pathways between sensory receptors and the brain:

1. Sensory receptors to spinal cord then to one of two ascending sensory pathways.
2. Vibration, light pressure and touch, and the kinesthetic sensations from stretching and movement of body parts are transmitted through the rapid transmission pathway.
3. Information about the body at rest, tickles, itches, sexual sensations, crude touch and pressure, temperature and pain are transmitted through the other pathway, arriving at the brain more slowly.

In the brain:

1. All information is transmitted through the brainstem to the thalamus for sorting and then sent to other parts of the brain.
2. The somatosensory cortex in the parietal lobes registers that part of the body is being stimulated.

3. The association, or memory cortex and existing neural connections relating to touch are stimulated. Existing patterns of responding to touch are activated.
4. The release of neurotransmitters affects the balance of the autonomic nervous system. The HPA axis reduces output of stress hormones.
5. If negative thoughts are acting as an internal stressor, a shift to more positive thinking also reduces sympathetic nervous system activity.

Pathways from the brain to the body:

1. Information is transmitted back to the body through the descending motor pathways in the spinal cord.
2. Motor neurons that have been firing persistently, and maintaining skeletal muscle fibres in a state of contraction, are inhibited and the degree of contraction reduced.
3. The parasympathetic nervous system is activated by the vagus nerve and heart. Respiratory, digestive, urinary and sexual functioning is affected.
4. Reduction of ACTH from the pituitary reduces adrenalin output from adrenals.

Effects of Massage on the Different Systems of the Body

Musculoskeletal

Massage that kneads and squeezes the muscles relieves stiffness, spasm, and tightness in the area massaged. The movements are detected by Golgi tendon apparatus and stretch receptors in muscle and tendons.

Fluid circulation is improved, wastes including lactic acid, the cause of muscle stiffness, are removed and oxygen and nutrients delivered to the muscles more effectively, and muscle functioning is improved. Light massage that interrupts the pain cycle may result in a decrease in muscular spasm. Percussive strokes cause an increase in muscle spindle activity in the immediate area, causing minute contractions in the muscle fibres and improved muscle tone.

Joint manipulations may facilitate production of synovial fluid in an under-used joint. Local massage around a fracture seems to facilitate formation of scar tissue and healing in bone.

Connective Tissue

Deep massage may flatten out adipose tissue in the skin temporarily. Restrictions and thickening in fascia, tendons and ligaments may be relieved. There are specific techniques for reducing adhesions from scar tissue in fascia.

Nervous / Endocrine

Depending on the techniques used, the autonomic nervous system is stimulated or soothed. Massage that relaxes stimulates parasympathetic activity, resulting in a decrease in anxiety, perceived pain and improved sleep. Pain is affected both by release of endorphins, neurochemicals that act as natural painkillers, and by the decrease in sympathetic nervous system activity, and by massage interferes with the nociceptive pain pathways in the spinal cord. Trigger point techniques relieve localised pain by improving fluid circulation in that area.

Cardiovascular

Draining and deep effleurage assists venous flow locally by mechanically pushing blood through the veins. The superficial circulation is increased by techniques that cause localised vasodilation of the capillaries. Both of these facilitate delivery of oxygen and nutrients and removal of waste.

Dilation of the capillaries temporarily decreases blood pressure. As sympathetic nervous system activity decreases, heartrate drops. There is some evidence that massage facilitates production of white blood cells and therefore ability to fight infection, the theory being that the body perceives massage as a micro-trauma and releases white cells to deal with it!

Lymphatic / Immune

Massage mechanically stimulates lymph flow in ducts and improves circulation of lymph through nodes. There is some evidence that massage facilitates production of white blood cells and therefore the ability to fight infection. Relaxing massage decreases sympathetic nervous system activity, and as levels of cortisol drop, allergic and inflammatory responses are restored.

Skin

The superficial circulation is increased by techniques that cause localised vasodilation of the capillaries. Sebaceous glands are stimulated and sebum improves texture and tone. The rise in superficial skin temperature results in improved evaporation of sweat from the surface, and removal of wastes. Certain massage techniques can reduce the formation of keloid and scarring in soft tissue.

Respiratory

Relaxing massage decreases sympathetic nervous system activity and respiratory rate slows. Massage of the intercostal muscles and diaphragm attachments can improve ribcage mobility and the mechanics of breathing. Compression, vibration or percussive techniques on the ribcage can loosen phlegm.

Digestion

Relaxing massage decreases sympathetic nervous system activity and improves digestive functioning. Clockwise massage on the abdomen may alleviate constipation mechanically and may stimulate peristalsis.

Urinary

Relaxing massage decreases sympathetic nervous system activity and improves urine output.

Gentle Massage

There are certain client groups for whom 'gentle massage' is recommended; with the very elderly, with people who are frail after long illness, or women in the late stages of pregnancy. Gentle massage may be suggested locally, even when the rest of the body can be treated normally; over thin skin or over areas of oedema. What does it mean? It is obvious that the holding and light contact strokes (light vibration, stroking, light effleurage) could be considered gentle massage, but all the other techniques could also be performed in a gentle way. Percussion with the fingertips and minimal pressure, as used on the face, for example is gentle massage. Kneading performed slowly and lightly could be considered gentle massage. The main points to remember is that the massage should not require a big response from the body, and should aim to activate the parasympathetic nervous system. The attitude and intention of the practitioner to perform a careful and caring massage is possibly as important as the choice of techniques and the degree of pressure employed.

Category of Stroke	Sensory Receptors and Tissues Involved	Possible Effects of Different Strokes
1. Holds – One or both hands in contact with the body, no or minimal movement, and minimal pressure.	Light touch: Merkel's discs, hair end organs in skin on limbs and free nerve endings. Heat: thermoreceptors and local capillaries.	Relaxing, decrease anxiety and perception of pain. Local dilation of capillaries.
2. Stroking, feathering, light effleurage, light vibration – strokes that engage the skin and subcutaneous tissue (superficial fascia, capillaries and lymphatic vessels).	Hair end organs in skin on limbs, Meissner's corpuscles in non-hairy skin and free nerve endings.	Increase flow in lymphatic ducts and veins in area massaged. Relaxing, decrease anxiety.
3. Deep effleurage, kneading, petrissage, compression (palming), trigger points – strokes that engage the muscles, using a rhythmical compression and release of the tissues.	Stretch receptors in muscles, Golgi bodies in tendons and Ruffini endings to deep pressure. Effect on fascia, shift from sol to gel states.	Resting muscle tone altered. Increase in motor neuron excitability during application.
4. Skin rolling, connective tissue massage, friction – techniques that address the connective tissues.	Effect on fascia, shift from sol to gel states.	Increased flow in lymphatic ducts and veins in area massaged. Immune system functioning improved. Decrease anxiety.
5. Percussion: hacking, cupping, tapping, pummelling – Techniques that use repeated rhythmical light striking, and affect the skin, connective tissue and muscles.	Paccini's corpuscles, Meissner's corpuscles to light percussion. Skin capillary dilation.	Increase arousal. Increase proprioceptive stimulation. May stimulate stretch receptors when applied to belly of muscle.
6. Passive movements: stretches, shaking, rocking, joint mobilisation – Techniques that involve movement of muscles in relation to bones or joints, or joints in relation to the torso.	Ruffini's endings and Paccini's corpuscles, in joint capsule, Golgi bodies in tendons, stretch receptors in muscles.	May alter resting muscle tone. Decrease joint and muscle tension. Generally relaxing but can be applied dynamically for energising effect.

Section 4

Maintenance, Growth and Repair

Introduction

Every single cell in our body needs an endless supply of two substances, oxygen and food, in order to function properly. Cells absorb and 'digest' nutrients, expel waste, divide to make new cells, and eventually die. Some cells have specialised work; for example, muscle cells contract, neurons transmit information, fibroblasts in connective tissue secrete ground substances and lymphocytes destroy foreign matter. Both oxygen and food are essential for maintaining life in the cell, and the body as a whole. On a cellular level, this is expressed as:

Food + Oxygen > ATP + Carbon Dioxide + Water

Food, after it has been broken down into glucose, fatty acids or amino acids, combines with oxygen, and a complex chemical compound called adenosine triphosphate or ATP is created. This is the energy currency of the body. There are two by-products, water and carbon dioxide, which are removed from the cell. This is part of the chemical process called cellular respiration.

When we consider this activity in terms of our whole body and its everyday activity, we are talking about breathing, heart beating, eating, urinating and defecating. Every breath that we take in brings a fresh supply of oxygen into the lungs, and every breath out removes carbon dioxide from the body. Every meal, snack and drink is digested and the nutrients absorbed into our blood whilst the waste is removed when we defecate. Excess water is removed when we urinate. Every beat of our heart pumps blood, the transporter of all these substances, around the body.

The systems involved in this activity are the respiratory, digestive, cardiovascular and urinary systems. The respiratory system is responsible for the transfer of oxygen and car-

244 Anatomy, Physiology and Pathology for the Massage Therapist

bon dioxide between the atmosphere, around the body, and the blood. The digestive system takes in food and breaks it down into small components. The useful parts are absorbed into the blood, and the waste is excreted.

The cardiovascular system transports the gases, food products and waste (as well as other substances) around the body. Excess water and salts are removed from the body by the urinary system.

The hormonal activity of the reproductive systems is responsible for the growth and maturation of the body from infancy to adulthood and into old age. Although not involved in repair or maintenance of the individual human body, the reproductive systems are concerned with maintenance of the human race as a whole. In this section, we consider the structure and function of each of these systems, with particular reference to their contribution to the functioning of skeletal muscle, common pathology and considerations for massage.

Chapter 14 The Respiratory System

The phrase 'do not hold your breath' implies that something is not worth waiting for, that it probably won't happen, and if you stop breathing you'll be dead long before whatever it is comes about. We talk about feeling suffocated, about 'needing room to breath', or about needing 'a breath of fresh air'. Everyday language reflects the importance of breathing as a basic life activity. The respiratory system, which is the part of the body responsible for this activity, consists of the nose, nasal cavity and the tubes that connect them to two lungs. It includes the diaphragm and the ribcage. The respiratory system is not just concerned with breathing and the exchange of gases, but also with speech and smell.

The process of breathing is called respiration, or external respiration, to distinguish it from internal, or cellular, respiration. Breathing in is called inhalation or inspiration; breathing out, exhalation or expiration.

Key Words

Structure and Function

Nasal cavity

Olfaction

Pharynx

Epiglottis

Tonsils

Larynx

Trachea

Lungs

Pleural membrane

Bronchus (**pl**. bronchi)

Bronchioles

Alveolus (**pl**. alveoli)

Oxyhaemoglobin

Gaseous exchange

Pulmonary vein and pulmonary artery

Diaphragm

Intercostal muscles

Disorders

Common cold

Influenza

Sinusitis

Laryngitis

Bronchitis

Pneumonia

Emphysema

Tuberculosis (TB)

Lung cancer

Asthma

Pleurisy

Structure and Function of the Respiratory System

Air enters the body through two nostrils of the nose, and/or the mouth, and passes immediately into the **nasal cavity**, which opens out behind the nose, above the roof of the mouth. The epithelial tissue lining this part of the respiratory tract is covered with fine hairs, or cilia, and also contains secretory cells, which produce mucus. The mucus traps unwanted material like dust, or pollen, and the waving motion of the cilia propel

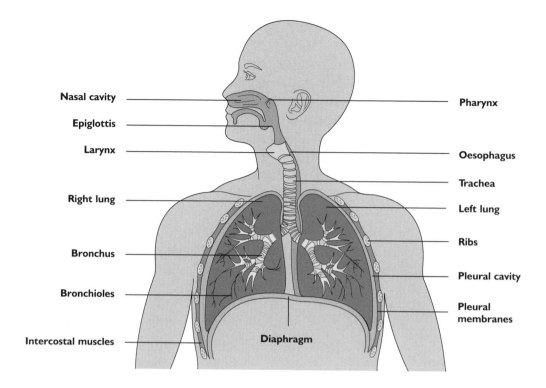

Nasal cavity

Epiglottis

Larynx

Right lung

Bronchus

Bronchioles

Intercostal muscles

Pharynx

Oesophagus

Trachea

Left lung

Ribs

Pleural cavity

Pleural
membranes

Diaphragm

▲ *Figure 14.1: The respiratory system.*

it back to the nostrils to be expelled, or down towards the throat to be swallowed. (These cilia are destroyed by smoking a cigarette, and take ten days to grow back). In the nasal cavity, the temperature of the air begins to adjust to body temperature before entering the lungs.

The lining of the nose also contains chemoreceptors, specialised sensory neurons which detect chemicals in the air entering the nose, transmit this information via the olfactory nerve to the brain, where it is registered as smell. The term for this process is **olfaction**.

The **pharynx** is the common channel for both food and air at the back of the mouth, where there is a small flap of tissue called the **epiglottis**. The epiglottis acts as a valve to regulate the flow of air to and from the larynx and food into the oesophagus, the tube connecting the mouth and stomach. Food or drink can sometimes go down the wrong way; coughing and sneezing are attempts to throw it back up. The **tonsils**, patches of lymphoid tissue, are attached to the wall of the pharynx, where they can trap and destroy foreign particles entering the body in the air.

The **larynx**, which contains the voice box, is made of cartilage joined by ligaments and membranes. Folds of tissue in the voice box vibrate and make a sound when air passes over them. A man's larynx is larger than a woman's, and is commonly called an Adam's apple.

The **trachea**, commonly known as the windpipe, can be felt easily at the front of the throat. It is a muscular tube reinforced by rings of cartilage. The oesophagus lies behind the trachea, and the thyroid and parathyroid glands are wrapped around the trachea at the level of the larynx.

The **lungs**, two sacs of smooth muscle, lie in the thoracic cavity, either side of the heart, extending from just under the clavicles to the diaphragm. Each is divided into lobes; the right lung has three, and the left two, there being less room in the left side of the chest due to the position of the heart. The lungs are covered with **pleural membrane**, which also lines the inside of the entire thoracic cavity. These pleura secrete a fluid to lubricate the tissues, and ease movement of the lungs against the ribs.

Just below the junction of the clavicles and sternum, the trachea divides into two tubes, also ringed in cartilage, called the **bronchi**. On entering the lungs, each bronchus divides into smaller and smaller tubes, with less cartilage and muscle, called **bronchioles**, which fill the lung, looking somewhat like the root system of a tree.

Alveoli and Gaseous Exchange

Each bronchiole ends in a little air sac, or **alveolus**, which is surrounded by a network of capillaries. The walls of the alveoli are elastic to allow for stretching and recoil as air enters the lungs and is expelled. They are also thin enough for gases to diffuse through into the capillaries and vice versa. Oxygen from the air breathed in diffuses through the alveolar wall into the blood in the capillaries, where it combines with haemoglobin, a chemical in red blood cells, to form **oxyhaemoglobin**. Blood that contains red cells carrying oxygen in this way is called oxygenated blood.

The capillaries around the alveolus also contain blood entering the lungs from the body, with the waste gas, carbon dioxide, dissolved in it. Blood containing carbon dioxide and not oxygen is called deoxygenated blood. Carbon dioxide diffuses from the blood in the capillaries through the alveolar wall into the alveolus, and leaves the body as air is expelled. This two way process is called **gaseous exchange**.

The rate of gaseous exchange determines levels of oxygen and carbon dioxide in the body. If more oxygen is needed during physical exertion, for example, we breathe faster, to bring more air into the lungs. In this way, the respiratory system has a homeostatic function.

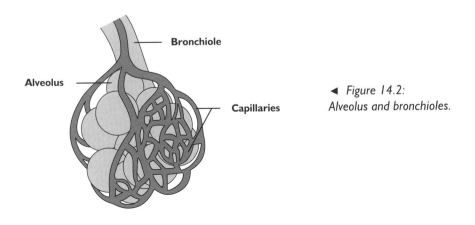

Bronchiole

Alveolus

Capillaries

◀ *Figure 14.2:*
Alveolus and bronchioles.

Inside each lung, the capillary system, also formed like tree roots, is linked to the **pulmonary vein**, which carries oxygenated blood from the lung to the heart, and the **pulmonary artery**, which brings deoxygenated blood from the heart into the lung.

Note: The pulmonary veins are the only veins in the body to carry oxygenated blood; all other veins bring deoxygenated blood from the tissues to the heart. The pulmonary arteries are the only arteries in the body to carry deoxygenated blood; all other arteries carry oxygenated blood away from the heart.

Mechanics of Respiration

How do we breathe? How does the oxygen needed by the cells get from the air around the body into the lungs? The mechanics of this process involve muscles; the diaphragm and the intercostal muscles.

The **diaphragm** is a dome-shaped muscle dividing the thoracic and abdominal cavities. It attaches to the internal surfaces of the lower ribs, the sternum, and the thoracic vertebrae, and posteriorly via two long extensions, the crura, to the lumbar vertebrae. The diaphragm is a mixture of smooth and skeletal muscle, with a central aponeurosis through which the oesophagus, the aorta and inferior vena cava (the main artery and vein) pass. When it contracts, the dome shape is flattened, pushing down onto the contents of the abdomen and creating space in the thoracic cavity (*see* also figure 8.34).

Between each pair of consecutive ribs are two **intercostal muscles**, with fibres aligned in opposite directions. When the external intercostals contract, the ribcage widens and the sternum lifts. When the internal intercostals contract, the ribcage is depressed, but only during forced exhalation or when the body is upside down.

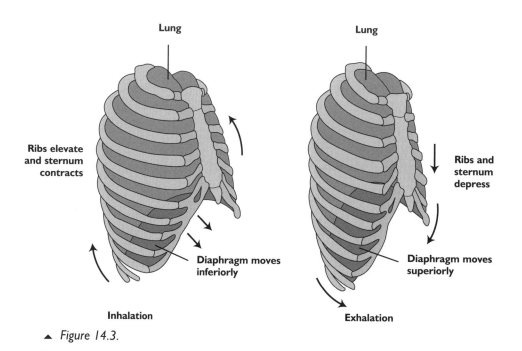

▲ *Figure 14.3.*

Inhalation

When the diaphragm contracts and flattens downwards, the space created in the thoracic cavity causes a vacuum in each lung. At the same time, the external intercostal muscles contract, the ribcage widens and the increased volume of the lungs means that the internal air pressure is reduced. Air is pulled into the lungs to fill the vacuum.

Exhalation

Normal exhalation is primarily the result of elastic recoil of the alveoli and the abdominal organs which were compressed, and relaxation of the diaphragm and external intercostals. These actions decrease the volume of the lungs, pushing the air out. Breathing out that is deliberately forced, during a long, loud shout, for example uses the internal intercostal and abdominal muscles as well.

Breathing and Exercise

After running up ten flights of stairs, you would probably find yourself breathing hard, with a pounding heart. Why? Because your leg muscles suddenly required extra energy for the burst of activity, including an increase in the supply of oxygen. As the available oxygen in your blood was used, your breathing rate increased to pull more air into your body. Extra carbon dioxide is produced as well, and the faster breathing rate means that this can be removed efficiently. Your heartbeats faster to pump these materials around your body, to and from your leg muscles.

Running up stairs, and exercise such as jogging, swimming, cycling, hill walking and energetic dancing is called aerobic (with air) exercise. These are designed to improve respiratory, cardiovascular and muscle functioning, and develop stamina and endurance. Other categories of exercise develop different aspects of fitness, although to some extent all affect the respiratory system. Strength exercises, such as weight lifting, focus on building muscle strength, and are usually intense over a short period. Flexibility exercises, such as yoga, develop muscle flexibility. The warm-up exercise routines of athletes, sports people and dancers develop muscle flexibility before performance, and help prevent injury.

Breathing and Relaxation

Breathing rate is determined not only by the physical requirements of the muscles, but also by the activity of the autonomic nervous system (ANS). Activation of the sympathetic branch and release of adrenalin from the adrenal glands stimulates, among other things, faster breathing. Activation of the parasympathetic branch slows breathing rate. Breathing is one of the activities of the body that we can have conscious control over. Can you control the activity of digestion in your stomach? No, but you can change how deeply you breathe, or how fast. And just as the ANS affects breathing, so can breathing affect the ANS. When we choose to breathe more slowly and regularly, sympathetic nervous system activity decreases. This principle is used in meditation, yoga, stress management training and by performers.

Our emotional states are linked to ANS activity; in high sympathetic nervous system states we tend to feel excited, alive, anxious, or afraid, depending on the situation. In parasympathetic nervous system states, we feel relaxed, calm and peaceful. Since we can consciously alter our breathing rates, it follows that we can affect our emotional states as well.

This two-way relationship can be applied to massage. We can observe the client's breathing becoming slower and gentler as a general monitor of their process of relaxing into the massage. We can observe sudden changes to the pattern, which may be an indication of discomfort – we commonly holding our breath as a reaction to pain – or a disruption to the process of relaxing. Teaching a client breathing exercises, or about the process of breathing, can be very helpful as part of a relaxation programme.

Respiratory Disorders

Disorders of parts of the respiratory tract are common, because of the direct connection with the environment and exposure to bacteria, viruses and pollutants. It is useful to remember that any medical term ending in *-itis* means 'inflammation of'; pharyngitis is inflammation of the pharynx, tonsillitis of the tonsils, bronchitis of the bronchioles, and so on. As a general rule, disorders of the upper part of the tract, from the nose to the larynx, are less serious than those affecting the lower part. Smokers have a much higher risk of developing respiratory disorders than non-smokers.

Upper Respiratory Infections

The **common cold** and **influenza** are both caused by viruses. There are hundreds of cold viruses around all the time, but 'flu viruses tend to come in epidemics. **Sinusitis** is inflammation of the air spaces in the head, causing pain and tenderness. **Laryngitis** causes a sore throat and hoarseness or loss of voice.

Other Disorders

Bronchitis refers to inflammation of the bronchi and/or bronchioles, resulting in overproduction of mucus. Acute bronchitis often follows an upper respiratory infection. Chronic bronchitis refers to a state of chronic inflammation of the lower bronchi after years of acute bronchitis. This disease is associated with damp, pollution, dust and cigarette smoking.

Pneumonia means inflammation of the alveoli and causes coughing, fever and chest pain. There are a number of causes, including bacteria, virus, chemicals or allergy. During the acute phase it is infectious.

Bronchitis can develop into **emphysema**. The walls of the alveoli are destroyed and breathing becomes very difficult.

Tuberculosis (TB) is a bacterial infection which once killed hundreds of people, and is on the increase again in the elderly, immigrant populations, the homeless and those who are HIV positive. It can occur in various body tissues. Only pulmonary TB can be transmitted by breathing in droplets from coughs and sneezes in the air. Other forms of TB are not contagious.

Lung cancer is the most common form of cancer in men, and there may be 2–3 years between the development of cancer and the appearance of any symptoms.

Asthma is a common condition, affecting one in seven people, and happens when the bronchioles are restricted, causing attacks of breathing difficulties. It is often an allergic reaction, worsened by stress. An asthmatic attack can be very frightening for the sufferer.

Pleurisy is a very painful inflammation of the pleural membranes, often connected with an underlying infection such as TB.

Recommendations for massage:

1. Many of the very common respiratory disorders are infectious; asthma is an exception. The decision to massage or not depends on the severity of the disorder – to catch a cold is very different from contracting pneumonia – and on the stage of the illness. Many are only infectious during the initial acute phase, including pulmonary TB, pneumonia and bronchitis. In these cases, medical approval should be obtained.
2. Massage of the muscles involved in breathing can be very helpful for people with respiratory disorders. Coughing, for example, puts unaccustomed pressure on the intercostal muscles and abdominal muscles. Emphysema results in tightening of all the respiratory muscles and those in the neck and throat. Asthma is associated with chronically tight intercostal muscles. Some disorders result in a build up of phlegm in the lungs, which can be loosened by percussion over the ribcage.
3. Breathing difficulties are often made worse by lying flat. If this is the case, it may be necessary to use supports to prop the client in a semi-sitting position, or in a side lying position.

Chapter 15 The Digestive System

The word digestion comes from two Latin words, one meaning 'dissolve' and the other meaning 'divide'. The digestive system does both these things; dissolves the food and drink we take in into very small particles, and then divides them into those useful to the body and those that can be eliminated. The whole digestive tract, a continuous tube from the mouth to the anus, is a bit like an assembly line in reverse; products are taken apart and broken down into their components. We usually know quite quickly when there are problems on the line. A faulty product gives us stomach ache, vomiting or diarrhoea; too long a gap and we feel hungry.

Digestion is a process associated with the parasympathetic nervous system, occurring when we are relaxed, and have energy available for the process, and ceasing in times of activity or stress, when energy is needed elsewhere in the body.

Key Words

Structure and Function

Alimentary canal

Peristalsis

Peritoneum

Ingestion

Mastication

Saliva

Bolus

Oesophagus

Stomach

Chyme

Pyloric sphincter

Small intestine: duodenum, jejunum, ileum

Portal vein

Large intestine (or colon or bowel)

Appendix

Faecal matter

Rectum

Anus

Liver

Gall bladder

Bile

Glycogen

Pancreas

Nutrition

Protein

Carbohydrate

Sugar

Fat

Minerals

Vitamins

Fibre

Water

Disorders

Nausea

Indigestion

Ulcers

Colitis

Crohn's disease

Diverticulitis

Hepatitis

Cirrhosis

Gallstones

Hernia

Anorexia nervosa

Bulimia

Structure and Function of the Digestive Tract

The **alimentary canal**, also called the digestive tract, is basically a tube of smooth muscle lined with mucus producing epithelium. The different parts vary in size and shape, and have slightly different roles according to their place in the digestive process. Various parts, for example the stomach, are sectioned off by rings of muscles called sphincters. Food is moved from one part of the tube to the next by a process called **peristalsis**, which is a series of wave-like contractions of the muscular walls that automatically sweep the contents along.

Below the diaphragm, the digestive tract and the other organs involved in digestion lie in the abdominal cavity. The entire cavity is lined with a membrane called the **peritoneum**, which produces a mucus to lubricate the movement of the organs enclosed within.

Ingestion is the process of taking food into the mouth (or oral cavity), and involves the lips and teeth. The epithelium lining the mouth contains chemoreceptors, sensory nerves that respond to chemicals in food, and transmit information to the brain that registers taste.

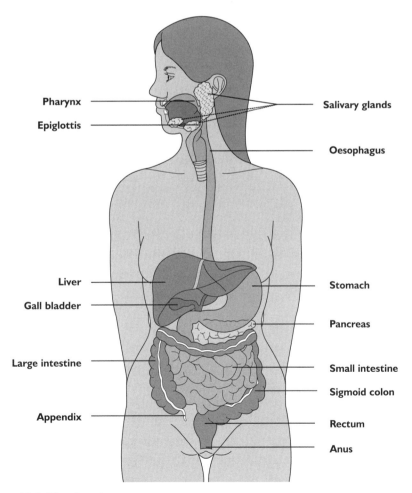

▲ *Figure 15.1: The digestive system.*

The four main tastes we are able to identify are salt, sweet, bitter and sour. Chewing, or **mastication**, involving the temporalis and masseter muscles, begins the process of digestion. Food is mixed with **saliva** from the salivary glands in the mouth. Saliva has a number of functions; it moistens food making it easier to swallow, it activates the taste receptors and it contains enzymes that begin breaking starches into sugars. (Try chewing a mouthful of rice without swallowing – eventually it begins to taste sweet).

Swallowing takes the moistened food ball, now called a **bolus**, down past the epiglottis into the **oesophagus**, a long tube that passes behind the trachea and the heart, and through the aponeurosis of the diaphragm, into the abdominal cavity where it becomes the stomach.

In common usage, the word **stomach** often refers to the whole of the abdomen. The proper use refers to a stretchable bag, the segment of the digestive tract immediately under and to the left side of the diaphragm, sectioned off by sphincter muscles at each end. Here gastric juice, containing hydrochloric acid and enzymes is mixed in with the food particles. The muscular stomach walls create a washing machine-like churning action to break down proteins and kill bacteria. If the top sphincter releases some of this acidic mix back up into the oesophagus, we experience heart burn, or acid reflux.

The food, now a thick liquid pulp called **chyme**, is squirted out of the stomach by the **pyloric sphincter** muscles into the next part of the tube, the **duodenum**, which secretes protective mucus, and receives digestive juices from the pancreas and the liver. The pancreas, also an endocrine gland, lies in the curve of the duodenum. Pancreatic juice neutralises the remaining acid, and splits fats, starches and proteins into smaller components. Bile, formed by the liver and stored in the gall bladder, helps break down fats and prepares vitamins for absorption. The duodenum is the first section of the small intestine.

The chyme then continues into the main, very coiled section of the **small intestine:** the **jejunum** and the **ileum** ('small' because of its small diameter, 2–3cms). This section is 6–7m long, and occupies the central area of the abdomen. This part of the tube has two layers of muscle, longitudinal and circular, to move food along, and an inner corrugated mucus lining to give maximum contact area for absorption into the network of lining capillaries.

The final breakdown of proteins and sugars is carried out by enzymes secreted by the walls of the small intestine. Nearly all food absorption occurs in this section. The useful nutritional elements – vitamins, minerals, starches, fats, and proteins – are taken into the blood circulation, all of which goes firstly via the **portal vein** to the liver, which filters out many substances; the rest continue into general circulation.

The small intestine enters the next section, the **large intestine** (or **colon** or **bowel**), low down on the right side of the abdomen just inside the right hipbone. The **appendix**, a vestigial worm-like tube, also joins the large intestine in this area. This section of the tube is 5–6cms in diameter and passes up to just below the liver in the ascending colon. It travels in the transverse colon across to the left side of the body to the underside of the spleen, just below the stomach, and down the descending colon to just inside the left hipbone. The walls do not secrete digestive juices, but instead absorb water from the contents as they pass along, becoming drier and harder **faecal matter**. Diarrhoea, in which wastes pass through this section too quickly to give up water, can severely dehydrate the body. The last part, the sigmoid colon is shaped like an 'S' bend, before becoming the rectum.

The **rectum** is an expandable holding sack located centrally at the base of the pelvic region. The sphincter muscle controlling elimination is the **anus**.

Associated Organs

The liver is a reddish-brown organ and is the largest solid organ of the body. It is situated directly under the diaphragm, protected by the lower ribs, with the largest part on the right and a wedge-like section projecting over to the left between the diaphragm and stomach. Tucked away underneath the liver is the **gall bladder**, looking like a small green pea. The liver has several hundred different functions; a few of the main ones are listed below. All blood from the small intestines passes through the liver via the hepatic portal vein before entering the rest of the venous circulation and returning to the heart, in order for nutrients and toxins to be removed and stored or broken down in the liver sinuses.

Functions of the Liver

1. **Bile**, a substance that breaks down fats, is produced in the liver and passed to the gall bladder for storage.
2. **Glycogen** is stored in the liver and released when there is a demand for energy for action, or to maintain body temperature or during stress. The release of the liver's store of glycogen to maintain the blood sugar level or to increase it in activity, is controlled by hormones from the pancreas. When all the glycogen stored in the body is used up, protein and fats are used instead.
3. Other foods that are stored include some vitamins and minerals.
4. Haemoglobin is produced, stored and broken down in the liver. Red blood cells at the end of their life are broken down.
5. Toxins from food, including alcohol and nicotine, are broken down for disposal.

The **pancreas** is a leaf-shaped organ and lies below the stomach and as well as its function as an endocrine gland producing insulin to regulate blood sugar, it also produces digestive enzymes that are passed into the duodenum.

Food and Nutrition

The three main categories of food essential for health are protein, carbohydrate and fat. Sugar is a form of carbohydrate. We also need small quantities of minerals and vitamins, as well as water and fibre.

Proteins, which are found in meat, fish, cheese, eggs, soya products and beans, are essential for building and repair of all cells and tissues in the body. If there is a shortage of fats and carbohydrates they can also be used to supply energy. We need more protein in our diets during growth, in pregnancy, during breast-feeding, and when convalescing. When there is not enough protein in a diet, wounds heal slowly, and resistance to disease is lowered. Some of the proteins found in red meats are too complex for our digestive systems to absorb, and get passed out of the body.

Carbohydrates are broken down to provide the fuel for cellular respiration. There are two sorts, starches and sugars. The latter are broken down and absorbed into the blood-stream very quickly, which is why we experience a 'sugar high' soon after eating lots of sweet foods. Starches are absorbed much more slowly, and are better for producing a sustained energy supply. Glycogen, the food used to enable muscle contraction, is derived from carbohydrates. Marathon runners often eat a large plate of pasta the night before a run. Starches are found in bread, potatoes and other root vegetables, grains, and pasta. **Sugars** are found in sweets, honey, fruit, jams, and many convenience foods. Alcohol is also a carbohydrate.

Fats yield twice as much energy as carbohydrates, but are digested much more slowly than other foods. If not used, they are stored in the adipose tissue under the skin and around the internal organs. High fat foods are dairy products, cheese, milk, cream, butter, foods that contain dairy products such as ice cream, oils, and nuts.

Minerals are important in the make-up of teeth, bones, muscles, other tissues, and the functioning of nerves. The main minerals needed by the body are sodium, potassium, calcium, iron and phosphorus.

Vitamins, required in small quantities, are essential for growth and general health.

Vitamin A. Helps produce a pigment important for vision, particularly night vision. Found in milk, green and yellow vegetables, and egg yolk.
Vitamin D. Essential for healthy bone growth. A deficiency of Vitamin D results in rickets (in children) or osteomalacia (in adults). Found in milk, butter, eggs and oily fish.
Vitamin E. May be important in reproductive functioning. A deficiency can cause blood disorders. Found in meat, cereals, and green leafy vegetables.
Vitamin B complex. A deficiency results in tiredness and nervous problems. Vitamin B complex is necessary for the body's ability to use glucose. Found in whole grain cereals.
Vitamin C. A deficiency results in scurvy. Found in citrus fruits and vegetables.

Fibre is the part of unprocessed foods that cannot be digested. It is essential for peristalsis throughout the digestive tract, particularly the colon. Fibre may prevent constipation, and some bowel disorders.

Water makes up 60% of our body, and is the essential fluid for all body processes and is found in all foods and liquids.

Diet

The term diet refers to the foods we normally eat. So everyone has a 'diet', even though we tend to use the term to refer to special diets. Although ideas about a 'good' or 'normal' diet vary a lot, several authorities on the subject, such as the Health Education Council, recommend a diet with lots of fresh vegetables and fruit, whole grains, fish, white meat, and limited amounts of fats, sugars, alcohol, caffeine and refined or junk foods.

There are many other types of diets that different groups of people follow for different reasons. Religious diets are those that forbid certain foods, and require other foods to be prepared according to certain rules. Islam and Judaism are examples of religions that have teachings about special dietary requirements. Exclusion diets are diets that consciously exclude certain foods. Some people are allergic to certain foods, such as shellfish, nuts or strawberries, and exclude them from their diets. Others decide not to eat some foods for moral, health or ethical reasons. Vegetarian and vegan diets are examples. Slimming diets are diets designed to facilitate weight loss, and range from simply reducing food intake to taking a wide range of commercially produced diet supplements.

The Digestive System and Massage

When doing firm massage on the abdomen it is essential to follow the direction of the large intestine, circling in a clockwise direction, so as not to risk pushing faecal material back into the small intestine. This may also assist the movement of faeces, and be helpful for relieving constipation.

With this exception, the digestive system is affected only indirectly by massage, and there are few direct contra-indications. But it is worth remembering the connection between digestive activity and autonomic nervous system activity, and the possibility that some disorders, such as colitis and ulcers may be linked to stress.

Massage may be very soothing in some cases of abdominal pain; period pain, for example, may be relieved by stroking (period pain originates in the uterus but can affect the whole lower abdomen).

Disorders of the Digestive Tract

Nausea can have many causes, including travel sickness, early pregnancy, food poisoning, and infection, and is not a contra-indication unless severe enough to cause vomiting.

Indigestion or heartburn can be worse after eating, so the client may be more comfortable to receive massage on an empty stomach.

All the following affect the stomach or intestines, and can be painful. Abdominal massage holds and gentle stroking only are suggested.

Ulcers of the stomach or duodenum happen when the balance of acid in the gastric juices is upset. Stress, diet, smoking and alcohol are all contributing factors.

There are two forms of **colitis**; ulcerative colitis refers to ulcers on the wall of the colon or rectum, and **irritable bowel syndrome (IBS)** refers to a situation where the peristaltic waves in the bowel become irregular.

Crohn's disease is a chronic inflammation of any part of the wall of the bowel, and is becoming more common. Like ulcers, it may be linked to a 'Western lifestyle'.

Diverticulitis refers to little pouches that protrude outward on the wall of the large intestine, and can become inflamed and painful.

Disorders of the Liver

Hepatitis can be caused by viruses, and, if so, is infectious in the acute stage. Massage is contra-indicated at that time for practitioner protection. Hepatitis means inflammation of the liver, and can also be caused by chemicals, or drugs. One of the symptoms is jaundice. People suffering from jaundice often have yellowish skin, from the excess of the pigment bilirubin in their blood. It can also be the result of a malfunction of the process that breaks down red blood cells.

Cirrhosis of the liver can also occur as a result of hepatitis, and is sometimes associated with alcoholism. The healthy liver cells die, and are replaced with fatty fibrous tissues.

Gallstones are hard little deposits in the gall bladder. A person with gallstones may not be aware of their existence; it is only when the stones try to pass down the bile duct that they cause severe pain.

Hiatus hernia refers to a condition where part of the stomach protrudes through the diaphragm into the thorax, and gastric juices may flow into the oesophagus (reflux). People with this condition are more comfortable sitting than lying, and should be massaged with their upper body raised.

Abdominal hernia occurs when part of the abdominal organs protrude through the muscles of the abdominal wall. This is most likely to happen in places of weakness; at the inguinal canal in the groin, usually in men, at the umbilicus, or where there has been abdominal surgery. Some hernias go back when the person lies down. An abdominal hernia is a local contra-indication – do not massage the affected area.

One of the characteristics of the eating disorders **anorexia nervosa** and **bulimia** is poor or distorted body image. Massage may be helpful, but sensitivity to the client's psychological state is important.

Chapter 16 The Cardiovascular System

The **cardiovascular system** refers to the heart and the blood vessels that carry blood in a closed circuit, to and fro between the heart and all the cells and tissues of the body. The **circulatory system** refers to the cardiovascular and the lymphatic systems, which together circulate blood and lymph. We become aware of the workings of this system on hearing our heartbeat; the familiar lubb-dubb ensures us that all is well in our chests, or, if beating hard, that we have been exercising, or if 'our heart is in our mouth' that something strange is happening. We are also exposed to its workings, literally, when we cut ourselves and the evidence seeps forth. But the moment to moment movements in the system and variations in composition of the blood are outside our consciousness, like many of the workings of the body.

Key Words

Structure and Function

Heart
Pericardium
Atrium (**pl.** atria)
Ventricle
Cardiac muscle
Sinoatrial node
Aorta
Systemic circulation
Vena cava (inferior and superior)
Pulmonary circulation
Hepatic portal system
Vasodilation / vasoconstriction

Artery
Arteriole
Capillary
Venule
Vein
Blood
Plasma
Erythrocytes (red cells)
Leucocytes (white cells): neutrophils / monocytes / macrophages / easinophils / basophils
Platelets
Coagulation

Disorders

Angina
Myocardial infarction (heart attack)
Heart failure
Blood pressure
Hypertension / hypotension (high / low blood pressure)
Arteriosclerosis / artheriosclerosis
Thrombosis / embolism
Deep vein thrombosis
Varicose veins
Phlebitis
Oedema
Anaemia: sickle cell / thalassaemia
Leukemia
Haemophilia

Functions of the Cardiovascular System

The two main functions can be summarised as transportation and defence.

1. Oxygen is transported from the lungs to the tissues.
2. Carbon dioxide is transported from the tissues to the lungs.
3. Products of digestion are transported from the small intestine to the liver for storage, and then spread throughout the body. This includes calcium salts for bones, and

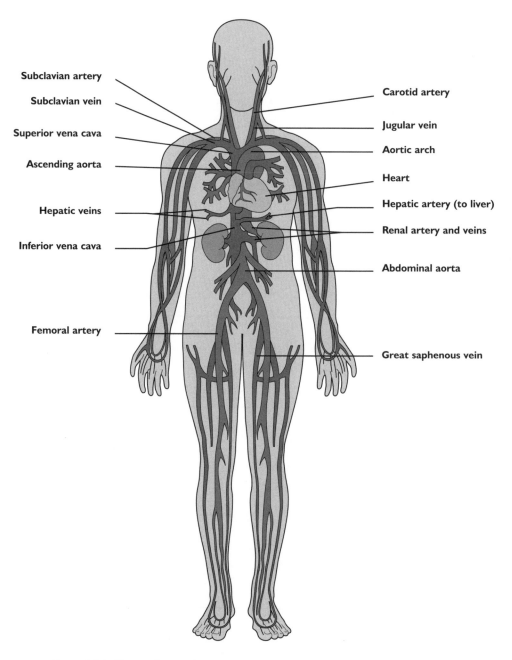

▲ *Figure 16.1: The cardiovascular system.*

glucose for energy for the cells, especially muscles cells.

4. Urea, a waste product from the breaking down of used proteins in all cells, is transported from the tissues to the kidneys, where it is made into urine.
5. Hormones are transported from the endocrine glands to their target organs.
6. Antibodies are transported to sites of infection.
7. Heat, the by-product of the numerous chemical reactions taking place all the time in the cells and tissues, is transported to the surface of the body if the internal temperature rises, or away from the surface if it falls. This is an important homeostatic function of the blood.
8. White blood cells are transported to sites of infection or inflammation, to fight disease, and generally remove waste and foreign material.
9. Clotting prevents blood loss in times of injury.

Structure of the Heart

The **heart** is a hollow organ, roughly the size of a clenched fist, situated in the chest, slightly to the left of centre between the lungs, resting on the diaphragm. It is surrounded by the **pericardium**, a layer of tough connective tissue which anchors the heart to the diaphragm and, via ligaments, to the ribcage. The inner surface of the pericardium secretes a fluid that enables easy movement of the heart as it expands and contracts. The muscular wall of the heart is highly specialised cardiac muscle. It is divided into two halves by a muscular wall, the septum, and each side has two chambers; the upper two are called **atria** and the lower two **ventricles**. Each upper and lower chamber is divided by valves that prevent back flow of blood.

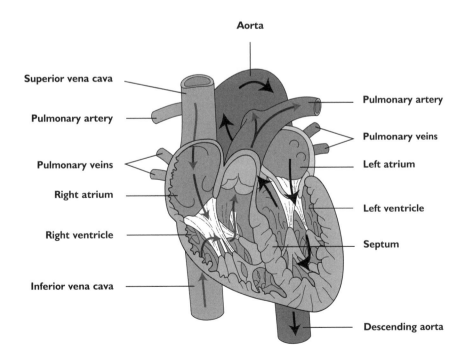

▲ *Figure 16.2: The heart.*

The specialised function of **cardiac muscle** is its ability to maintain regular contraction without motor nerve input from the brain, through a built-in pacemaker, the **sinoatrial node**, in the wall of the right atrium. This node receives input from the vagus nerve, part of the parasympathetic nervous system, which maintains the resting heart-beat, usually 70 beats per minute in adults. Other nerves to the heart, the cardiac nerves, are innervated by sympathetic nervous system activity to increase heartrate.

The heart, being a constantly working muscle, also needs a good blood supply. The coronary blood vessels that encircle it arise from the first part of the **aorta**, bringing blood out of the heart and directly to the heart muscle.

Functions of the Heart

The heart's purpose is to pump blood from the body to the lungs for a fresh supply of oxygen, and then to pump this blood from the lungs to the rest of the body. Both atria contract together, then both ventricles contract together; there is a simultaneous shutting of the valves. Deoxygenated blood which has circulated through the tissues and lost its oxygen supply, enters the right atrium, which contracts forcing the blood into the right ventricle and shutting the valves. The right ventricle contracts, forcing blood out into the pulmonary artery, which carries it to the lungs. Simultaneously, oxygenated blood from the lungs enters the left atrium, is forced into the left ventricle, then out into the aorta, the main artery in the body.

Circulation of the Blood

Within the whole circulation system there are some sub-circuits which have particular functions:

1. The **systemic circulation**. This is the circuit that carries blood from the heart in the aorta, through a network of finer and finer vessels to all the cells in the body, and returns it to the heart in the **inferior vena cava** from the lower body or the **superior vena cava** from the upper body.
2. The **pulmonary circulation**. The circuit that transports blood from the heart to the lungs and back again is called the pulmonary circulation.
3. The **hepatic portal system**. Blood from the small intestines carrying the products of digestion is taken to the liver before being returned to the venous system for return to the heart. This detour is to enable nutrients and toxins to be removed from the blood for storage or destruction in the liver.

Blood Vessels

All blood vessels are hollow tubes forming the pipework of the system. The walls have an outer layer of connective tissue, a middle layer of smooth muscle, and an inner layer of epidermal tissue. Expansion of the central cavity is called **vasodilation**; when it contracts it is called **vasoconstriction**.

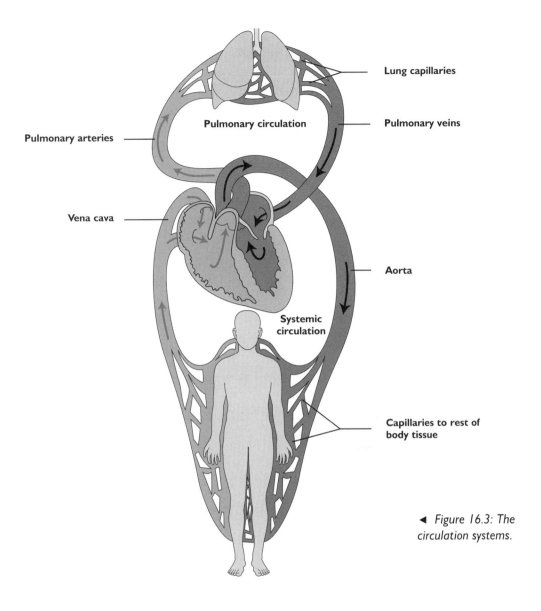

Lung capillaries

Pulmonary circulation

Pulmonary veins

Pulmonary arteries

Vena cava

Aorta

Systemic circulation

Capillaries to rest of body tissue

◀ *Figure 16.3: The circulation systems.*

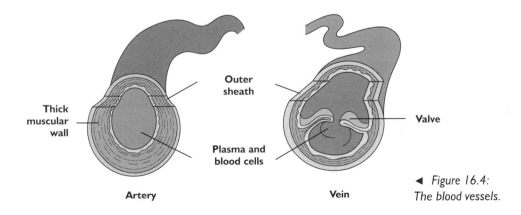

Outer sheath

Thick muscular wall

Valve

Plasma and blood cells

Artery

Vein

◀ *Figure 16.4: The blood vessels.*

Arteries are the vessels that carry blood away from the heart. (A tip to remember: arteries and away both begin with a). The smooth muscle layer is much thicker than in the other blood vessels, because these vessels need to expand and withstand the pressure of blood as it is pumped from the heart. The recoil of the muscular walls also helps to propel blood along. If an artery is damaged, a lot of blood can be very quickly lost, often with fatal results. Hence, they tend to be in the safest areas of the limbs to minimise this risk – passing on the inside of joints as in the armpit, elbow, wrist, or back of the knee, often together with the nerves which are similarly protected. They also tend to be deep in the body, except for a very few places; in the wrist and throat the pulse can be easily felt in the radial or carotid artery respectively. The largest artery leading out of the heart is the **aorta**. As they branch out into the tissues, arteries become smaller in diameter, and are called **arterioles**.

Apart from the pulmonary artery going to the lungs, all of the arteries in the body carry oxygenated blood.

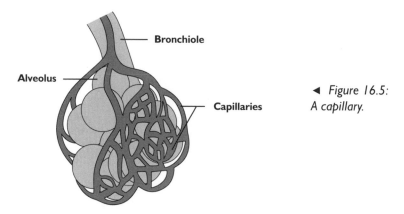

Bronchiole

Alveolus

Capillaries

◄ *Figure 16.5: A capillary.*

The vessels continue to decrease in size until they become **capillary** networks. These are found in all tissues with the exception of the epidermis of the skin, hair and nails. Some tissues, such as skeletal muscle, have very extensive capillary networks; others, like connective tissue, have very little. Capillaries are very thin walled vessels, so thin that they are permeable, and the nutrients, hormones, antibodies and other large molecules in the blood, as well as white blood cells, can pass through into the intercellular fluid, and waste material can pass into the capillaries.

As it begins its journey back to the heart, blood passes first into **venules** then into the similar but larger **veins**. Veins have thinner walls than the arteries, and another important feature; one way valves. As the blood passes through, the valves shut to prevent the back flow. Blood moves much more slowly back towards the heart; there is no force to pump it back and often it is working against the pull of gravity. So what moves it? To some extent, it is pulled back by suction, as blood empties from the two venae cavae into the heart. Another important factor, especially in the legs, is the effect of muscles squeezing the blood vessels as they contract for action, thereby pumping blood back through the veins. Unlike arteries, veins are often close to the surface in the limbs, which is why heavy massage strokes that squeeze the muscles need to be done 'towards the heart' when working on the limbs.

The Lymphatic System (*see* figure 11.5)

In the capillary networks, the fluid part of the blood, plasma, filters through into the tissues, becoming intercellular fluid. Not all of this is reabsorbed into the capillaries. The rest is picked up by the lymphatic ducts and returned to the blood supply in the subclavian veins, under the clavicles, having been filtered through the lymph nodes. Flow of lymph, like venous blood, depends on suction and muscle pumping (*see* Chapter 11).

Blood

Blood consists of 55% liquid plasma and 45% blood cells and materials dissolved in the water, which are being transported round the body.

Plasma is a straw-coloured liquid that is composed of water, minerals, proteins, hormones, waste which includes urea, and nutrients.

The precursors of all blood cells are made in red bone marrow, and differentiate into three main groups.

Red blood cells, or **erythrocytes**, give the blood its colour. They are biconcave and are unusual in having no nucleus. Their function is to transport oxygen around the body from the lungs; in the alveoli, oxygen attaches to a chemical called haemoglobin in the erythrocyte. Once it reaches the tissues, oxygen is released for use in cell metabolism. Erythrocytes have a life span of about 120 days and are destroyed in the liver or spleen.

Leucocytes, or white blood cells, are all involved in defending the body. They live for a few hours to a few days and have the ability to change shape, leave the blood by squeezing out of capillary walls, and to migrate through the tissues.

There are five different kinds: **neutrophils** and **monocytes** are able to engulf and destroy bacteria, viruses and foreign material through a process called phagocytosis. Monocytes are called **macrophages** when in the tissues rather than the circulation; the lymph nodes are full of macrophages. **Easinophils** and **basophils** are the white cells involved in allergic responses, and **lymphocytes**, which include T cells and B cells, are involved in the adaptive immune response.

Red blood cells (erythrocytes)

Platelets

White blood cells (leucocytes)

▲ *Figure 16.6: Blood cells.*

Platelets are small cells that are responsible for clotting blood. When exposed to air or objects that have penetrated the blood vessel, they stick together to plug the hole in the vessel wall, and combine with one of the proteins in the plasma, fibrinogen, to form a clot. The latter process is called **coagulation**.

Massage Considerations

In healthy people, there are two considerations for massage relating to the cardiovascular system:

1. Never put heavy or prolonged pressure on the major superficial arteries. These are the two arteries where you feel for a pulse, the carotid at the side of the neck and the ulnar on the inner surface of the wrist, and the arteries on the inner surface of the elbow joint, and the back of the knee.
2. When massaging the limbs with firm pressure, work towards the heart. If you massage firmly in the opposite direction, there is a danger of turning the valves in the veins inside out and permanently damaging them.

Disorders of the Cardiovascular System

The different kinds of cardiovascular disorders are those that affect the heart, those that affect the circulation, and those that affect the blood.

Disorders of the Heart

About a third of all deaths in the UK are related to coronary heart disease, and it is the main cause of death in people over 35 in industrialised countries. Heart disease is linked to smoking, lack of exercise, high blood pressure and excessive cholesterol in the blood. This last factor may be related to high fat diet, or may be inherited.

Heart disorders can be caused by a restricted supply of blood to the heart, or by faulty heart structure, or by disease of the heart tissues.

Angina is a condition caused by inadequate blood supply to the heart muscle. The symptoms are cramp-like pains in the chest which are made worse by exercise or stress, and relieved by rest. One particularly severe form of angina is called unstable angina, and this can be a precursor to a heart attack.

Recommendations for massage – Relaxing massage is beneficial for people with angina because it can reduce stress. Massage for anyone with unstable angina should only be carried out with permission from the person's doctor. Keep the client warm, since cold can bring about an attack.

A **myocardial infarction** (or **heart attack**) occurs when part of the heart muscle dies due to inadequate blood supply, caused by blood clots, or **artherosclerosis**, which are lumpy fatty deposits that accumulate on the inner walls of the arteries if there are excessive levels of cholesterol in the blood. These deposits clog the vessels, and can break free. The symptoms of a heart attack are sudden severe pain in the chest and, sometimes, the left arm.

Recommendations for massage – Because there is a very high risk of a reoccurrence in the two to three months after the attack, massage is contra-indicated for practitioner protection, and after that given with advice from the person's doctor.

Heart failure occurs if the heart is unable to perform its function as a pump properly, and fluid can back up in the lungs, causing pulmonary oedema, also called 'water on the lungs' or oedema in the ankles and legs. Heart failure can be caused by a number of different factors, including previous heart attacks or chronic high blood pressure.

Recommendations for massage – Get medical permission, and give gentle massage to avoid stressing a weak heart.

Blood pressure depends on the ability of the heart to pump blood round the body, the volume of blood to be pumped, and the size of the arteries, whose muscular walls can dilate or constrict. These factors interact to adjust blood pressure to the different needs of the body over time, but sometimes this mechanism goes wrong.

Hypertension, or **high blood pressure**, is common, and although in the majority of cases there is no known cause, and no symptoms, it has been linked to stress, smoking, lack of exercise and inheritance. Long-term hypertension can lead to damage of the heart or brain, and is usually controlled with medication.

Recommendations for massage – Deep abdominal massage is contra-indicated, but relaxing massage is probably beneficial for someone with high blood pressure, to keep stress levels down. If someone has high blood pressure that is not controlled by medication, diet or exercise, it might be advisable to get medical permission, for practitioner protection.

In the UK, **hypotension**, or **low blood pressure**, is not considered a medical problem. When massaging someone with low blood pressure, take care helping them off the table because the change in position from lying to sitting when relaxed may cause them to faint.

Disorders of the Blood Vessels

Blockage of blood vessels occurs when a blood clot forms on the wall, or when an obstruction such as a clot, or air bubble, or dislodged bit of plaque is moved in the bloodstream to another site. The first type of blockage is called a **thrombosis** and the second, an **embolism**. Anticoagulants are given to prevent clots growing larger.

Arteriosclerosis, or thickening of the arteries, refers to a general hardening and loss of elasticity of the walls. **Artherosclerosis** is caused by a build-up of plaque in the arteries, which could lead to clot formation.

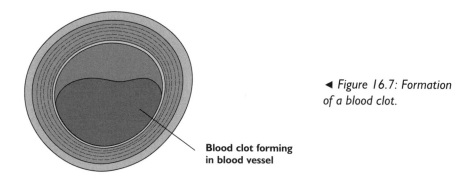

◄ *Figure 16.7: Formation of a blood clot.*

Blood clot forming in blood vessel

Recommendations for massage – Seek medical permission first, and give gentle massage only.

Deep vein thrombosis (DVT) is a much more serious condition, where a blood clot forms in a vein, often when someone has to stay in bed after surgery, a stroke or child-birth. It can also arise from immobility on long haul flights. If the clot breaks lose it can travel through the system to the lungs, with fatal results.

Recommendations for massage – Massage is totally contra-indicated for 3–6 months after diagnosis, for practitioner protection. After that period, seek medical permission, and give gentle massage only.

Varicose veins, usually in the legs, are the result of valve failure in the veins, and accumulation of pockets of blood. The vein walls, being thin, stretch and become flabby. Pregnancy and obesity are risk factors.

Recommendations for massage – Massage is contra-indicated in the area directly over, or immediately below the veins. The affected area can be held gently while the rest of the leg is massaged. Support under the legs to aid drainage back to the heart during massage is recommended.

Varicose veins can become red, tender and inflamed. This painful condition is called **phlebitis**, and there may be a risk of clots. However, it affects the superficial veins only, with virtually no risk of clots entering the circulation.

Recommendations for massage – Massage of the affected area is contra-indicated.

Oedema is an accumulation of lymphatic fluid in the tissues, caused by failure of the lymphatic system to drain properly. The resulting swelling may be localised; for example the swollen ankles commonly experienced by pregnant women, or general, if associated with an underlying disease such as heart failure.

Recommendations for massage – Massage with most common types of oedema is probably beneficial, if it can help stimulate a sluggish lymphatic circulation. Supports under affected limbs to assist drainage are recommended. Massage of someone with generalised oedema resulting from a serious condition should only be carried out with the doctor's advice. Anyone with chronic oedema is likely to have thin skin in the affected areas – use gentle massage and be sensitive to the person's feelings about their condition.

Disorders of the Blood

Anaemia results from a lack of red blood cells, or haemoglobin, and the capacity of the blood to carry oxygen to the tissues is reduced. It is a sign of an underlying disorder.

Sickle cell anaemia is an inherited condition found in peoples of Black African descent, in which the red cells are deformed, and the ability to carry oxygen reduced.

Thalassaemia is another inherited form of anaemia common to people of Turkish or Cypriot descent. Symptoms of all the anaemias are fatigue, headaches, insomnia and joint pain.

Recommendations for massage – The level of vitality of the anaemic person at the time of massage would determine the quality of treatment; when very fatigued, give gentle massage only. Seek medical condition in severe cases.

Also known as 'cancer of the blood', **leukemia** develops when immature white blood cells multiply excessively, interfering with the ability of normal white cells and platelets to do their work.

Recommendations for massage – Get medical permission and use gentle massage.

Haemophilia is an inherited disorder and is a failure of the blood to clot properly. The condition ranges from mild to severe; sufferers bruise and bleed easily.

Recommendations for massage – Gentle massage is fine for people with mild haemophilia. Take care to help the person on and off the table to prevent accidental bruising. Seek medical permission for someone with severe haemophilia.

Chapter 17 The Urinary System

Some of the end products of chemical processes in the cells are toxic to the body, and need to be removed before they begin to cause damage. There are four systems that contribute to the removal of metabolic waste; the digestive system removes the solid waste products of digestion, the respiratory system removes carbon dioxide, the skin removes some waste in sweat, and the urinary system removes urea and uric acid, as well as excess fluid.

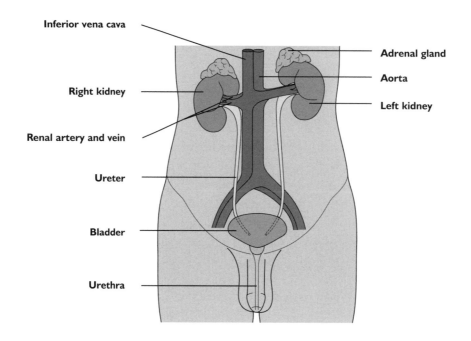

▲ *Figure 17.1: The urinary system.*

Body cells use protein in their chemical activities. Urea and uric acid are the most common waste products from this process. The two kidneys filter these and other substances out of the blood, producing urine which is passed through two long tubes called the ureters to the bladder, where it is held until ready to be passed out of the body through the urethra.

Key Words

Structure and Function

Kidneys
Antidiuretic hormone (ADH)
Ureter
Bladder
Urethra
Urine

Disorders

Incontinence
Cystitis
Kidney stones
Renal failure
Gout

Functions of the Urinary System

This system has many important homeostatic functions:

1. Removal of waste matter; urea and uric acid, and other toxic substances such as drugs.
2. Regulation of the fluid content in the body; in adults, water makes up about 60% of the body. If this level falls, the kidneys excrete less fluid, to maintain the right level.
3. Regulation of blood pressure and the acidity of the blood.
4. Maintenance of the balance of minerals such as sodium and potassium in the body.

Structure of the Urinary System

There are two **kidneys**, situated high up at the back of the abdomen, one on either side of the spine, partly protected by the lowest ribs and partly protruding below them. The right kidney is slightly lower due to the presence of the liver on that side of the body. They are about 11cms (4ins) long and about 3cms (1in) thick, and shaped like large kidney beans. The kidneys are outside the peritoneum, the connective tissue wall that encloses the rest of the abdominal organs, and their position renders them susceptible to injury, particularly through contact sports, and to the cold, although to some extent they are protected by the layer of fatty adipose tissue surrounding them.

On top of each kidney sits an adrenal gland. The ureter, and the renal artery and vein bringing blood into the kidney directly from the aorta and out to the inferior vena cava, enter the kidney on the indented side. The outer part of the kidney is composed of millions of units that filter blood.

At each heartbeat, a proportion of the blood coming through the aorta is pumped into each kidney via the renal artery. Because it is under pressure, much of the plasma and the small particles floating in it are pushed from the capillaries into tiny, but very long, adjacent tubules, filtering units in the outer part of the kidneys. As this fluid slowly passes down the tubules to collect in the central renal cavity, the salts, minerals, sugars and fluid that are needed by the body are filtered back into the blood vessels and hence returned to the main circulation via the renal vein. 90% of the water filtered through the kidneys is reabsorbed into the body. The remaining 10% of the filtrate is passed into the ureters.

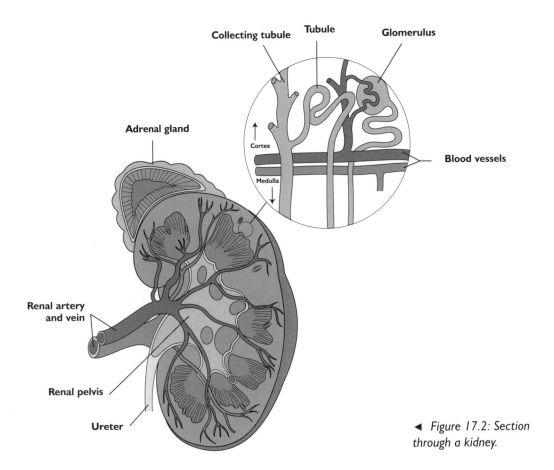

◄ *Figure 17.2: Section through a kidney.*

Regulation of the Kidneys

The rate of activity in the kidneys is controlled by a hormone called **antidiuretic hormone** (**ADH**). When water levels in the body fall, the blood becomes more concentrated. The brain registers this and the pituitary secretes ADH into the bloodstream that results in the kidneys slowing their rate of activity and secretion of water. The **ureters** are two long thin tubes, about 30cms long, with walls of smooth muscle that carry the urine from the kidney to the bladder. The urine is pushed through the ureters by peristalsis.

The **bladder** is a sac of smooth muscle at the front of the pelvis just behind the pubic bone, slightly lower in women than in men. The walls of the bladder contain sensory receptors that monitor the amount of stretch in the muscle, and relay the information to the brain where it is registered as the need to urinate.

The tube to the outside of the body, the **urethra**, differs in men and women. In men it is 15–20cms (6–8ins) long, travelling through the penis, where it forms a common duct for the passage of **urine** and sperm. In women it is only 2–5cms (1–2ins) long, following a straight course from the bladder to the exterior, making women more prone to urinary infections. Internal and external sphincters govern the excretion of urine.

Disorders of the Urinary System

Incontinence is involuntary urination, and is more common in the elderly and in women who have had children. Stress incontinence occurs through laughing, running or strenuous activity.

Urinary tract infections are common and include inflammation of the bladder and **cystitis**, which is more common in women, and causes burning pain when urinating.

Kidney stones are small hard deposits found in the kidneys, similar to gallstones in the gall bladder. They can be very painful, especially when they are passing down the ureters.

Renal failure is a rare and dangerous condition, and means that the kidneys have stopped functioning. Treatment is with dialysis on a kidney machine.

Gout is due to a build-up of uric acid in the body and affects the joints, most often the big toe joint. An attack of gout is extremely painful.

Recommendations for massage:

1. Massage is contra-indicated for those with acute urinary tract infections, acute or chronic renal failure, acute stages of gout, or a kidney stone attack.
2. It is locally contra-indicated for joints affected with gout or on the abdomen in non-acute stages of urinary tract infection.
3. Sensitivity to embarrassment, or frequent need to urinate, is important if working with someone with cystitis or incontinence.
4. Due to the exposed position of the kidneys, avoid heavy percussion on the back between the ribcage and pelvis.

Chapter 18 The Reproductive System

The reproductive systems are the only systems that are very different, both in terms of structure and function, for men and women. The sex organs, the ovaries in a woman and the testes in a man, are also endocrine glands, so there are also sexual differences in the functioning of the endocrine system. The sex hormones are responsible for the development of the secondary sexual characteristics at puberty, sexual and parenting behaviours, and changes in the mother's body during pregnancy and childbirth. This system is also the only one that undergoes particular changes at certain times during an individuals' life, coming to maturity at puberty, and, for women, ceasing to function in the same way after the menopause.

In acknowledging this difference, the structure and function of the female and male reproductive systems will be discussed separately. Because massage has a long and unfortunate association with sexuality, there is a brief discussion of the issues that can occur concerning sexuality. And although menstruation, pregnancy and childbirth, and menopause are normal events in a woman's life, and not pathological conditions, it is important to mention the special considerations for massage at each of these stages, as well as for the complications that can arise.

Female Reproductive System

Key Words

Structure and Function

Vulva	Oestrogen
Labia	Progesterone
Vagina	Conception
Clitoris	Pregnancy
Cervix	Amniotic fluid
Uterus / womb	Placenta
Ovary	Umbilical cord
Fallopian tubes	Colostrum
Ovum (**pl.** ova)	Menstruation
Menstrual cycle	Menopause

Disorders

Chlamydia	Endometriosis
Thrush	Pelvic inflammatory infection
Non-specific Urethritis (NSU)	Prolapse
Fibroids	

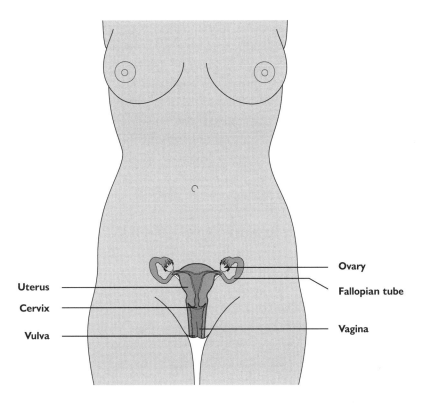

▲ *Figure 18.1: The female reproductive organs.*

Structure of the Female Reproductive System

The external genitalia, between the pubic bone and the anus, are collectively called the **vulva**. There are a pair of fleshy lips, the **labia**, which protect the openings to the **vagina** and the urethra. The **clitoris**, at the front of the vulva, is a highly sensitive organ that, like the penis, becomes erect when excited.

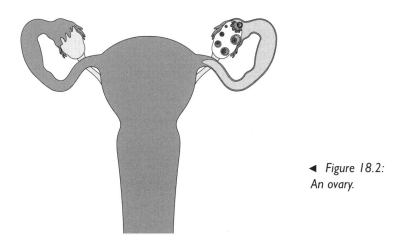

◄ *Figure 18.2:
An ovary.*

The vagina, with walls of smooth muscle lined with membranes that secrete a lubricating mucus, connects to the uterus at a small opening called the **cervix**. The **uterus**, or **womb**, lies in the lower part of the pelvic cavity, between the bladder and the rectum, and also has walls of smooth muscle that can enlarge significantly during pregnancy. The **ovaries** are two small almond-shaped glands about 3cms long that lie in the pelvic cavity on either side of the uterus out towards the hip bones. Leading from the uterus, one on each side are the narrow **Fallopian tubes**. The feathery open ends of these tubes are situated just below each ovary, ready to catch the **ova**, or eggs. The secondary sexual organs of the female reproductive system are the breasts (mammary glands), which develop at puberty, and produce milk after childbirth for the baby.

Function of the Female Reproductive System

Control of the **menstrual cycle** involves a chain of hormonal reactions; the hypothalamus releases certain hormones to the pituitary gland (the master gland), which in turn releases two others into the bloodstream, which stimulate the ovaries to produce **oestrogen** and **progesterone**. Fluctuations in the production of all these hormones over the course of on average, 28 days, causes an ovum to mature and be released from one of the ovaries. This causes the lining of the uterus, the endometrium, to thicken and become engorged with blood, in preparation for the implantation of the ovum.

When this fails to happen, this blood rich lining is shed and a new lining built-up. The first two weeks of the cycle is the building-up phase; then comes ovulation, the release of the ovum, and then, if fertilisation fails to occur, the lining is broken down and expelled. After a further fortnight, menstruation occurs, and the process begins again.

Conception, the joining of an ovum with a sperm from a male partner, takes place in the Fallopian tube. The gestational process, comprising the growth and development within a woman from conception to birth is known as **pregnancy**. The fertilised cell begins to divide and grow straight away, and moves towards the uterus. Around the sixth day it burrows into the wall of the uterus, where it remains for the next nine months, inside a sac filled with protective **amniotic fluid**. The **placenta**, connecting the foetus and uterus through the **umbilical cord**, is a special organ that becomes the route of nourishment between the mother and the developing foetus. It also sends out a hormone to stop further ovulation during the pregnancy. In late pregnancy, another hormone (relaxin) causes softening of all ligaments in the body; in the pelvic area this is needed to allow for expansion of the pelvic girdle at birth. The baby settles in a head down position, and in late pregnancy the head engages with the pelvic bones.

When the baby is ready, the cervix gradually expands and opens up and the muscular walls of the uterus and the abdominal muscles contract rhythmically to expel the baby out through the vagina. Soon after the baby comes out, the placenta is also expelled as the afterbirth. Immediately after birth, a nutritious and disease resistant fluid called **colostrum** – 'first milk' – is secreted from the mother's breasts, followed by the true milk after a few days. Milk production is stimulated by a reflex initiated by the baby sucking at the breast. Over time, the uterus gradually shrinks back to normal, and hormones cause resumption of the menstrual cycle.

During the first three months of pregnancy, there is a high risk of miscarriage, and all massage on the abdomen is contra-indicated, for practitioner protection. After that stage, deep abdominal massage continues to be contra-indicated throughout pregnancy and for several weeks after birth.

Positioning and supports are important: during the initial stages, a women can receive massage in the usual positions, but in the later stages she cannot lie on her stomach, and needs to lie on her side, or to be supported in a sitting position. When lying on her back, she needs good support under her knees. Avoid the supine position for too long, because of pressure of the foetus on the abdominal blood vessels.

In late pregnancy, hormonal changes loosen all ligaments and tendons in the body, so avoid, or take particular care with joint manipulations and stretches.

Menstruation is the periodic (typically 4–5 days) discharge through the vagina of a bloody secretion containing tissue debris from the shedding of the endometrium from the non-pregnant uterus. During the two weeks before menstruation, many women experience some of the signs of pre-menstrual syndrome (PMS); fluid retention, sore breasts, irritability, sugar cravings, fatigue, or headaches. Soothing massage may be helpful.

During a period (menstruation), some women experience abdominal cramps, or sensitivity in the abdomen, lower back or thighs. Massage of these areas may be helpful or completely unwanted; negotiation is important, and proper use of supports is needed for sore breasts or abdomens. Avoid deep abdominal massage. Sensitivity is also needed for women who bleed very heavily, and need to wear heavy feminine protection, or to change during a treatment. Constipation is not uncommon before a period. There is some evidence that abdominal massage may help.

At around the age of fifty, the ovaries cease to produce ova, and falling levels of oestrogen produce the signs of **menopause**; hot flushes, cessation of menstruation, thinning of the vaginal walls, weight gain and increased risk of osteoporosis. The menopause involves adjustment on an emotional as well as physical level, and massage may help ease the transition.

Disorders Specific to the Female Reproductive System

Discharge from a vaginal infection such as **chlamydia**, **thrush** (a fungal infection) or **non-specific urethritis** (**NSU**) is not a contra-indication to massage.

Fibroids are slow growing, benign tumours of the uterus wall. They are rarely painful but can cause heavy periods, and a dragging sensation in the abdomen. They can sometimes be felt through the abdomen, but they are not a massage contra-indication, although sensitivity to a woman's feelings is important.

Endometriosis means the presence of tissue from the inside of the uterus growing in other places in the body, usually in the abdominal cavity. Periods are very painful, and there may be abdominal tenderness. Deep abdominal massage is contra-indicated.

Pelvic inflammatory infection, which is infection of the uterus and ovaries is extremely painful, and a major cause of infertility. Deep abdominal massage is contra-indicated.

In women who have had children, the pelvic floor muscles can lose their elasticity, particularly after the menopause. **Prolapse** involves the uterus or vagina falling, and possibly protruding outside the body. Abdominal massage is contra-indicated.

Male Reproductive System

Key Words

Structure and Function

Testes	Epididymis
Scrotum	Vas deferens
Spermatozoa / sperm	Seminal vesicle
Penis	Seminal fluid / semen
Urethra	Prostate gland

Disorders

Prostate cancer

Structure of the Male Reproductive System

The two **testes** hang outside the body, each in a sac called the **scrotum,** either side of the penis. They produce **spermatozoa** or **sperm**, the male germ cells, as well as being endocrine glands producing the male sex hormones. The **penis** consists of columns of spongy tissue, surrounding the **urethra**. Erection is a fast influx of blood into the tissues of the penis, squashing shut the outgoing veins. The urethra is a common duct for sperm and urine; the flow is controlled by a valve so that it is impossible to secrete both at the same time.

Sperm cells formed in the testes initially pass slowly along a long coiled tube, the **epididymis**, which lies just behind each testis, as they mature. The tubes that carry sperm to the root of the penis, looping up through the lower abdomen in the region of the groin, are called the **vas deferens**.

Each vas deferens passes through a sac like gland called a **seminal vesicle**, which secrete most of the fluid component of the **seminal fluid** or **semen**, before joining with the urethra after it leaves the bladder. Finally, the urethra passes through another gland, the **prostate gland**, which secretes more of the seminal fluid, before entering the penis.

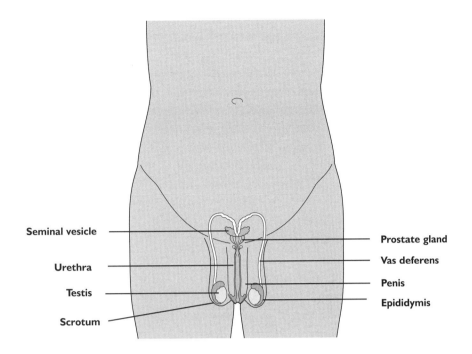

Seminal vesicle

Urethra

Testis

Scrotum

Prostate gland

Vas deferens

Penis

Epididymis

▲ *Figure 18.3: The male reproductive organs.*

Function of the Male Reproductive System

The function of the male reproductive organs is to produce sperm, and to transmit them to a female body for the fertilisation of an ovum. Sperm are made and stored in the testes. Each sperm has a cap of enzymes, with which to penetrate the egg, and a tail to swim on its journey through the vagina, uterus and Fallopian tube towards possible fertilisation of an egg. There are usually millions in each ejaculation.

During sexual arousal, the spongy spaces in the penis become engorged with blood, which causes the organ to become erect. When ejaculation occurs, sperm and seminal fluid are propelled through the tubes and out through the tip of the penis.

Disorders Specific to the Male Reproductive System

Prostate cancer is a form of cancer common in elderly men, and rarely fatal if treated in time. Not a contra-indication to massage, but note that there can be a need to urinate more frequently.

Massage and Sexuality

The connection between massage and massage parlour in the public mind is decreasing, as the massage therapy profession develops rigorous standards for training and registration of its practitioners, and claims its place as an important complementary therapy. Unfortunately, there are still some individuals who book a massage treatment expecting sexual services, and therapists need to know how to deal with this.

Since both non-sexual massage and sexual contact involve touch and the nature of the touch can be very similar, even though the context – treatment room rather than bedroom – and the intention of the giver – massage therapist rather than lover – are different, a body could be forgiven for interpreting long, slow effleurage strokes as sexual caresses, even when the mind knows full well that this is not the intention. On occasions, sexual arousal can occur innocently during massage, more obviously in men, who are usually very embarrassed by an unwanted erection. The therapist also needs to know how to deal with this.

Sexually Transmitted Diseases

These include syphilis (which if untreated eventually causes central nervous system damage), gonorrhoea, non-specific urethritis, genital herpes, and genital infestations such as pubic lice and scabies. Genital scabies may indicate the presence of scabies on the hands too – don't massage.

While sexually transmitted diseases are not of direct concern in a massage treatment, there is an Act of Parliament from 1917 prohibiting the use of complementary therapies to treat syphilis, gonorrhoea or soft chancre (genital sores). Massage does not claim to treat, in the sense of diagnose and cure, medical conditions, but practitioners should be aware of this law.

Bibliography

Andrade, C-K., and Clifford, P.: 2001. Outcome-based Massage. Lippincott, Williams and Wilkins, New York.

Bray, J. J., Cragg, A. C., Macknight, A. D. C., Mills, R. G.: 1999. Lecture Notes on Human Physiology, fourth edition. Blackwell Science, Oxford.

Calais-Germain, B.: 1993. Anatomy of Movement. Eastland Press, Seattle, USA.

Clemente, C. D., Urban and Schwarzenberg: 1975. Anatomy – A Regional Atlas of the Human Body. Munchen, Berlin.

Crouch, J. E.: 1978. Functional Human Anatomy, third edition. Lea and Febiger, USA.

Damasio, A.: 2000. The Feeling of What Happens: Body, Emotion and the Making of Consciousness. Vintage, London.

Evans, P., Hucklebridge, F., and Clow, A.: 2000. Mind, Immunity and Health. Free Association Books.

Field, T., Morrow, C., and Valdeon, C.: 1998. Touch Research Institute Studies, USA.

Gorman, D.: 1981. The Body Moveable. Ampersand Press, Canada.

Gosling, J. A. et al.: 1985. Atlas of Human Anatomy from Manchester University Department of Anatomy. Gower Medical Publishing, London.

Grisigono, V.: 1984. 'Sports Injuries: A Self-help Guide. John Murray, London.

Hildebrand, M.: 1988. Analysis of Vertebrate Structure, third edition. John Wiley and Sons Inc., New York.

Juhan, D.: 1987. Job's Body – A Handbook for Bodywork. Station Hill Press, USA.

Kapandji, I. A.: 1982. The Physiology of the Joint, Vol. 1. Churchill Livingstone, Edinburgh.

Kapandji, I. A.: 1988. The Physiology of the Joint, Vol. 2. Churchill Livingstone, Edinburgh.

Kapandji, I. A.: 1974. The Physiology of the Joint, Vol. 3. Churchill Livingstone, Edinburgh.

LeGros Clark, Sir W. E.: 1971. The Tissues of the Body – An Introduction to the Study of Anatomy, sixth edition. Oxford University Press, London.

McMurtie, H., and Krall Rikel, J.: 1991. The Coloring Review Guide to Human Anatomy. Wm. C. Brown, USA.

McNeill, Alexander, R.: 1994. Bones – The Unity of Form and Function. Weidenfeld and Nicholson, London.

Marieb, E. N.: 2000. Essentials of Human Anatomy and Physiology. Addison Wesley Longman, Inc. (published under the Benjamin/Cummings imprint), USA.

Panskepp, J.: 1998. Affective Neuroscience: the Foundations of Human and Animal Emotions. Oxford University Press, London.

Pansky, B.: 1979. Review of Gross Anatomy, fourth edition. MacMillan Publishing Co., Inc., New York.

Parker, S.: 1994. How the Body Works. Dorling Kindersley, London.

Penner, Dr. C.: 1996. Behold Your Body – Anatomy and Physiology Anyone Can Enjoy, Volume 1: Dry Bones or Wet Noodles. Rose Bud Publishing, USA.

Salvo, S.: 1999. Massage Therapy: Principles and Practice. W.B. Saunders Co., New York.

Smith, L. K., Lawrence Weiss, E., Lehmkuhl, L. D.: 1996. Brunnstrom's Clinical Kinesiology, fifth edition, revised. F. A. Davis Company, USA.

Smith, Dr. T. (ed.): 1995. The British Medical Association – Complete Family Health Guide. Dorling Kindersley, London.

Thompson, C. W., Floyd, R. T.: 1994. Manual of Structural Kinesiology, twelfth edition. Mosby (Mosby-Year Book Inc.), USA.

Trew, M. and Everett, T. (ed.): 1997. Human Movement – An Introductory Text, third edition. Churchill Livingstone, Edinburgh.

Vickers, A.: 1996. Massage and Aromatherapy: a Health Guide for Professionals. Chapman and Hall, London.

Werner, R.: 1998. A Massage Therapist's Guide to Pathology. Lippincott, Williams and Wilkins, USA.

Williams, P. (ed.): 1995. Gray's Anatomy, thirty-eighth edition. Churchill Livingstone, Edinburgh.

Wirhed, R. 1984. Athletic Ability and the Anatomy of Motion. Wolf Medical Publications Ltd., London.

Index

Muscle Index